The Pacific Alliance

United States Foreign
Economic Policy and
Japanese Trade
Recovery, 1947–1955

William S. Borden

The University of Wisconsin Press

Published 1984

The University of Wisconsin Press
114 North Murray Street
Madison, Wisconsin 53715

The University of Wisconsin Press, Ltd.
1 Gower Street
London WC1E 6HA, England

First printing

Printed in the United States of America

For LC CIP information see the colophon

ISBN 0-299-09550-9

To Matthew

Contents

Preface

In 1973, I set my interest in the postwar European recovery aside temporarily to study American policy toward Japanese trade recovery under the Occupation. John W. Dower, a leading scholar of the Occupation and possessor of a virtual library of primary materials on the Occupation from the Japanese Ministry of Finance Historical Collection, graciously shared his knowledge and materials with me. Unlike the European Recovery Program (ERP) drama, with its four major and numerous lesser nations as actors, policy toward Japan seemed a manageable topic. Initial research convinced me that Japan's "dollar gap" (trade deficit with the United States) became the primary problem for the Occupation after 1947. From an economic viewpoint, I found most interesting the American policies to economically integrate Japan and Southeast Asia and to subsidize Japanese purchases of American products by contracting with Japanese industry to produce war materials for American and Allied armies in Asia. The strategic value of Southeast Asian integration with Japan seemed to provide a convincing rationale for American intervention in Indochina from 1950 to 1954. American procurement of military materials in Japan contributed significantly to Japan's emergence in the late 1950s from the structural trap of insufficient foreign demand for its industrial production. These two subjects form the heart of this present work.

In 1974, under the sophisticated guidance of Thomas J. McCormick, I took to a study of European policy the perspective on American policy gained from my studies of the occupation of Japan. The similarities in policy toward Japan and Europe could not have been more striking. The Economic Cooperation Administration (ECA) also emphasized increasing trade with Europe's "dependent territories," and European purchases of American products were also subsidized by American military expenditures long after the ERP had ended. The idea of performing a fundamental economic analysis of the European and, in more detail, the Japanese recovery programs became irresistible.

My research plan took me in 1976 and 1977 from Professor Dower's archives and a reading of Congressional hearings on Europe and Japan and ECA and OEEC (Organization of European Cooperation) documents from 1947 to 1955 to the extremely intimidating repository for the records of the Supreme Command for Allied Powers (SCAP)—the Occupation—in Suitland, Maryland. These largely unorganized and massive (over ten thousand cubic feet) files grudgingly revealed the character of the Occupation's preoccupation with Japanese recovery, foreign trade, and American aid. More conventional sources such as the files of the Departments of State and Army and of the National Security Council and the Truman and Eisenhower Library Collections filled in many more gaps. Thanks to Professor Dick K. Nanto's extreme generosity, I was able to use his collection of materials from the Japanese Ministry of Finance in 1978. Also in 1978 I filed Freedom of Information requests with the Departments of State and Treasury for access to materials from the forbidden post–Korean War era. The State Department assured me it could not comply with the requirements of the law and that the archives for the 1950–54 period would soon be available (that is, in the fall of 1978). The Department of Treasury, historically the most tightfisted protector of its files, took its legal obligations more seriously and eventually granted me access to secret files of my choice through 1959, provided my notes were approved by the department's gracious Japan desk officer. Thus, despite the absence of State Department files, I was able to view excellent primary material postdating June 1950 from SCAP, Japanese Ministry of Finance, Treasury, and Truman and Eisenhower collections.

Japanese colleagues have assured me that the basic themes of this work are old hat in Japan and so well accepted that, were it not for the previously unviewed archival substantiation for those themes, this work would produce no more than a yawn among most Japanese historians. I assured them that many cold-war-oriented and less economically astute American diplomatic historians would find unduly one-sided my insistence that economic policies loomed very large in

American policy toward Europe and Japan, the core of American diplomacy, in the postwar period. The goal of this work is to provide an overall understanding of the environment within which American foreign economic policy developed. American diplomatic historians need such an understanding to analyze the close relationship between strategic anti-Communism and economic multilateralism.

I owe untold thanks to Takeshi Matsuda, who strongly influenced my approach in 1973, and to Yoichi Miura, Eichi Shindo, Yoko Yasuhara, Joe Moore, Bob Marks, and Ikuhiko Hata. Nathan Godfried and Michael Schaller encouraged and helped me after reading early drafts of the manuscript. Howard Schonberger, like Professors Dower and McCormick, has educated me through the high quality of his work as well as through his original ideas on the Occupation. Tom Good's excellent editing of the original manuscript and the patience of typists Hally Abbott, Carole Morand, Denise Dunn, and Donna Fersch are also extremely appreciated. The Aigners and many other friends have helped me in my travels. Finally, without my wife, Carla, and parents this work would never have been written.

Abbreviations

ECA	Economic Cooperation Administration
ECAFE	Economic Commission for Asia and the Far East (United Nations)
ECC	European Cooperation Committee
EROA	Economic Recovery of Occupied Areas
ERP	European Recovery Program
ESS	Economic and Scientific Section (SCAP)
FEC	Far Eastern Commission
FOA	Foreign Operations Administration
GARIOA	Government Aid and Relief for Occupied Areas
IBRD	International Bank for Reconstruction and Development
IMF	International Monetary Fund
JIP	"Japan's Industrial Potential"
MDAP	Mutual Defense Assistance Program
MITI	Ministry of International Trade and Industry
MSA	Mutual Security Administration
MSP	Mutual Security Program
NAC	National Advisory Council for International Financial and Monetary Affairs
OEEC	Organization of European Economic Cooperation
POLAD	Political Advisor to SCAP
SCAP	Supreme Command for Allied Powers

The Pacific Alliance

Introduction

The Allied Occupation of Japan, 1945 to 1952, was initially designed to reform Japan's militaristic culture and democratize her quasi-feudalistic political and economic order, symbolized by the so-called emperor system. Washington issued occupational directives through 1946, mandating impressive social reforms, establishing a Western-style constitution, and seeking to dismantle the monopolistic control of industry. The Japanese public eagerly embraced these reforms to overthrow their discredited leadership and its antidemocratic ideology. The Occupation has been heralded as one of the great social experiments in history—and, for the most part, one which succeeded (although the entrenched Japanese political elite subtly resisted and watered down the reforms).

Through 1947 and 1948, however, Washington and SCAP (the Supreme Command for Allied Powers, which was the Occupation bureaucracy headed by General MacArthur) shifted their emphasis from sociopolitical reform to economic recovery, reflecting both the cold war conflict with the Soviet Union in Asia and the failure of American economic recovery policies in the postwar world in general and in Japan specifically. This "reverse course" enabled traditional Japanese business bureaucrats and political elites to remain entrenched in political power and ended the attempt to diversify ownership of industry. By 1949 the United States instituted a full-blown "Japanese recovery program," which closely paralleled the European Recovery Program (otherwise known as the Marshall Plan).

Scholars have traditionally viewed the "reverse course" as a product of the cold war. Indeed, strategic planners in Washington were primarily concerned with preserving the postwar alliance with Japan to preserve a favorable balance of power. Actual war with the Soviet Union over Japan would have rendered insignificant any other con-

3

siderations regarding American policy toward Japan. Yet, although the Joint Chiefs of Staff and other strategic planners had to concern themselves with Japan's vulnerability to Soviet assault, the likelihood of such an event was known to be remote. Military policy to arm Japan, with both American troops and local "defense forces," served not only to deter the Soviets but also to strengthen the conservative social and political fabric of Japan.

The Japanese themselves were concerned primarily with their nation's extreme economic frailty. In the absence of a direct threat of a Soviet assault, American officials sought primarily to gain the voluntary allegiance of conservative Japanese officials to the alliance with the United States. Occupation officials had to assure Japan that its economy could prosper within the American-led capitalist bloc and without extensive trade with Communist Asia. By 1948, American officials agreed that the sole means of assuring Japanese loyalty to American strategic objectives in Asia was to revive Japan's industrial plants. Thus, the primary means of preserving the Pacific alliance and the balance of power in Asia was to promote vigorous economic recovery. Even though the goal was the Asian balance of power, the primary tactics of American policy were economic. Beyond even the cold war and balance of power, American goals of a multilateral economic system with large foreign markets for American production also required the revival of Japanese industry and trade. Strategic and economic goals were mutually reinforcing.

American and Japanese political and economic cooperation had been the rule rather than the exception before World War II. Both nations had similar interests in free trade, in the economic development of Asia on terms favorable to the industrial nations, and in stifling Communist revolution in Asia. Japanese and American leaders and corporations had strong ties and similar world views. It was Occupation policy to reform Japan that was the aberration in twentieth-century American policy toward Japan, not the later recovery policies.

The "Pacific alliance" between the United States and Japan thus came to depend heavily on economic aid—that is, on the Japanese recovery program. Only through a long and costly modernization process could Japan fulfill its latent economic potential—so obvious in retrospect from the remarkable industrial skills, energy, and discipline of its people today. In the postwar decade, however, Japan faced great obstacles to recovery. Cut off from her vital trade outlets and dependent upon American products but with no means to pay for them, Japan depended on economic aid to survive the dissolution of her empire. As an interim solution to the lack of industrial modernization, the United States subsidized Japanese purchases in the United States and sought to strengthen Japanese ties with non-Communist Asia. Fears of Chinese Communist influence in Japan, however, led the United States to oppose the revival of Japanese trade with North China and Manchuria.

The Japanese recovery program proved to be as monumental and far-reaching as the more familiar plan to democratize Japanese society and politics. Indeed, the Japanese recovery program, largely overlooked by scholars of the Occupation and postwar American foreign policy, was a decisive force in shaping the modern world economy.

In 1947 and 1948 the "reverse course" spawned a series of studies and commissions that were to recommend instituting economic aid to "prime the pump" of Japanese production and thus to increase her exports. From 1949 through the end of the Occupation, and on a less formal basis through the 1950s, the United States subsidized and promoted Japanese trade and successfully overcame numerous Japanese economic crises that threatened the alliance. The recovery program significantly contributed to the reemergence of Japan as an economic power in the 1960s and formed a vital link in American global economic policy—indeed, the recovery program was developed within that larger policy and hence cannot be understood without first comprehending the formation of overall American policy objectives after the war.

American foreign economic policy after World War II was shaped by a decisive paradox: the sheer economic supremacy of the United States also caused a tremendous imbalance in the world economy that threatened both the prosperity of the United States and its foreign policy objectives. Thus, the most knowledgeable and influential American policymakers, whose sophistication and broad outlook reflected the nation's maturity as a world power, faced the challenge of reducing the domination of the world economy by American producers. Otherwise, foreign nations would become insolvent vis-à-vis the United States and would be unable to purchase American goods. The global trade imbalance took the form of a "dollar gap" in world trade—that is, a shortfall in foreign dollar accounts caused by an annual $10 billion surplus of American exports over American imports. For reasons stemming partially from the war, but more fundamentally from the uneven structural development of international capitalism and the decline of formal colonialism, the foreign demand for American goods far outstripped the American demand for foreign goods.

On a purely commercial, theoretical basis, the dollar gap could not have existed. No American exporter would have shipped goods abroad, since his customer could not have obtained sufficient dollars for payment, foreign supplies of dollars being so scarce that governments were forced to ration them carefully to secure vital food and raw material imports. The dollar gap, therefore, existed only at the sufferance of the American Congress, whose foreign aid appropriations financed the export of American goods: terminating foreign economic aid would have meant that foreigners would have had to slash their purchases from the United States to the level of their meager dollar earnings; that world trade would have collapsed (it was already at depression levels); and that multilateral exchange in the world economy would barely have existed. Barter and state trading would have dominated international economic relations.

American officials feared a cutoff of foreign economic aid not only because it would have had immediate and serious implications for American employment, income, profits, and production, but also because it would have destroyed their plans for an American-controlled, multilateral, international economic system. Multilateralism (i.e., the absence of barriers to the transfer of goods and capital across national borders) had been the goal of American foreign policy officials since the Wilson Administration. Roosevelt's secretary of state, Cordell Hull, championed free (multilateral) trade, and his postwar successors at the State Department took up the banner of multilateralism, determined to apply the full force of American political and economic power to achieve a viable international economic system. Multilateralism in American plans, however, came to mean "capitalist-bloc multilateralism." American leaders sought to minimize economic ties with the Soviet sphere to avoid having the

Allies come to depend on Soviet-controlled materials. The philosophy of free trade had long appealed to economic theorists in economically dominant nations, notably Great Britain in the nineteenth century and the United States in the twentieth. More than a sacred principle, multilateralism was a doctrine of convenience for American leaders, who sought to impose international laws which would allow powerful corporations to operate abroad unhindered by foreign government restrictions. Protectionism (i.e., the use of government-imposed restrictions on trade) would help only weaker nations and weak American industries that lacked the political power to influence foreign economic policy.

The postwar dollar gap posed a nearly insurmountable threat to the State Department's multilateral goals. Multilateral relations were impossible in conditions of global economic disequilibrium—in which one nation dominated world trade. Only if commercial transactions produced relatively balanced trade, requiring only traditionally acceptable adjustments (such as currency devaluations and deflationary policies in deficit nations), could the dreaded exchange and trade controls, tariffs, and quotas—the bane of multilateralists—be avoided.

In the postwar economy, with the huge dollar gap, multilateralism was no more than a pipe dream. The world economy was sharply divided into soft- and hard-currency areas. Hard currencies (the dollar, the Swiss franc, and those Western Hemisphere currencies tied to the dollar in the "dollar area") were in great demand, while soft currencies (the pound sterling, other European currencies, and the yen) were of less value because the nations that issued them had relatively few products which could compete with dollar-area products in world markets. Soft-currency nations traded relatively freely among themselves, although they set limits to ensure balanced trade. They traded with the dollar area only with great caution, however, in the fear of squandering scarce dollars necessary to purchase vital imports. Foreign nations sharply limited the freedom of their citizens to spend dollars, by imposing tight trade and exchange controls on trade with the dollar area. The alternative was bankruptcy and a total breakdown of trade with the dollar area. The greatest American fear was the total breakdown of economic relations between the soft- and hard-currency areas, which would effectively close off European, African, and Asian markets to American manufacturing corporations and food and raw material producers. At times the threat of a collapse of American exports and resulting economic depression was explicitly used as a rationale for aid. More often, however, the need for continued high exports to ensure domestic prosperity remained implicit in official statements and conversations. Indeed, it is often overlooked that the very prosperity of the United States after World War II was significantly dependent on earnings from exports.

The balance-of-power struggle isolated Europe and Japan from prewar markets and sources of raw materials in Eastern Europe and China. This increased the dependence of Europe and Japan on dollar-area supplies and thus exacerbated the imbalance in the world economy. The conflict with the Soviet Union also lent great urgency to recovery policies in Europe and to policies to stabilize the turbulent Third World. The cold war did not otherwise alter the economic crisis which would have faced American officials even in the absence of a Communist threat. Indeed, the cold war gave the United States great power over its allies through their increased dependence on American capital and goods—the result of capitalist bloc trade patterns. Most important, the cold war enabled the Truman Administration to obtain vast foreign aid grants from Congress in the name of anti-Communism and provided the rationale for continued dollar transfers to Europe and Japan in the form of military expenditures after foreign aid declined.

By making dollars available through a transitional period, the United States sought to finance the export surplus in order to sustain American exports, maintain American control of overseas markets, and minimize foreign restrictions on trade with the dollar area. The more fundamental and long-term response was to correct the massive structural disequilibrium in world trade by rebuilding the "workshop" economies of Europe and Japan and restoring their economic ties with primary producing areas in Asia, Africa, and Latin America. Restoration of colonial trade patterns, in which Europe and Japan could exchange manufactured goods for food and raw materials, would greatly ease the strain on American production.

Both policies of foreign economic assistance and foreign economic recovery, however, proved too fragile in the face of the tremendous imbalance in the world economy. In addition, the Truman Administration badly underestimated the depth of the global economic disequilibrium and, for political expediency, couched its appeals to Congress for foreign aid appropriations in anti-Communist rhetoric (instead of tutoring the economically unsophisticated congressmen in the complex, contradictory, and potentially divisive nuts and bolts of international economics). For both these reasons, the Administration found itself unable to sustain congressional foreign economic aid appropriations for a sufficient period of time to cover the longer-than-expected transitional period to a nearly balanced world economy. A series of crises subsequently engulfed the State Department, beginning with the Marshall Plan emergency of 1947 and ending with the crisis of the Japanese dollar gap in 1954. This is not to imply, however, that the State Department had any choice but to rely on anti-Communism instead of economic realities, or that—given the American goal of multilateralism—the crises could have been avoided. Remarkable boldness characterized the aggressive American attack on the dollar gap; without such a concentrated effort, there might have been a single but larger crisis and a far different world economy than that which emerged in 1955. Dean Acheson set the pattern of postwar policy when he conjured up the image of Russian barbarians overrunning Western civilization to frighten congressional leaders and gain their approval for the Marshall Plan in 1947. From that point on, there could be no severing of the link between the fear of Communism and large foreign aid appropriations. Congressional leaders clearly did not react as immediately to the dollar gap as to the perceived Russian threat.

Five themes are central to understanding postwar foreign economic policy. First, ruling circles were divided between (1) those who advocated "international-Keynesian stimulation" of the world economy through foreign economic aid until a solution was achieved, and (2) those who supported balanced budgets, low taxes, low inflation, and adherence to classic economic doctrine, even in the face of the world economic crisis. Foreign economic aid stimulated world economic demand in a Keynesian manner; the government-appropriated dollars raised world economic activity through the Keynesian "multiplier effect" (each dollar spent is respent several times, which stimulates further production).

Second, the dual and contradictory nature of the American effort to rebuild the world economy pitted local/corporate interests against

American foreign policy interests in international trade and investment. The global recovery policy—dictated by the decisive paradox of American strength as the cause of international weakness—sought to protect American markets at home and abroad; at the same time, it helped foreigners expand their markets to overcome American domination of trade. It also preserved the capitalist power structures of the industrial nations. It is important to remember that *not until 1962* did an American Congress support Keynesian spending policies to stimulate economic growth. Congress was, in the main, composed of locally oriented politicians, not economic theorists or cosmopolitan lawyers and business executives with foreign trade interests. It is true that many "liberal" senators and congressmen were very sympathetic to "internationalism"—an aggressive foreign policy—and interested in foreign trade. Local interests, however, had less to gain (international markets) and more to lose (local markets and the drain of taxes to pay for foreign aid) than the emerging multinational corporations. Most congressmen were thus tied philosophically to pre-Keynesian economic doctrine and undisposed to sacrifice short-term local interests for long-term international interests. Anti-Communism provided the emotional rallying point for congressmen, editors, and the public, casting the economic struggles into the shadows and giving the State Department a magic wand to command congressional approval of foreign aid and public approval of American influence abroad.

A third theme is that the policymaking elite created a global framework to realize their multilateral goals: Europe (especially West Germany) and Japan played a key structural role in American plans, and the European and Japanese recovery programs were of pivotal importance. American policy sought an alliance of industrial, capitalistic states with three poles: the United States as the center of Western Hemisphere production, Japan as the center of Asian production, and Europe as the center of European/African/Middle Eastern production. All else would flow from the structural relations among the three productive poles and between them and their peripheral areas. The "Atlantic alliance" depended on West Germany's cooperation and satisfaction with its global economic prospects, and the "Pacific alliance" relied on Japan's choosing to fulfill its economic ambitions within the American-dominated international capitalist bloc.

"Economic cooperation" marked American policy to cement the two alliances; the concept symbolized a series of grants and other measures to facilitate European and Japanese foreign trade recovery.

Thus, the Pacific and Atlantic alliances were intended to guarantee both the "balance of power" and a favorable global economic climate for American producers. The latent productive capacity of Germany and Japan could readily be converted into military capacity, since factories and skilled labor forces form the bases of military power. The United States sought at all costs to preserve its superiority over the Soviet bloc by retaining the loyalty of the two defeated enemies. Balance-of-power considerations were paramount; the loss of Germany and Japan to the Soviets would irrevocably tip the balance in the Soviet favor. Yet the key to retaining their loyalty was the success of the economic cooperation programs. Although it was also important for Japan's rulers to have American military support—against potential invaders but more important against the threat of internal social upheaval (especially the general strike of 1947)—nevertheless the global ambitions of the United States would live or die with the policy to satiate German and Japanese economic desires.

That the industrial-capitalist alliance had implications for the non-industrial, underdeveloped states as well forms the fourth key theme. To satisfy Europe and Japan, to end the dollar gap, and to restore the traditional world economic order required the United States to revive the system whereby Europe and Japan traded manufactured goods to Asia, Africa, and Latin America in return for vital food and raw materials. Because this system restored the economic relations of formal colonialism, without the burdens and counterproductive effects of formal colonial rule, it can best be termed "neocolonial." The industrial nations viewed colonial trade patterns as the "natural" form of international economic relations. Moreover, neocolonialism was essential to reduce the extreme dependence of Europe and Japan on American primary materials—a major cause of the dollar gap. But where the Europeans sought control of their traditional trade outlets in the Third World (or nonindustrial) nations, the United States sought to realize its longstanding goal of multilateral relations between the industrial and nonindustrial states. A relative latecomer to the business of colonialism, and benefiting from competitive advantages in an "open door" system, the United States had long sought to crack open the European empires and provide access for American corporations to primary producing areas. In the American scheme, Third World political independence would not affect traditional patterns of trade (now on a multilateral basis), and control over Third World economic policies by the International Monetary Fund (IMF) and World Bank would limit the new nations' choices about development strategies.

Finally, the fifth critical theme: the recovery plans formulated in 1947 and 1948 failed to provide reasonable assurance that the dollar gap would be ended by 1952—the date set for the congressionally mandated cutoff of foreign economic aid. This failure led Secretary of State Acheson and his aid, Paul Nitze, to replace "international Keynesian stimulation" of the world economy with "international military Keynesian stimulation of the world economy."

The fall of 1949 marked the low point in postwar policy for the United States. The confident and boastful attitudes of 1948 and early 1949 based on the "miraculous success" of the European Recovery Program and the defeat of European Communism changed to anxiety in top circles in late 1949. The dollar gap had proved stubbornly resistant to reviving foreign production; it seemed impossible to end it by 1952. Moreover, the economic vulnerability of the American bloc was aggravated by the stubborn and consistent growth of Communist ideology (especially in the Third World) in the face of the Truman Doctrine prohibition on such movements. Since military production and foreign military aid serve practically the same economic function as Keynesian domestic stimulation and foreign economic aid, massive foreign aid programs could continue past 1952 but only under a military heading. And, indeed, a military boom would quicken the economic pulse and ease the fierce competition in world markets that made conventional solutions to the dollar gap politically impractical in early 1950. The "new cold war" of the 1950s, marked by massive rearmament, thus provided the means to loosen congressional purse strings to continue the flow of dollars abroad. The new Mutual Security Program (MSP), born of the NSC 68 doctrine conceived by Acheson and Nitze in early 1950, served to cover the dollar gap through the extended transition period.

Fears of Communist gains and world economic collapse were two sides of the same coin. Socialist state trading practices, opposition to neocolonial economic relations, and influence over Third World development strategies, as well as fears on the part of foreign investors that their property might be confiscated or nationalized—all crippled the world recovery program. Likewise, the halting economic recovery fueled Communist propaganda about the obsolescence of capitalism and the ill effects of participating in the American-dominated capitalist bloc, and increased the likelihood of leftist revolts and electoral victories. Capitalist economic deterioration and Communist ideological strength were mutually reinforcing, and together they combined to form a far more deadly threat to American goals than a less likely Russian invasion of Western Europe or Japan. Congress and the public feared Communism and supported the Mutual Security Program; in official policy papers, however, the most sophisticated leaders primarily feared economic deterioration. To argue the primacy of either the Communist threat or the internal threat of economic deterioration, however, is to argue the primacy of the "chicken or the egg." Military alliances strengthened the economic alliances and erected armed shields for economic recovery. Strong military and police networks discourage internal revolt (even political radicalism) as effectively as they deter armed invasion.

The contradiction of the United States' fostering foreign export expansion while concurrently seeking to prolong and extend American market domination offers a key to understanding the evolution of international capitalist relations in the twentieth century. The United States and other capitalist industrial powers were both competitors and economic allies. Whereas some economic groups within each nation would lose from foreign competition, other groups, usually more powerful, would gain from profitable deals with foreign corporations. There was a recurrent tension between these competitive and cooperative strains within the capitalist bloc.

In one sense, the use of American state power to finance the American export surplus and to break down barriers to market penetration by American corporations in foreign nations affirmed the competitive strain—the domination of the world economy by one nation and its incessant need to expand. But without huge dollar grants to foreigners, giant American oil, manufacturing, mineral, and agricultural interests would lose foreign markets to soft-currency producers. Although foreign competitors could not compete with American producers after the war, the dollar gap could force the suspension of purchases from the United States, and the resulting vacuum could quickly be filled by enterprising foreigners. Thus the policy of economic cooperation (rebuilding the industrial allies to provide long-term equilibrium) reflected the mutual interests of the industrial nations—the supercartelization of the world economy. Huge banks and other corporations became bound by patent agreements, interlocking investments and financial consortiums, marketing agreements, and syndicates. National government finance ministers met often to discuss mutually beneficial means to ameliorate the distortions in world economic relations. And the Bretton Woods institutions (the IMF and the World Bank) formed a global umbrella controlling currencies, payments agreements, and investment. Moreover, the industrial states had a common interest in anti-Communism and in intensifying development of the Third World to spur primary production and to expand markets. The 1945–55 dollar gap era was dominated by economic cooperation: the world economy was so imbalanced that the United States was forced to subsidize its greatest rivals. However, as the dollar gap disappeared at the end of the 1950s, the competitive strains of capitalist rivalries emerged once again. The latent competitive strain explains why so many American interests feared German and Japanese revival (the memories of the economic wars of the 1930s had not died) and resisted foreign economic aid and the liberalization of American import policies.

The tension between the cooperative and competitive strains in American policy led to a fascinating factionalization within the American bureaucracy. The Economic Cooperation Administration (ECA), charged with overseeing the European Recovery Program (ERP), and the Department of Army, through its civil affairs division and its Occupation bureaucracy in Japan, formed the "foreign recovery bureaucracy." Traditionally, of course, Washington had represented nationalistic interests; the Commerce, State, and Treasury departments used export promotion and other policies to further American corporate interests against those of foreign competitors. The dollar-gap-created "foreign recovery bureaucracy," however, represented the economic interests of Europe and Japan in Washington deliberations. Their role was to end the dollar gap and usher in an era of multilateralism; only by promoting European and Japanese export expansion could they close the dollar gap and end the demeaning annual parade to Congress for foreign economic aid. In the transition period, these officials put foreign economic interests ahead of some immediate American interests, with long-term American interests, of course, constantly in mind. They attacked American protectionism, an embarrassment to the ECA and SCAP when the United States ran a massive trade surplus, and fought for subsidies for foreign interests. There existed, moreover, a divisiveness within the foreign recovery bureaucracy itself, between those representing Europe (ECA) and those representing Japan (SCAP and the Army). When SCAP supported "coordinated aid," in which the United States would subsidize Japanese exports to Southeast Asia to further Japanese penetration of this critical region, the ECA claimed that this violated the rights of European industries to bid competitively for the aid-generated markets. The tripolar cooperative/competitive system—between American, European, and Japanese interests—was thus re-created in microcosm within the Washington hierarchy.

The role of Japan, in contrast to that of Europe, has been woefully overlooked by historians. Japan formed the Asian equivalent of Germany—the "engine" or "spark plug" of European production and trade—and also the Asian equivalent of Europe as a whole, since Japan was the sole industrial center in East Asia. Further dramatic parallels existed between Japan and Germany: each was occupied by American troops and administrations; each was a defeated enemy with great latent potential for expansion from its industrial skills, energy, discipline, and genius; and each retained fierce national pride, only slightly tempered by defeat. The difference was that Germany was only the pivot of the larger ERP, while the Japanese recovery program formed the sole large-scale American effort in Asia. For strategic planners, the two countries formed the key to the balance of power; for economic planners, they formed the bases of world production and the strongest allies of multilateralism (Germany and Japan had no empires after the war and, like the United States, were able to compete effectively in multilateral world markets). If Germany and Japan failed to spark European and Asian recovery, the world economy would develop along more exclusive, self-sufficient, and nationalistic lines. Finally, for Occupation officials, the success of the occupations depended on voluntary German and Japanese adherence to American policy. The two occupied nations would not long tolerate the stifling of their economic power, and would resist American plans to tie them firmly to the American bloc if they felt that their economic interests required a more independent posture.

The American policy to integrate Third World, primary producing economies with the capitalist industrial economies dictated the pattern of postwar American intervention in South and Central America, the Caribbean, the Middle East, Africa, and, most noticeably, in Southeast Asia. The American intervention in Indochina in the 1950s reflected cold war anti-Communist ideology; more concretely, however, it reflected the perception that Southeast Asian markets and materials were needed by the capitalist bloc to expand and balance world trade. Japan, especially, required Southeast Asia as a trading area and this need was continuously recognized by the National Security Council, Dulles, SCAP, and the Joint Chiefs of Staff. At the low level of State Department desk officers and Saigon embassy officials, the story of intervention is one of intrigues with the French and Vietnamese officials the United States counted on to defeat the Communists. The highest levels of the Truman and Eisenhower administrations, however, saw Asian policy as a whole, and viewed a procapitalist Southeast Asia, specifically Indochina, as vital to preserve the Pacific alliance with Japan, which far outweighed the importance of any other nation in Asia. This work does not focus on the details of intervention, but demonstrates that Japan was the key to all Asian policy and that intervention in Southeast Asia was central to the success of policy in Japan. It will explain why the United States nurtured Japan's recovery after World War II and how American officials coped with the economic challenges to the task of cementing the "Pacific alliance." More generally, it will explore and analyze the dual American response to the dilemma of achieving multilateral goals in a badly unbalanced world economy. But since American cognizance of the "Communist threat" has been well documented, it will instead emphasize the threat of economic deterioration and its impact. Chapter 1 analyzes the global framework of American policy, particularly the ERP, NSC 68, and the MSP. Chapters 2 through 6 examine in detail the Japanese recovery program, especially the efforts to revive Japanese foreign trade. The global dollar gap was too pervasive, the parallels between European and Japanese structural problems and American solutions too dramatic, and the links between the ERP and the Japanese recovery program too developed to explain the Japanese policy without first presenting the global framework.

1. Multilateralism, the Dollar Gap, and Mutual Security

Senator Fulbright: Is it not true that a further reason which supports this program [Mutual Security] . . . is that unless we give some aid of this sort a very serious situation would be created with regard to the dollar balance in many of our friendly countries?

Secretary Dulles: Yes that is true; however, that is a subsidiary reason, and not a primary one.

Fulbright: That is right. It is not the primary reason, but it is an important subsidiary. Is it not true that since the last war somewhere in the neighborhood of $40 billion, $40–50 billion have been spent abroad in one form or another, loans or grants? That has had the effect—you have already mentioned it with regard to the Marshall Plan, which is a very clear case—but in many other cases in many other areas, has had the effect of enabling these countries to make purchases which were absolutely necessary for their survival; is that not true?

Dulles: It is.

Fulbright: So that this program, in addition to the primary purpose of defense and prevention of spread of communism, also has a very great effect upon our own economy in the sense that it gives the purchasing power to these countries to purchase many of our products, that is our raw materials and our manufactured articles; is that not true?

Dulles: It is.

Fulbright: There would have been a great contraction in our own economy had we not carried on the aid program that we have during the past ten years?

Dulles: I agree with you.

—Senate Foreign Relations Committee Hearing on the Mutual Security Act of 1955, May 1955

The Collapse of the World Economy

Postwar American foreign economic policy sought to create a successfully functioning and multilateral global economic system. Prosperity was also essential to the political cooperation among the capitalist states that was vital to American strategic policy. American leaders were haunted by the failure of the United States between the two world wars to stimulate world trade; indeed, America had raised its tariffs and exported its depression to Europe. The rise of protective nationalistic policies had led to global economic disintegration, from which world trade never recovered. World War II finally convinced American officials that a multilateral world economy, based on durable institutions to regulate trade imbalances and outlaw extreme protectionism, was necessary to prevent destructive nationalistic political conflicts. Prosperity was the requisite to peace. Economists had long argued that free trade was theoretically best for economic efficiency, but for the United States it was also a doctrine of convenience. For efficient U.S. corporations and farmers, the logic of free competition was inescapable; they could outproduce and undersell *all* foreign competitors. Moreover, they relied on foreign markets for profits from maximum production and efficiency. Their very supremacy was, paradoxically, the greatest obstacle to global economic equilibrium and multilateral trade.

Like the United States in 1945, nineteenth-century Britain had dominated the world economy and had run a large trade surplus. British bankers, however, had used investments, loans, and currency reserves to settle their trade imbalances and to sustain the capacity of foreigners to purchase British manufactures. They thus maintained conditions of free, or multilateral, trade. Because American policy was to achieve multilateralism, which had not functioned successfully since the nineteenth century, American economic planners in 1946 glorified the British liberal economic world order; it "afford[ed] the only promising basis, the only sound principles for a durable peace."[1] America's dilemma, however, was that it could not duplicate Britain's almost total control of world finances and strategic alignments. Britain ruled many areas directly through colonial administrations and controlled other areas through the gold standard and the power of the British navy. To re-create this system, the United States had to maximize its control over other nations' economic policies and to exert its military power.

The gold standard was the foundation of nineteenth-century multilateralism. The value of each currency in gold was determined by its trade balance—that value rose if the area exported more than it imported, and fell if it ran a trade deficit through surplus imports. If the value of the currency fell, the nation suffered a loss of purchasing power as foreign goods became more expensive. And when gold flowed out of the nation, the money supply declined and incomes and prices fell, again discouraging imports and encouraging exports. Currency devaluation was the classical deflationary remedy for payments imbalances, not government intervention to restrict imports, which would have violated free trade. The gold standard enforced deflation and austerity on deficit nations, causing their relative impoverishment while preserving unhindered access to world markets for British exporters. By 1900, however, Europeans had erected nationalist, protectionist barriers against imports in order to protect their wealth, markets, and jobs. As the hardships and violent fluctuations of the global economic cycle increased, and as labor parties increased their political power, protectionism grew more sophisticated; competing blocs formed and the resulting political conflicts helped lead to World War I.

Liberal economists and businessmen blamed nationalism, not the market system, for economic stagnation; they blamed the symptoms for the disease. The collapse of Wilsonian multilateralism after World War I revealed the failure of idealism, economic theory, and cooperative intentions to overcome depressed markets and fierce international industrial competition. Nationalism achieved new heights during the Depression.[2] The thrust of American policy after World

War II was to overcome nationalism by enforcing global economic integration, using international institutions to regulate market imbalances along multilateral lines.

Economic integration can vary in degree, from economic cooperation (negotiations over lower tariffs) to complete integration, or multilateralism. Two nations that trade heavily with each other have well-integrated, highly interdependent economies. In classic colonial trade, the sale of manufactured goods in the colony forces the colonial economy to depend on the advice, capital, technology, and spare parts of the metropolitan economy. In turn, the metropolitan economy depends on the colony for markets and food and raw materials. Classic colonial trade was bilateral; under multilateral trade, the unrestricted trade rights formerly available only to the metropolitan nation are enjoyed by all industrial nations. The United States sought to achieve maximum economic integration both among the industrial states (in order to allow unfettered trade in manufactures and access to European and Japanese agricultural markets) and between industrial and primary producing states (in order to revive the vital flow of food and raw materials to Europe, Japan, and the United States, and to increase the West's export markets). The very concept of "economic integration" was largely born and popularized with American officials and economists in the 1940s.[3]

International institutions to regulate trade practices—the International Monetary Fund and the International Bank for Reconstruction and Development (IBRD)—were established at the 1944 Bretton Woods conference. Lord Keynes, who best anticipated the depth of the impending economic crisis, sought a huge international stabilization fund with automatic withdrawal privileges. The United States Treasury Department, however, limited the size of the IMF and made withdrawal conditional on deflationary policies by the borrower. The IBRD and IMF proved inadequate to fund the massive disequilibrium in world trade caused by the American export surplus. The IMF would have been rapidly depleted in the 1940s. Thus, until 1955, it played little role in overcoming the dollar gap;[4] it could neither finance the imbalance nor use its power to force deflationary policies on borrowers—hence, the Marshall Plan was designed to assume these functions.

The United States historically had run a trade surplus with Europe and balanced it with raw material imports from European colonies. Europe earned the dollars sent to the colonies through exports to its dependencies and billions of dollars per year in profit from colonial investments. Europe, however, liquidated much of its investment to pay for the war and was thus forced to increase its exports to compensate for lost profits. Europe had paid for 70 percent of its prewar imports through exports; after the war, however, its exports paid for 90 percent of its imports.[5] The decline of colonialism destroyed the triangular trade system upon which the shaky prewar equilibrium rested. To further compound the structural problem, Europe, especially Germany, had formerly relied on Eastern European markets and primary products which were inaccessible after the war and their incorporation into the Soviet sphere of influence.

In short, Europe had to secure vast new export outlets to balance its postwar trade. The long-term structural disequilibrium was so severe (from 1939 to 1947, U.S. exports increased by $15 billion, while European exports fell by $2 billion) that classical deflationary remedies were hopelessly inadequate. Moreover, if severely enforced, these "remedies" might have plunged Europe more deeply into depression. Since the American demand for European goods was relatively price inelastic, devaluation and reduced prices would not sufficiently increase the American demand for European goods. Conversely, since European demand for American exports was also relatively price inelastic, increased prices of American goods would not curb the European demand for them. (The American economy was highly self-sufficient, and this self-sufficiency increased during World War II, when dollar-area sources of materials, including South America, substituted for Asian supplies.) Only a bold American initiative could hope to overcome the structural imbalance which prevented world trade recovery and harmonious political relations.

Indeed, it is useful to view postwar American foreign policy as shaped by the twenty-five-year economic crisis which began in 1930. Overproduction, insufficient demand, and nationalistic policies all stifled commerce. The war simultaneously created great productive capacity in the United States and a limitless reservoir of demand elsewhere. There were, however, no means for the purchasers to compensate the producer. From this problem sprang a plethora of artificial mechanisms to finance the purchase of American goods by foreigners. These mechanisms, which became increasingly sophisticated and bold, served multiple ends and preserved American market domination. The dollar gap was the expression of the contradicting economic forces after World War II and the most single important phenomenon in American foreign economic policy. Few noneconomists understood it at the time and not all historians have understood it subsequently.

Obstacles to Multilateralism

The large dollar gap made multilateral trade and payments impossible. The gap was $7.8 billion in 1946, $11.6 billion in 1947, and $6.9 billion in 1948. Indeed, had Europe not restricted dollar exports, the gap could have been much higher. Without import and exchange controls, European currencies would have collapsed and trade would have ceased. By 1947 the situation was grave. ECA administrator Paul Hoffman said that fifty years of economic nationalism had "reached the point of ultimate absurdity"; tariffs and controls had "finally almost completely fouled the lines of trade." Without American grants and loans, other nations would have to increase their controls, which would "tend to break the world into trading blocs."[6] American officials vowed to forestall such a disaster at all costs.

The size of the disequilibrium created economic conditions which favored either nationalism—that is, economic disintegration and emphasis on self-sufficiency—or socialism. The task facing the United States was to overcome existing economic conditions and create patterns of liberal economic integration. Since liberal integration was possible only if relative equilibrium existed, the United States sought to create equilibrium artificially through dollar grants until balanced commercial trade was realized. The State Department had to convince Congress and business that the United States should "take bold and cooperative steps to try to reverse the trend toward bilateralism and control, to help friendly nations back to their feet, and to start trading nations moving again in the direction of open multilateral international trade."[7] If patterns of multilateral trade and payments were not created, either planned, socialist integration (planned state-to-state trading) or disintegration (economic nationalism) would result, and multilateral goals would be shattered.

Without compensatory dollar grants, economic disintegration would freeze American products out of world markets: nations would have insufficient means to pay for them. The postwar world economy was divided into "soft" and "hard" currency areas. Soft-currency nations protected their currency by not allowing it to be converted into dollars. Thus, they were forced to trade primarily within the soft-currency area, not with the United States. Inconvertibility forced foreign buyers to limit their dollar imports, regardless of price or quality, in order to preserve the few dollars they received from the sales of goods and services to the United States for their essential imports. As the deputy assistant secretary of state for economic affairs, Paul Nitze, explained to American businessmen:

> Good markets are basic to sound trade. To be good markets, they must be accessible and they must be able to pay for the goods they receive. Goods can be disposed of by gift or barter deals, but neither provides what we could consider a sound market.
> Through the ERP, European countries are being helped to restore their production and hence their capacity as sound markets for each other, for us and for the rest of the world.

Business, he added, needed the "freedom, security and calculability of the conditions of doing business across national frontiers."[8] The latent psychological threat or restrictions tended to hinder world trade.

International economists understood the obstacles confronting multilateralism and equilibrium in 1945 and 1946. They knew that the United States had to grant dollars to Europe, because loans led only to a vicious cycle of repayment. They assumed that Congress, in gestures of enlightened self-interest, would lower tariffs and encourage imports as the soundest solution to the dollar gap. The Congress, however, operated on nationalistic principles, not international economic theory. A Canadian economist and a devout Keynesian, R. B. Bryce, was thus both naive and insightful when he urged Americans to pursue "true internationalism" by maintaining an import surplus and sending dollar aid abroad untied to purchases in the United States.[9] It was naive to believe that Congress would sacrifice marginal American industries for foreign interests, but insightful to realize the advantages of multilateral aid, which could finance an entire series of international transactions before the dollars finally returned to the United States to purchase American goods and services. American officials grew to appreciate the benefits of "coordinated aid"—using tied dollar grants to stimulate non-dollar trade—for overcoming the dollar gap. Indeed, such aid represented the most sophisticated mechanism in American foreign policy.

The State Department's task in solving the dollar gap was complicated by two problems. First, Congress had to appropriate the massive funds necessary to balance the dollar gap, and the lack of congressional and public understanding of the perplexing international economic crisis limited the department's ability to secure such funds. Large segments of Congress and the business community adhered to the classical economic doctrines of balanced budgets, low taxes, and primacy over foreign industrial rivals. Second, the threat of leftist ascension in economically weak and vulnerable Europe made it of utmost urgency to overcome congressional opposition to long-term foreign aid and budget deficits. The socialist/Communist threat to pro-American governments made the Administration unwilling to risk plunging Europe into depression by limiting dollar grants and relying on deflationary policies. Yet, ironically, the ubiquitous "Communist threat" ultimately enabled the State Department to overcome congressional economic orthodoxy by incorporating foreign economic aid into ever larger foreign military aid programs.

The rise of socialism and Communism as solutions to economic distress paralleled the rise of economic nationalism in the twentieth century. The Soviet Union posed a dual threat to multilateral goals. Its control over Eastern Europe imperiled Western European recovery, because the East was a traditional export market and a source of food and raw materials (for which Western Europe now had to turn to the dollar area). Soviet ideology and state trading practices, moreover, represented "sinister" influences on foreign nations, since they contradicted capitalistic multilateralism. In many nations, both industrial and nonindustrial, socialist and Communist parties threatened conservative rule. Global or local economic deterioration would greatly enhance their prospects.

The European Recovery Program

In 1947, European dependence on the dollar area increased, and gold and dollar reserves ran low. Bilateral restrictions proliferated, and stability and multilateralism seemed remote. The European Cooperation Committee (ECC) reported: "If the flow of goods from the American continent to Europe should cease, the results would be calamitous, [and] life in Europe would become increasingly unstable and uncertain; industries will grind to a gradual halt for lack of materials and fuel, and the food supply of Europe will begin to diminish and disappear." The dollar gap had quickly exhausted interim financing funded through the UNRRA (United Nations Relief and Rehabilitation Agency) and the 1946 British Loan.[10]

The Marshall Plan, or European Recovery Program (ERP), formed the American response to the dollar gap in 1947 and 1948. The ERP had four objectives: (1) to increase European production and investment through dollar grants; (2) to stabilize prices for export competitiveness and sound currencies, through American pressure for balanced budgets, reduced social expenditures, and lower wages to reduce domestic consumption and import demand; (3) to increase exports, the sine qua non of the ERP, in consequence of increased production, competitive pricing, and restricted domestic consumption; and (4) to develop nondollar sources of food and raw materials in European colonies. Only intensified colonial trade and development could substitute for European dependence on American primary materials. Of these objectives, only increased European production could easily be obtained. Europe was amply blessed with skilled labor and industrial infrastructure. Yet the dollar gap proved stubbornly resistant to increased European production.

A prime function of the ERP was to exert American control over European domestic economic policies in order to curb inflation. The United States imposed austerity policies on Europe, especially Germany. The ERP was also an investment program designed to finance European recovery through net additions to European resources. The United States used the mechanism of "counterpart funds" to control European investment patterns and limit European economic autonomy. Counterpart funds were created with the local currency proceeds from the sale of American-aid goods. Thus, few dollars changed hands internationally under the aid programs; the dollars went to American producers, and the goods were sold to the European public for lire, marks, or francs, which formed the counterpart funds.

Another vital function of the ERP was to help revive colonial trade patterns to provide nondollar sources of materials for Europe. Postwar European imports from nondollar areas were $3.5 billion less than prewar imports, owing to the loss of Eastern Europe and the decline of colonialism. The Organization of European Economic Cooperation (OEEC) reported:

> A rapid development of supplies in non-dollar areas is of vital importance not only for the primary producing countries themselves; it is also a necessary condition for a solution of Western Europe's dollar problem. It is essential if both the United States and Western Europe are to be provided with the basic products they need.[11]

Although the United States sought to gain equal advantages for American companies in European colonies, the dollar gap dictated that Europe revive its colonial trade to ease its dependence on American imports. Moreover, Europe's export competitiveness relied on cheap colonial raw materials. Paul Hoffman told the American Management Association that if Europe could not obtain non-dollar-area raw materials, it could not afford to purchase American manufactures.[12]

The decline of formal colonialism, however, unleashed powerful nationalistic forces in areas which had never experienced the nationalistic phase of development so indispensable to social, political, and economic maturity, strength, and independence. Colonies began to cherish independence from both their monocultural economies and unstable world markets for primary goods; they vowed to diversify their economies, to industrialize and gain control over their own economic fate. The United States, on the other hand, sought to retain the economic relations developed under colonialism, albeit on a multilateral basis and without the drawbacks of formal political control. Colonial areas would still sell primary products in exchange for manufactured goods in the world division of labor. The United States had sought multilateral development of the Third World since 1900, when it urged the cooperative development of China by the imperialist powers.

Europe required low-cost and plentiful raw materials to compete with American manufactures. Postwar industrial production increased much more than primary production, which increased the price of primary goods and limited their availability. To stimulate the development of colonial resources and trade, the ECA set up a colonial development division in March 1949 and created the Aid to Dependent Territories Program, which sent counterpart funds to colonies as investment capital. This "coordinated aid" helped cover the dollar gap when the aid dollars were transferred to Europe to pay for manufactured goods.[13]

One of the most perceptive advocates of innovative mechanisms to rebuild the world economy was Walter Salant, a brilliant foreign economic policy expert on the staff of the Council of Economic Advisors. As a Keynesian, Salant recognized the deep fundamental nature of Europe's need for extensive trade with primary producing areas. He recognized that high exports were vital to American prosperity and that only by reviving European colonial trade patterns and triggering a world trade boom could the United States "avoid a sharp contraction in United States exports . . . such as appears bound to occur," because "Europe will still have a substantial deficit with the United States for years after the ERP is scheduled to end." Salant connected the dollar gap and the colonial development problem, suggesting aiding the colonies to enable them to produce more for Europe and Japan and thereby increase their capacity to absorb European and Japanese exports. The White House shaped the idea into the famous Point IV in Truman's 1949 inaugural address. The State Department stressed the technical assistance rather than the more expensive capital investment aspect of Point IV aid, and formed the Technical Cooperation Administration to administer Third World aid. As with any large-scale economic transformation, years of investment and trade were required to create sufficient substitutes for American raw materials in the colonies. The ERP, however, had only three years remaining after July 1949. Colonial development was a long-term solution to a short-term problem.[14]

The 1949 Dollar Gap Crisis

Because the ERP sought mainly to revive productive capacity damaged by the war, it was doomed at its inception to fail in its primary goal of ending the dollar gap by 1952. Pessimistic European economic projections exposed the inadequacy of the ERP soon after it was implemented.

In December 1948 the OEEC figures showed that projected congressional aid would not enable Europe to achieve dollar balances by 1952. The OEEC reported that the 1953 dollar gap would be $1–$3 billion, to which the *Economist* added that it would "likely be nearer three billion." The OEEC "Interim Report" revealed that

> Western Europe cannot achieve a balance by 1952 on the basis of its present plans, its present standards of living, and on the existing conditions of world trade. If no further action is taken, the shock to the European economic system caused by the ending of foreign aid will bring such economic and social dislocation that political stability will be undermined. This means, of course, that the Marshall Plan, in the rather simple form originally conceived, cannot succeed within time originally set. . . . [The] malady is more obstinate and deep seated than was thought.[15]

Washington insiders realized that the ERP would not succeed by 1952. The *Marshall Plan Letter,* an organ to inform American business about ERP developments in Washington, reported in January 1949 that ECA officials were privately agreeing with the OEEC that there would be no end to aid in 1952, even though the form of the aid might shift: "More and more it becomes obvious that the ERP, *in one form or another* . . . is to become a *long-lived* device to aid in the omnipresent struggle for world peace . . . [and] to stave off business depressions. *Make no mistake about it* the Marshall Plan WILL continue beyond 1952." The projected dollar gap of $2.5 billion in 1952 "means a drastic cut in imports from the U.S. . . . an outlook that frightens American business." American officials could not accept or publicly acknowledge the fact that the plan would fail and boasted of the success of the Marshall Plan in defeating Communism. To conceal economic realities and maintain a positive attitude toward the ERP in Congress, the administration spokesmen became mere "boosters" for the ERP.[16]

In late 1948 the American economy slipped into a recession. The recession was significant not for heralding a postwar depression (since a postwar boom, domestic government subsidies and transfer payments, foreign aid, and military spending made a depression unlikely) but for creating a dramatic impact on the dollar gap. The small drop in GNP wiped out up to half the dollar exports of some European countries and revealed the structural self-sufficiency of the U.S. economy: "Now, in 1949," the *Economist* reported, "the underlying maladjustment between Europe and the United States is emerging like a reef hidden for a time under a spring tide." Foreign gold and dollar reserves plummeted. The United States forced a devaluation of the pound in September 1949, exhausting classical remedies. The *New York Times,* terming the crisis "Democracy's Economic Marne," warned that American exports to Britain would be cut by $250 million and that a world depression might ensue from downward-spiraling trade.[17]

Theoretically, the ERP could have financed the dollar gap until global economic equilibrium was restored by extending dollar grants indefinitely. The fatal obstacle in the plan, however, was the required annual congressional approval of foreign aid appropriations. Congress limited both the amount and the duration of aid; indeed, congressional obstruction of long-term dollar gap financing became one of the most significant influences in American foreign policy after World War II. The Truman Administration found itself with a far more serious dollar gap problem than it originally perceived, and could not convince Congress of the vital economic necessity for long-term foreign aid, and therefore rarely tried.

From the beginning, Congress had been misled about the function of foreign aid. Congress was told that the war had damaged European production and that, unless aid revived its production, Europe would turn to Communism, thereby imperiling American security. This was easier than explaining the structural problem of fundamental disequilibrium in the world economy. Indeed, Congress would have had to shed its inherent nationalism to accept that thesis. Acheson realized in 1947 that only by raising the spectre of Russian barbarians overrunning Western civilization could he get Congress to approve massive aid programs. Moreover, Congress was little disposed to finance industrial competitors with American tax dollars. Thus, after hailing the instant success of the Marshall Plan in defeating European Communism and raising production in 1948 and 1949, the Administration could not reveal that the problem was more complex and long-lasting and would require foreign aid for an indefinite period. As long as humanitarianism and immediate anti-Communism were served by aid, Congress would lend support, but international and domestic Keynesian stimulation contradicted all conventional economic wisdom and led many in Congress to fear massive deficits and rampaging inflation.[18]

A group of influential and conservative congressmen kept the Administration on the defensive. To gain ERP funds, the Administration had to pledge that aid would decrease each year and would not continue past 1952. Thus, Administration spokesmen praised the great progress made against the dollar gap and repeatedly affirmed the 1952 deadline, even after post-ERP aid had been planned. Fiscal conservatism and local-oriented economic nationalism made Congress highly skeptical of Keynesian deficit spending and massive international aid programs. Some believed that cold war expenditures would destroy the economy through inflation, that "victory by bankruptcy may be the Machiavellian aim of the Kremlin." Such skeptics were not awed by the high-powered businessmen who ran the ECA. When Paul Hoffman threatened to resign as ECA administrator if Congress did not approve the full amount of ERP aid in 1949, Senator Kenneth McKellar bluntly replied: "I think the sooner you would resign, the better it would be for America."[19] By 1950, Congress had tired of extensive foreign aid and was determined to make "Europeans stand on their own feet."

Arkansas Senator William Fulbright understood the OEEC report and saw through the superficial explanation of the dollar gap as a product of the war. He charged that the ERP would fail unless it cured the underlying structural disequilibrium. Paul Hoffman assured him that European economic integration would cure the gap by increasing the size and efficiency of European corporations so that they could compete with American corporations. He added that integration would prevent nations from applying separate, nationalistic solutions to exchange crises, and thereby preserve multilateralism. The ECA used the policy of European economic integration to provide Congress with a "solution" to the dollar gap. Congress, eager to compel aid recipients to toe the American line, sought to force unity on Europe to soothe its own anxieties that Europeans were not doing enough for themselves. Hoffman flattered congressional leaders by echoing their belief that only by insisting that all economic aid would end by 1952 would the Europeans unite to end the dollar gap. The reality was the opposite.[20] Europeans feared that the looming aid cuts would trigger currency crises and were more determined to resist integration and retain their right to save their national currencies by implementing protectionistic measures. The State Department realized that European integration, like colonial trade, was a long-term solution to a short-term problem; it would take years for European firms to grow as large as American companies and for Europe's tastes and buying habits to become standardized enough to support mass production.[21]

Other possible solutions to the dollar gap included American foreign investment and increased American imports. Foreign investment would be a painless, indeed profitable, way to solve the dollar gap. The catch was that if it were too profitable, and profit remittances exceeded new investments, it would actually aggravate the dollar gap. Business came to support the concept but did not invest overseas significantly until the mid-1950s, when the postwar domestic investment boom, fueled by military expenditures, finally slackened. The ECA campaigned for increased American imports in late 1949 in response to the fall dollar gap crisis. The ECA's Wayne C. Taylor issued a report on American imports and tariffs in October 1949. He warned that without imports, foreign investment, and ongoing aid programs the dollar gap "would damage our export industries and cause world trade to stagnate again," as in the dreaded 1930s. The Taylor report added that if tariff cuts did not increase American imports by $2 billion per year, American exports would "dwindle to a mere trickle." Even increasing imports was not a sure solution. Because of the state of "depressed equilibrium," an increase in imports would provide more dollars to the world and automatically increase exports,[22] leaving the dollar gap unchanged.

The OEEC succinctly described the equation of European export recovery. It noted that world trade had increased 5 percent since 1913, while world production had increased 46 percent; thus, bitter trade competition resulted: "If the size of the market remained the same as at present, Western Europe's share would have to rise from under two-fifths to over three-fifths; unless the nature of the demand is changed, this is most unlikely. If its share remained the same, the market would have to increase by two-thirds."[23] Conservative American economists, and the Congress, believed that the dollar gap was caused by the fact that Europe and the world were living beyond their means and encouraging inflation through government credit and spending. The British, however, disagreed. The *Economist* charged: "The problem of the dollar gap is now an essentially American problem. . . . If it expands its purchases or lends consistently, the major disequilibrium in world trade will vanish. Otherwise it will not."[24] The only alternative to continued aid or an economic boom was decreased trade.

According to the OEEC, "the solution of the dollar problem . . . calls for action extending far beyond the fields of responsibility of the OEEC countries themselves." European exports and colonial dollar-earning exports were

largely determined by the level of demand in the United States. If United States demand is strong, primary producers everywhere earn large amounts of dollars (which partly accrue indirectly to the OEEC countries) and there is an expanding market for participating countries' products; if United States demand weakens, the primary producers' dollar earnings rapidly fall away, and it becomes impossible to develop sales of quality products. The same forces work on invisibles. The sort of expansion of dollar earnings which the OEEC countries contemplate is inconceivable in conditions of declining business activity in the United States.[25]

Postwar, Keynesian economic theory suggests that disequilibrium in world payments is cured by expanding the economies of surplus countries to encourage their imports, rather than by deflating deficit economies to curb their imports. Deflationary policies can lead to downward spirals of trade and to depression, while stimulation of surplus nations can lead to upward spirals of trade that can absorb the increased exports required by deficit nations.[26] The year 1950 was the critical one for putting this theory into practice.

World anticipation of an American depression (or lack of sustained American growth) posed serious political and propaganda problems for the State Department. Psychology formed a powerful weapon in the cold war. If foreigners doubted the ability or willingness of the United States to stimulate its economy (especially since the Russians encouraged such doubts), the psychological gains the ERP had made against Communism would be canceled. Indeed, such doubts were justified, because fiscal restraint, not boldness, characterized the Administration and Congress in 1949. Congress had already gutted the Employment Act of 1946, which was designed to put a floor under American and world economic activity.[27]

The pro-Keynesian forces in the Administration faced the considerable challenge of overcoming the natural inertia in economic thinking that bolstered the conventional economic wisdom. Truman himself came from a noncosmopolitan background and shared the key economic tenets of his generation. He was anxious about postwar budget deficits. He told the National Security Council in July 1949 that foreign expenditures were too high, that domestic programs had been deferred long enough. He ordered them to review all programs, while the Budget Bureau was required to establish "tentative fiscal limits" for foreign expenditures. He assured his chairman of the Council of Economic Advisors, Edwin Nourse, that he would curb spending increases by "preventing the large prospective rise in the military area." Nourse, an influential fiscal conservative, stood in the way of a Keynesian takeover of economic ideology on the council. His solution to recession was to tell businessmen to "solve it with [your] wits": the government would step in only if necessary. He later recalled, "If the Korean War had not intervened at that time we would have had to face that possibility." Nourse said deficit spending would hurt business confidence in the long run, despite short-run stimulation of the economy. He insisted that if it became necessary to spend the nation out of recession, then funds would be best spent on domestic welfare rather than on arms production. Truman determined the military budget by subtracting all other programs from revenues and allotting the balance to the military. His $13.5 billion defense ceiling in 1950 was backed by the National Security Council, the

Budget Bureau, the White House staff, and Defense Secretary Louis Johnson. Nourse, however, resigned because of Keynesian Council of Economic Advisors member Leon Keyserling's growing influence in the White House through Clark Clifford, which opened the door for more expansive policies.[28]

The Threat to American Prosperity

The 1949 dollar gap crisis, congressional determination to limit and terminate foreign aid, and Administration opposition to large budget deficits, combined to threaten the future of American exports. The dream of multilateralism might be replaced by the American nightmare of the development of a strong soft-currency bloc to exclude American exports from world markets. Truman warned in his midyear economic report in July 1949: "If a severe shrinkage in the flow of dollars abroad occurred, it would not only reduce our exports now, but would also force other countries to try to save dollars by making discriminatory trading arrangements that would adversely affect the long run future of our foreign trade." Willard Thorp warned that pressures for nationalistic policies would grow on both sides of the Atlantic now that the "honeymoon period" of the ERP was over and the struggle for markets was on. Even the American-sponsored integration of European economies would threaten American exports. Paul Hoffman explained that it "creates the danger that a soft currency area insulated from dollar competition will thereby be created in which discrimination against the dollar would tend to be self-perpetuating." Indeed this permanent ostracizing of American goods was a goal of nationalists in Britain. The staff of the American embassy in London warned in August that the British and European desire to slash dollar imports as a means of survival would "hurt important and influential sectors of American agriculture and industry," especially cotton, tobacco, and oil. The problem was so severe that American officials had to abandon full-scale multilateralism as a short-term goal. Acheson advised Ambassador to Britain Lewis Douglass that the United States would accept discrimination against American products only if austerity and devaluation were implemented in Europe. He advised that such acceptance of discrimination would last only for the length of the "emergency situation" in the "transitional period" predating multilateral relations.[29]

Concurrent with its fear over the crisis in Europe and its effect on American freedom to export, Congress became alarmed about the effect of the termination of the ERP on American agricultural exports. Agricultural interests sought to increase aid to facilitate the removal of agricultural surpluses. This contradicted the interests of manufacturers whose exports would be reduced to the extent that foreigners remained dependent on American agricultural products. Similarly, agricultural producers would gain if Europe purchased fewer manufactured goods and saved its dollars for food. Nathan Koenig, assistant to Agriculture Secretary Anderson, raised the issue in June 1949, warning that a severe agricultural crisis would occur with the inevitable drop in agricultural exports. Pressure mounted in Congress for a bipartisan commission to plan ways of guaranteeing a minimum level of agricultural exports. White House staff officials agreed, but recognized that Congress would impose protectionist solutions like the Peril Point Clause in the Reciprocal Trade and Tariffs Act of 1949. The White House staff recommended instead a plan to subsidize American industries hurt by increased American imports and sell the policy to the public via a committee of distinguished businessmen and men of affairs such as the Harriman Committee on the ERP.[30]

The State Department recognized by late 1949 that the ERP would not succeed by 1952. On November 23, Thorp told the ECA in Paris that an increase in imports and falling exports were inevitable because of the dollar gap. Thorp's Division of Economic Affairs estimated on December 6 that American imports would remain at the $7.1 billion level in 1953, the same figure as in 1948. American exports, running at $12.5 billion, could be cut by $3.7 billion at most, and this meant losing $2.4 billion in markets in Europe and Latin America alone. The remaining dollar gap in 1953 would thus be between $1.7 and $2.3 billion for essential goods that foreigners could find no substitutes for outside the dollar area. The study concluded that American agricultural exports would remain high because foreign demand would be relatively inelastic. Thus, "the impact of this diversion will be primarily on U.S. durable goods industries." The agricultural sector too, however, would suffer lost markets of "considerable magnitude." Hoffman advised Acheson at a December 8 meeting that the dollar gap problem was now of "great urgency." Thorp presented his position to the under secretaries' meeting on the 12th, but met with opposition from the Policy Planning staff. Thorp contended that the only solution was to give up markets, lower tariffs, and continue to enforce traditional remedies in Europe, such as devaluation. The Policy Planning staff argued that a reduction in aid would reduce European dependence on the American economy, allow Europe to become dependent on the Soviet bloc for vital imports, and rend the Atlantic alliance. Thus, the Policy Planning staff concluded, "unconventional" methods of dealing with the dollar gap (i.e., continued foreign aid) had to be employed.[31]

The White House staff was also critical of the conventional approach of Thorp's office. George Elsey, a thirty-year-old presidential advisor, wrote that increasing imports had implications for domestic producers that required the approval of many agencies other than the State Department. Moreover, it was in the United States' interest to maintain the highest possible level of exports, especially agricultural exports. He agreed with the basic theme of the Policy Planning staff: if the flow of aid dollars were halted, the resulting instability abroad would present political problems for the United States that would reach "crisis magnitude," and would "wreck" multilateral goals "in a very short time." If conventional approaches were unacceptable for strategic and domestic economic reasons, what policy would work? Elsey was critical of Thorp's office for not exploring public foreign investment under the Point IV program to aid underdeveloped nations as an alternative to currently rumored plans for post-ERP foreign aid.[32]

On January 26, the State Department finished its draft of a dollar gap memo for the president for Acheson's review. It said that the end of the ERP in 1952 would endanger United States security, as well as the economy:

> But we now know, without much doubt, that in the absence of a
> vigorous alternative program developed in advance, stoppage
> of the ERP in 1952 is likely to precipitate economic problems at
> home and abroad which may approach crisis proportions. United
> States exports, including the key commodities on which our most

efficient agricultural and manufacturing industries are heavily dependent, would be sharply reduced, with repercussions on our domestic economy. European countries and friendly areas in the Far East would be deprived of basic necessities which we now supply, to an extent that would threaten their political stability.

It said further that if Europe and the world lacked the dollars to buy a high level of American exports, this might "weaken, and perhaps jeopardize, the efforts we are making . . . to promote the political strength and economic well-being of the free world"; a "successful economic system among the free nations" was vital to U.S. national security: "It is important we face the future now. We cannot delay until the end of the ERP period. As ERP grants are diminished, the new pattern will take shape."[33]

The fear of a "new pattern" of trade was significant. If the world sought nondollar sources of vital goods, in the East or through alternative sources in the West, the United States would find it difficult to regain its accustomed markets and exert the accustomed degree of influence over its allies. The suggested remedies for the dollar gap would all antagonize Congress. Increased imports would require sacrifices on the part of particular economic groups in the United States. Thus, any solution "will be a major undertaking of the United States Government and will undoubtedly involve legislative and administrative problems of the greatest difficulty."[34]

The State Department discussed three means of organizing the Administration's attack on the dollar gap. It rejected the National Security Council as a forum for the new policy because "public and congressional and foreign reaction . . . might be quite unfavorable, with criticism centering on what would be regarded as another move to envelop domestic and foreign policy in an atmosphere of military security." It also rejected the NAC (National Advisory Council on International Financial and Monetary Affairs) because of its narrow financial scope. The State Department recommended presidential assistant Sidney Souers to coordinate a group under Acheson's leadership.[35]

The next day Acheson revised the memo to reflect his view that the economic crisis was a critical factor in the strategic review of

American policy being undertaken in January, which resulted in NSC 68:

> The economic strength of the free nations of the world, and their hope for economic progress, are among the strongest forces that can be brought to bear against Soviet Communist aggression. Our present economic policies are designed in the long run to build this strength and provide this hope. Existing plans are inadequate to meet the needs of the present situation . . . the political consequence will be a substantial shift of power from the democratic to the Soviet sphere. This possibility gives real urgency to the problem of the dollar gap.[36]

There followed a period of discussion between Acheson, Truman, Treasury Secretary John Snyder, and other officials before the formal presentation of a third draft of the memo to the president on February 16. The State Department warned Truman that imports would have to increase and that some mechanism of transferring dollars abroad had to be found to replace foreign economic aid, which itself would have to continue past 1952. An aid cut would enhance the bargaining position of the Soviet Union with weak European economies and thus imperil American security. Foreign investment would not cover the gap, because it was limited and itself tended to increase capital goods exports, decreasing the net dollar flow abroad.[37]

Truman appointed his aides George Elsey, Charles Murphy, and John R. Steelman to coordinate the dollar gap effort in the White House. The Administration considered W. Averell Harriman and Will Clayton to head a public committee, but ultimately settled the dispute with Acheson by selecting Gordon Gray, former secretary of the Army, a New York lawyer and scion of the R. J. Reynolds Tobacco Company, to prepare the public for the unpleasant antidotes to the trade crisis. Gray made up a list of standard topics such as tariffs and foreign investment for the executive agencies to consider. The State Department, meanwhile, having been denied an interdepartmental forum from which to control policy, established the Departmental Dollar Gap Working Group to coordinate department studies on the gap for Gray's consideration. The lack of action on the problem on Gray's part disappointed State. Gray explained to Thorp on April 10 that he had not yet considered the problems of his task and was waiting to see what opposition arose to the program. The White House staff, on the other hand, complained that Gray was being upstaged by Hoffman's and others' public statements on the problem.[38]

The Administration greatly feared drawing public attention to the problem until they had designed a strategy to overcome American economic nationalism in the name of national security. When New Mexico Senator Clinton Anderson presented a bill for a commission on foreign trade it alarmed the White House staff and the State Department, each of which brought pressure on Truman and Gray to announce the appointment of a public advisory board under Gray's control to "take the wind out of the sails of the unsound Anderson proposal" and "allow Mr. Gray and the Department of State to make a more positive reply to the numerous letters of inquiry which they are receiving on the dollar gap problem."[39]

In March the State Department looked to imports to bear the brunt of the trade adjustment in 1953. Thorp's office planned to continue foreign aid of $1 billion in 1953, increase imports by $3.2 billion, increase net foreign investment by $300 million, and increase purchases of foreign gold by one-half billion. With a $400 million decrease in exports, these adjustments would offset the decrease of $4.1 billion in foreign economic aid. Salant advised Thorp that by setting his priority on maintaining exports, he had overlooked the benefits of foreign aid to European prosperity and the political problems which would ensue were aid to be cut. Salant criticized the policy of increasing imports to maintain exports, noting that such a dramatic increase in imports was no more feasible than an equally dramatic increase in foreign investment, and that increasing imports would negate the benefits to American producers of maintaining a high level of exports by reducing domestic markets for American products.[40]

The State Department concentrated on increasing imports rather than on decreasing exports because export cuts would seriously hurt sensitive industries like agriculture, while an increase in imports would hurt many more producers to a much lesser degree, thereby minimizing political damage. Salant argued, however, that Europe, which re-

ceived the bulk of foreign aid, but which would have the most difficulty in earning dollars through increased sales to the dollar area (most
of the increased imports would be in the form of raw materials), would
no longer be able to absorb the vast quantities of agricultural products
it received under the ERP. Thus, agricultural producers would still be
hurt despite the overall high level of exports. Salant argued for expanded public foreign investment as a more sound method of resolv-
ing the problem.[41]

In April the State Department lowered its target for imports in 1953
by 10 percent. Salant advised the Council of Economic Advisors and
Thorp that with the domestic economic expansion planned by the newly
Keynesian Council of Economic Advisors, such an import target could
be met without "creating protectionists and general isolationists in the
effort to attain it." Thus, the State Department should let the sleeping
dogs of American economic nationalism lie, by deemphasizing increased imports and shifting "its main effort toward stronger support
for the attainment of maximum employment on foreign policy grounds,
relating it both to general foreign policy (our leadership position and
Russian expectations of collapse here) and to imports." According to
Salant, a general expansion of the U.S. market was "a far more sale-
able article than an expansion of the U.S. market for foreign products" of a kind which would displace American production. Salant
advised Thorp that maximum employment was critical to American
foreign policy because foreigners looked to American economic growth
to solve their own economic problems: "If we cannot maintain maximum employment, any assistance that we do continue to give to other
countries . . . is subject to the charge of ulterior motives. This charge
was in fact made abroad—and believed—to an astonishing degree even
in 1948, much more so now . . . [and] is associated with hostility and
distrust of the U.S." A U.S. economic boom would disappoint the
Russians and strengthen American foreign policy. One of the solutions being considered was trade adjustment assistance to industries
hurt by increased imports, a policy that became significant two decades later. Salant told Thorp to "drop entirely the idea that there will
be any special need for protecting industry and labor against injury
from increasing imports." Such a policy would "concentrate people's
attention on the danger of such injury," which would damage efforts
to reduce tariffs.[42]

George Elsey distributed Salant's memo to the rest of the White House staff and to Gray, calling it "the most important single document relating to the foreign economic policy I have seen in the past six weeks." Elsey advised the staff that the Administration now "should drop entirely the idea that there will be any special need for protecting industry and labor against injury from increasing imports" and avoid "alarmist cries about imports."[43]

Salant also criticized the shortsighted view of the ECA toward underdeveloped countries. Like the State Department, the ECA counted heavily on Europe's earning dollars through a trade surplus with the Third World to trim the dollar gap by 1952. The ECA viewed the primary producers merely as sources of nondollar production and dollar earnings for Europe. Salant advised Gray, however, that underdeveloped countries were equally part of the global problem and indeed were more vulnerable to Communism and thus deserved special attention, not neglect. He warned that the ECA and European policy of forcing underdeveloped countries to forego industrialization in order to provide more exports for Europe would hinder their economic development, reduce the long-term availability of nondollar supplies for Europe, and threaten American foreign policy goals of stability.[44]

Salant's concern for development in the Third World meshed neatly with his Keynesian and radical approach to the dollar gap. He believed that private foreign investment was a necessary but limited solution, but he placed great emphasis on public foreign investment. He envisioned Point IV's growing to replace the ERP and truly solving the dollar gap. Much like planners in Japan, Salant sought to link the excess capacity and idle labor in Europe and Japan with the need for manufactures in developing areas as interrelated problems.[45]

Paul Hoffman had to tread a fine line before Congress in early 1950 because of the rumors of secret planning swirling around Washington. On the one hand he contended that the ECA would end on schedule. On the other he said that in special situations the State Department might desire aid after the ERP had ended. When Nebraska Senator Kenneth Wherry asked about the reports on post-ERP aid planning, Hoffman denied them. In February he emphasized that the United States would have to forego exports to solve the puzzle in 1952, but by June he emphasized that continued aid was vital to subsidize American exports and that ending aid "would destroy our chances to rebuild in Europe a customer of American goods."[46]

The Strategic Crisis: NSC 68

While he was ultimately concerned with the balance of power, Dean Acheson knew that the primary strategic threat to American interests was not military. He concluded in late 1949: "The most immediate risks facing the security of the free world and ultimately of the United States are in the ideological, economic, and political aspects of the cold war." He based American strategy very clearly on the premise that the Russians would not attack; he believed that their plan was to wait for the international economy to collapse, plunging Europe into chaos. They would then have only to "pick up the pieces."[47] Acheson believed that economic strength and social-political stability were the best means to control the Communist threat. American policy, of course, had been based on rebuilding European economic strength since the war. But the 1949 dollar gap crisis, and the strength of European neutrality, convinced Acheson that massive rearmament was necessary to crystallize European anti-Communism and ensure investors that revolution would not threaten their property.[48] Soviet and European socialist strength combined with Western economic fragility required aggressive American policies in late 1949 and early 1950. Acheson sought to bring the economic might of Europe, America, and Japan into full play in the cold war.

Acheson and his associate Paul Nitze represented the brilliance and boldness of the cosmopolitan foreign policy elite. Acheson was a leading international corporate lawyer and a devout Wilsonian multilateralist. He admired nineteenth-century British imperialism, and he thought, a biographer noted, that the "British managed their world role with great responsibleness. Acheson perceived the willingness of the British to transfer great amounts of their capital overseas as the root of England's greatness and the basis for a prolonged era of world peace and stability." He blamed nationalism for the breakdown of capitalism in the twentieth century and attacked British Imperial Preferences by writing Article VII into the wartime Lend Lease agreement. He helped create the Bretton Woods institutions and there battled Keynes, who enlightened Acheson about the depth of the impending economic imbalance. Using the Russian domination of Eastern Europe to arouse Congress to pass the ERP, he realized that public and congressional fears mitigated their stubborn support for low taxes and normalcy. He exploited the cold war as a vehicle to overcome fiscal conservatism—although he knew that "if the Soviet Union had not existed, the problem would still have been there."[49]

Paul Nitze was an ideal associate for Acheson. A brilliant success on Wall Street, vice-president of Dillon Read, he moved to the State Department after serving on the Board of Economic Warfare during the war. He worked on international trade and economic affairs before replacing the less economically astute George Kennan as head of the Policy Planning staff in 1949. He had analyzed European import needs in 1947 and wrote the ERP legislation for Congress. He also recognized early that military aid could cover the dollar gap: "If the portion of assistance so linked is made available in dollars rather than military aid items," he reported in January 1949, Europe could produce weapons and cover the dollar gap at the same time.[50] No two men were better suited to solve the puzzle created by the dollar gap, the congressional limitations on aid, and the need to militarize the vulnerable Western political framework.

Acheson "welcomed" the Russian atomic detonation of late 1949, because it enabled him to prompt an Administration review of strategic policy, which he expanded to encompass all foreign policy. With Nitze, he decided that full-scale rearmament, including a $50 billion defense budget, was needed to overcome Communist ideology and Western economic vulnerability. They planned to "bludgeon the mass mind of government" with a frightening portrayal of the Communist threat, in order to overcome public, business, and congressional desires for peace, low taxes, and "sound" fiscal policies. The task was formidable. There was complacency about any Russian threat: the Budget Bureau, the White House staff, the secretary of defense, the president, and Acheson's own Russian experts opposed such massive escalation of the cold war. When Kennan explained that Russian policy was essentially defensive, the secretary termed the argument "sterile" and removed him.[51]

Knowing that his policy would not survive if taken through normal channels, Acheson set Nitze to work secretly through the National Security Council together with a Defense Department official on the foreign policy review mandated by Truman in January 1950. The military requested an $18 billion budget and expected less; when Secretary Johnson, who was wedded to a $15 billion defense budget ceiling, finally saw the new plans, he blew up at Acheson's audacious ideas and methods. Truman read the document in April and buried it until after the fall elections, in the hopes that it might then be possible to broach it to the public. Premature leakage would expose the Democrats to charges of extreme fiscal irresponsibility.[52]

NSC 68 revolved around three themes: moral abhorrence of the Soviet Union, the threat of potential Soviet military might, and the political/economic vulnerability of the West. The rambling and lengthy sections on Soviet "slavery" served to horrify and galvanize top officials. Acheson relied on starkness and hyperbole to create fear. The Budget Bureau commented that the freedom and slavery dichotomy was simplistic, very poor, and a travesty on the word "freedom." The bureau criticized the analysis of American problems as being a result of Communism as simplistic: "The gravest error of NSC 68 is that it vastly underplays the role of economic and social change as a factor in the underlying conflict." The threat was not primarily military, but rather that "today many peoples are striving actively to better themselves economically and politically and have thus accepted or are in danger of accepting the Communist movement." This critique strikes at the heart of our understanding of the NSC 68 ideology and subsequent American foreign policy. Third World nationalism and socialism threatened the goal of integrating the primary producing areas and industrial Europe and Japan and thus threatened multilateral goals and the capitalist bloc itself. Acheson knew also that internal "subversion" formed the greatest threat, but couched his argument in terms of Soviet aggression as a tactic to make Americans unhesitatingly support his efforts to militarize the cold war.[53]

NSC 68 used carefully phrased calculations to show that the Soviet Union could challenge the American military by 1954, if it ap-

plied its entire economy to arms production. Willard Thorp, however, charged that the case for a Russian military advantage was
"clearly not proven. . . . In fact all the evidence in the report points
the other way, that the actual gap is widening in our favor." Psychological, social, and economic trends, however, posed a legitimate
threat to American security and multilateral goals. The "gravest dangers" were Allied doubts about American capacity and willingness
to intervene militarily, as well as about the recovery of world trade
if the United States economy slipped into a recession. Thorp commented: "I feel we cannot emphasize enough the disaster which an
economic depression would be. This could destroy the entire structure even though we might weather the storm ourselves. . . . This is
not only the hope of the Kremlin but the fear of our friends." Robert
Lovett, temporarily back on Wall Street between top Administration
posts, advised that rearmament would help stimulate the economy.
And when a senator asked Acheson whether the Soviet plan was to
force the United States into bankruptcy through deficit spending, the
secretary replied that Russia viewed arms production as a safety valve,
not a burden, for capitalism.[54]

The failure of the ERP laid the foundation for NSC 68. "The political, economic, and military situation of the free world is already
unsatisfactory and will become less favorable unless we act to reverse present trends," the document warned. The economic problem
in 1950, identical to that facing the United States in 1947, posed a
threat to American political power:

> There are grounds for predicting that the United States and other
> free nations will within a period of a few years at most experience
> a decline in economic activity of serious proportions unless more
> positive governmental programs are developed than are now
> available. In short, as we look into the future, the programs now
> planned will not meet the requirements of the free nations . . .
> the present foreign economic policies and programs of the United
> States will not produce a solution to the problem of international
> economic equilibrium, notably the problem of the dollar gap,
> and will not create an economic base conducive to political sta-
> bility in many important free countries . . . perhaps most impor-
> tant, there are indications of a let-down of U.S. efforts under the

pressure of the domestic budget situation, and disillusion resulting from results of our assistance programs.[55]

Washington insider James Reston best explained Acheson's cataclysmic view of the world in the critical spring of 1950. Acheson's goal, he reported, was to make permanent the temporary, stopgap programs of military expansion and foreign aid developed in the 1940s, to "provide machinery to replace the ERP in the middle of 1952." According to Reston, Acheson's anxiety was fed by European fears of a depression and an end to American aid.[56] The crux of the problem, Reston continued, was integrating Germany with the West; Germany would not accept an inferior commercial and military status, and France would not accept Germany. The much-acclaimed policy of European integration as a solution to both the dollar gap and German problems had failed. Reston concluded that Acheson was frustrated by the limits imposed by the White House, the Allies, the Pentagon, and, of course, Congress on his actions to solve these problems with boldness. He wanted matters "tidied up" at home and abroad to increase the speed "with which he can deploy the power of the United States. . . . The official line now is that the Soviet Union is not merely an annoyance but a pestilence."[57]

Acheson sought both to establish permanent institutions to replace the fading ECA and to arm all anti-Communist nations against revolutionary change. By subsuming economic vulnerability and economic aid within a single strategic/military program, he successfully simplified complex economic problems into issues of patriotism and the cold war. He channeled the United States away from economic nationalism toward military nationalism, negating at a stroke the unfavorable competitive implications of helping the Allies rebuild.

While the link between the dollar gap crisis and the military escalation of the cold war remained largely implicit, one man waged a relentless campaign to use American military expansion to cure the dollar gap. Tracy S. Voorhees had discovered the remarkable benefits of expending military funds abroad for the dollar gap while serving as under secretary of the Army in 1949. As a Republican, Voorhees was an outsider in the Truman Administration. Responsible for convincing Congress that large-scale aid to Japan was needed, Voorhees sought to show increasing progress against Japan's dollar gap to warrant congressional enthusiasm for Japanese aid. When Japanese instead of American contractors were used to build military facilities in Okinawa, Japan received the dollar value of the project for its treasury and thus could survive with that much less direct economic aid. The intricacies of military aid and the dollar gap are fully developed below in my examination of Japan. In the spring of 1950, Voorhees also sought to convince the Administration to give Europe dollars to arm themselves and thus contain Communism and finance the export surplus simultaneously.[58]

Voorhees was an enthusiastic cold warrior. Indeed, he was a founder of the ultramilitaristic Committee on the Present Danger in 1951. He merged this warrior adventurism with an understanding that the ERP would fail to cure the dollar gap. Europe could not rearm with the relatively modest $1.2 billion MDAP (Mutual Defense Assistance Program) or through its own insufficient budgetary revenues. Voorhees boldly called for merging the ECA and the MDAP and using counterpart funds to finance European production of arms: "Increased military production would also assist in sustaining the Western European economy by providing a market which it needs."[59] He said that the NSC 68 plans "could furnish a dollar market for Europe through its production of defensive weapons." As much military material as possible should be made by the Europeans: "Since these nations would probably be otherwise unable to earn the dollars they need to purchase our wheat, cotton and tobacco, we can make one dollar do almost the work of two." Voorhees proposed that all aid be under one program on a global basis to assure that as few of the aid dollars as possible were spent in the United States. This idea represented the antithesis of tied aid; indeed, Voorhees was suggesting that the aid be tied to *non-American* producers rather than American producers.[60]

Voorhees claimed that his proposal was approved by Gordon Gray and Defense Secretary Johnson and, orally, by Truman. Paul Hoffman, however, strongly resisted any military role for the ECA and, according to Voorhees, temporarily blocked the program. Voorhees said he discussed the situation with Hoffman, who told him that ECA funding was supported by many groups "which did not believe in war, and he felt that the public was not prepared for the tying up of economic and military assistance." When congressmen asked

Hoffman why Europe could not produce arms with counterpart funds, he replied that there had to be a "rigid separation" between military and economic programs.[61]

Soon after Gordon Gray was appointed by Truman, he told Voorhees that Truman had read Voorhees's proposal "very carefully and thought it was a good idea . . . and wanted this aspect considered as one of the possible courses of action in the study of the dollar gap problem." The Bureau of the Budget, closely representing the views of the White House staff, also encouraged Gray to consider using military aid to close the gap. Stating that the goal was to "win the cold war by non-military means," the bureau advised Gray that foreign economic policy had to serve strategic goals and that without aid foreign nations "would become dangerously vulnerable to Communist pressure." Reflecting the influence of both Salant and Voorhees, the bureau said that the net addition to European resources was the key, not the balance of trade as emphasized by the ECA and the State Department's office of economic affairs. It urged Gray to consider how foreign aid could be used for help to Europe and at the same time "for security purposes (e.g., military aid, ideological warfare, U.S. defense establishment)." Finally, the bureau urged "thoroughgoing coordination between our military and economic aid programs," especially using the MDAP to produce material in Europe.[62]

The concept of "offshore procurement" of military material, the basic theme of Voorhees, and mentioned by Nitze in January 1949, was incorporated into the first year of the MDAP. The Administration proposed spending $155 million of the $1 billion MDAP for "arms production abroad," using the funds as ERP-style balance of payments aid in order to save taxpayers' dollars. The Administration argued that Europe had requested arms production to employ its idle industrial capacity.[63]

Voorhees's proposals and other similar ideas circulating that spring gained some public recognition. A British economic intelligence report said in April that U.S. domestic expansion was the key to increasing U.S. imports and that the boom could be sustained by using the "almost limitless" cold war military demands. American officials on both sides of the Atlantic had been suggesting "for some weeks" prior to the Korean War that Europe should receive its dollar aid in the form of military orders.[64] The stage was set for the Korean War and the transformation of American aid policies.

International Military Keynesianism: The Korean War and the Dollar Gap

Until North Korean forces crossed the border on June 25, 1950, the Administration had little to show for its concerted nine-month campaign to militarize the cold war and put the ERP on a semipermanent footing. By confirming the desperate forebodings of NSC 68 and Acheson's anticipation of a Soviet provocation, the attack facilitated the implementation of the new policy. The United States would find its global power eroding unless it assumed a more aggressive posture and backed it up with dollars and weapons. Acheson led the move to intervene in Korea over military doubts and, with the realization of NSC 68 rearmament goals assured, commented that it was the greatest four weeks in American history. With Congress more concerned with international assertiveness than fiscal conservatism, Acheson had attained the power to militarily stem the tide of Communism and militant nationalism.[65] The war not only freed American policy from fiscal and military constraints, but also had a profoundly positive effect on the creation of a multilateral world economy.

Korean intervention spurred a flood of congressional appropriations to rearm Europe and the United States and to finance the French reconquest of Indochina. Moreover, it touched off a massive speculative buying boom by business, transforming the world buyer's market to a seller's market and helping Japan and Europe sell their surplus production. The American economic boom, sparked by military spending, created the great demand for imports, especially primary materials from European dependencies, that the OEEC had long hoped for. During the boom, American imports from Europe and its colonies increased by $1.4 billion while exports fell by $3.2 billion, temporarily bringing trade into balance.[66]

The boom brought windfall profits to raw materials producers because military demand drove primary commodity prices up as much as 150 percent. This spurred triangular trade and so increased the dollar earnings of the sterling area that ERP aid to Britain was temporarily eliminated in 1951. The most significant beneficiaries of the boom, however, were Germany and Japan. These two strategic linchpins in American foreign economic policy had the only significant unused industrial capacity to fill orders and seize expanding markets, while Britain and France were turning productive facilities to rearmament. The Korean boom more than compensated for the American recession of 1949; world gold and dollar reserves increased by $5 billion from July 1950 to July 1951. *Business Week* asked, however, "Is the dollar gap bound to reappear when the military emergency ends and more normal world trading conditions resume?"[67]

The Korean War marked the beginning of the end of the twenty-five-year economic crisis of stagnation, economic nationalism, and war, which had stricken the West in 1929 and which ended with the global trade boom after 1954. The Korean War boom and the flood of congressional defense and foreign aid appropriations assured that the dollar gap would no longer threaten the very survival of the American-led capitalist bloc. Gordon Gray's November report to the president optimistically called for reduced foreign aid. When the war broke out, Gray had still planned to attempt to convince labor and business groups to help solve the dollar gap by relaxing protectionist pressure on Congress. By mid-July, however, Gray and his staff realized that war-related spending would channel dollars to primary producers, thus spurring the triangular trade boom needed to solve the gap. Following the concept agreed upon prior to Korea, the Gray Committee planned to integrate military and economic aid in a post-ERP program to finance the dollar gap. The two main themes of the report, foreign military aid and increased Third World production, reflected the influence of NSC 68, Voorhees, and Walter Salant. In July, Salant proposed a $750 million aid package for primary producers, not tied to purchases in the United States, and $4 billion in Export-Import Bank credits. He argued insightfully that the short-term drawbacks of Third World development on American producers were outweighed by the long-term markets which would follow.[68]

Salant quickly understood the crux of the problem created by the Korean situation. On the one hand there existed a fixed amount of industrial capacity in North America, Europe, and Japan. On the other hand, the West faced booming demand, both from the primary producing areas, flush with skyrocketing proceeds from their exports, and from rearmament itself. A generation of leaders now returned to the economic mentality of World War II, as fear of depression and trade collapse once again gave way to fear of inflation, industrial bottlenecks, and overstrained industries. Salant posed the key question: how would the industrial nations divide the combined spoils/burden of booming demand? Would the United States arm the world itself and leave Third World markets to Europe and Japan, or would it subcontract its weapons production to Europe and Japan and share in the growth of commercial markets?[69] Either road was a sure solution for the dollar gap: American focus on arms would greatly stimulate triangular trade and reestablish the prewar basis of equilibrium; giving dollar-earning arms contracts to Europe and Japan would directly subsidize the dollar gap. Ultimately, the United States both subcontracted weapons manufacture abroad and shifted its own industry to defense production.

Under the pressure of wartime fiscal policies, the debate between Keynesian expansionists and more conservative elements assumed new fervor. With Korean spending, the Keynesian Council of Economic Advisors now had only to defend the bold existing economic expansion based on military spending instead of pleading in vain for minor government stimulation. Leon Keyserling explained the key tenet of Keynesianism to the Economic Joint Committee in January 1951: If "a very high level of defense outlays becomes fixed over a period of years, then the dynamic character of the American economy is such that in the long run it will build up to meet the additional strain." Supported by fellow Keynesian cold warriors like the Americans for Democratic Action, Keyserling urged Congress to unleash the productive capacity of the American economy against the Soviet Union. Though largely oblivious to the conventional economic wisdom, Keyserling still shared conservative fears of overly large deficits and inflation.[70]

Fiscal conservatives, like the First National City Bank, still stood by classical liberal economic theory. Declaring the military budget "untouchable," First National City called for eliminating expenditures for social welfare, health, security, education, general research, housing, and community development. These "paternalistic" programs were "havens of a growing rash of socialistic enterprises."[71]

In April 1951 the war boom subsided and demand slackened. The testing time of military Keynesianism had arrived. The floor under the economy that the liberal Keynesians had supported in the form of the Full Employment Act of 1946 was now in place in the form of huge war spending. The *Magazine of Wall Street* reported that there was "no question that the prospect of peace is altering the thinking of economists, businessmen, and investors . . . the cease fire came at the wrong time. . . . On the other hand, the very high continued rate of arms production will greatly tend to support the economy." It added that arms spending had become "the most important dynamic element of spending in the economy." The Korean War, however, despite its overwhelmingly positive effects, was not a panacea for Europe; the demand for primary products still outstripped the supply, and the consequent inflation hurt Europe worse than the United States. In 1951 the dollar gap reappeared and necessitated continued economic aid. The "hard core" dollar gap, caused by Europe's continuing dependence on American goods, would persist until Europe could compete with the United States and raw materials production increased.[72] Thus, although the Korean War helped Europe, it had not solved the underlying structural disequilibrium— the ERP in its original form remained doomed.

The State Department well learned the lessons of manipulating Congress during the ERP struggles and the subsequent huge military appropriations following Korea. Department thinking on continuing dollar gap aid programs within a larger military aid package was set by November 1950: "Congress is more likely to be sympathetic to a program based upon military security than one in which part of the justification is based on continued economic recovery." Through early 1951 the Administration debated the merits of a single-umbrella foreign aid program. The Gray, Rockefeller, and Brookings reports supported the combined military and economic aid strategy. In April Acheson called for repealing the termination date of the ERP because the program had to continue. Acheson and new ECA head William Foster agreed in June that pressuring the House Foreign Affairs Committee to prolong the ERP was, however, "the surest way of bringing the Committee to the decision to end it." Indeed, congressional critics of foreign economic aid remained determined to see the ERP expire on schedule in mid-1952. The military's increasing share of the budget left little room for foreign economic aid in the minds of fiscal conservatives.[73]

By combining military and economic aid in a single program, the Administration could put the onus of the appropriation on "defense" spending, while the benefits of foreign economic aid would continue apace. The simplest, if least frank, way of defusing the anti-foreign-economic-aid and anti-ERP sentiment in Congress was to declare the ERP a success and to rename foreign economic aid as "defense support" under the newly formed Mutual Security Agency, which embodied the concept of the integration of military and economic aid. There was, indeed, confusion within the Administration about the dollar gap, with some mistakenly believing that the problem was over in mid-1951. The Gray Report had been overoptimistic, both because Gray's staff had been aware of the beneficial effects of an economic boom on the dollar gap prior to the Korean War, and because the Administration came to realize that confronting protectionists with the necessity of increasing imports would only stiffen their resistance. The emergency of early 1950 had been greatly eased by the Korean boom and the loosening of congressional military purse strings. Administration spokesmen like Harriman and Richard Bissell told Congress of the "miracle" of the ERP, a success "far ahead of what was projected." They argued that European production had so increased by 1950 that exports could conceivably pay for Europe's imports, were it not for the "burden" of rearmament which absorbed plant and labor otherwise available to produce exports. And indeed, rearmament proved a significant burden for Great Britain, which mounted the largest effort with the least ability to afford it, and to a lesser extent for France. Overall, however, the boom was highly beneficial; Germany and Italy profited greatly from the business the arms boom provided to their idle plants and labor.[74]

To thoroughly explore the impact of rearmament on Europe and the global dollar gap would require a detailed economic investigation beyond the scope of this work. The debate would hinge, however, on Keynesianism. Keynes's significant contribution to economic theory was to disprove Say's law, that supply creates its own demand. Keynes maintained that demand created its own supply. Europe lacked sufficient dollar markets without rearmament to balance its dollar trade in spite of increased production. Indeed, European production had "recovered" to only depression levels and had leveled off after 1948. The full realization of military Keynesian demand stimulation on an international scale would come with the offshore procurement program launched in 1952. The initial Mutual Security Agency (MSA) legislation, from an economic standpoint, was limited to continuing economic aid in a package palatable to Congress.[75]

Despite Administration claims that the Marshall Plan was a past success rather than a present and future drain on the treasury and taxpayer, congressional skeptics saw only prolonged foreign economic aid. When Congress passed the Mutual Security Act, the ECA became a semipermanent institution. The *New York Times* reported that "the only difference between the ECA and the MSA is a new letterhead." The ECA's hierarchy, led by Richard Bissell, remained intact in the new agency. Texas Senator Tom Connally, head of the Foreign Relations Committee, said of the Marshall Plan: "Instead of completing it we are just adopting the device of saying we have to give them all this economic aid to help the effort of defense." New Jersey Senator Alexander Smith advised the Administration and his colleagues that "since we are going to use 'defense support' in place of the old economic and Marshall Plan type of thing, we had better use the words 'defense support,' which we can defend on the floor better than when somebody says here you have got the word 'economic' in it." To exploit the military/economic confusion even further, the Administration requested authority to transfer 10 percent of the funds between the economic and military aid programs, and routinely shifted 10 percent to the economic side to help cover the dollar gap.[76] Indeed, the Europeans complained in 1951 about the predominance of military over economic aid, and the MSA transferred $500 million. Moreover, Fulbright turned congressional opposition to economic aid under the Mutual Security Program on its head, by requesting the Administration to send more economic aid and fewer manufactured goods to Europe. He argued that the United States had to finance its agricultural exports with economic aid to prevent Europe from turning to the Soviets for trade.[77]

Some Administration spokesmen were frank about the continuing dollar gap, and the attempt to portray the ERP as a success did not fool everyone. Harold Stassen said that dollar aid subsidized American exports and helped multilateralism: "The defense support assistance most correctly reflects what might be called the follow through from the original Marshall Plan." And the Detroit Chamber of Commerce complained: "In spite of attempts by the Administration to convince people to the contrary, the Marshall Plan, or ECA has merely been continued under a new name. . . . We cannot escape the fact that the ERP has failed to accomplish most of the objectives set forth when the Marshall Plan was first conceived." Indeed, they noted, despite massive dollar transfers, the gap was so wide that European tariffs were 35 percent higher than in 1948. And the United States Chamber of Commerce charged that Bretton Woods, the British Loan, and the Marshall Plan had all been hailed as solutions, but actually had "fallen far short of expectations" and "failed to dent the balance of payments problems of Europe."[78]

The United States finally solved the dollar gap problem through the mechanism of "offshore procurement," or the purchase of military goods in dollars from Europe. Offshore procurement represented the ultimate integration of military and economic aid and the logical Keynesian mechanism to stimulate foreign economies with congressional funds. First discussed prior to the Korean War, and supported most vociferously by Voorhees, the concept was a frequent topic throughout 1951. Ludwig Erhard, the German foreign minister, appealed to Acheson in July for military orders to increase production and employment in Germany's underutilized industrial plants. General William Draper launched the program in Italy in March 1952. He explained to Congress that offshore procurement "gives work and it does help the dollar situation of these countries." By June 1953, the United States placed $2.2 billion in orders, primarily in France, Britain, Italy, and Belgium. The Administration advised Congress that in addition to providing foreign supply bases for military action, the orders lessened the need for "defense support" economic aid. Offshore procurement head Tracy Voorhees told Congress that the program had strengthened the military positions and, "as a valuable byproduct, the economic positions of Europe. . . . The OSP program has been one of the principal factors in reducing the need for economic grant aid to the European nations." He explained that American employment was also stimulated by off-shore procurement, since dollars sent abroad were "homing pigeons" which returned to buy American goods.[79]

The Failure of the ERP

Again in 1953, as in 1947 and 1950, the United States faced a dollar gap crisis. Although the gap seemed permanent, military expenditures and economic aid were scheduled to decline in 1956. The gap stood at $2.6 billion in 1953. Through the 1950s the export surplus of the United States totaled $24 billion, which was more than offset by over $20 billion in economic aid and $20 billion in military expenditures abroad.

The failure of the ERP was best explained by the United Nations' Economic Commission for Europe in 1953. The report brilliantly reached the heart of the problem, stating that the ERP was misnamed from the beginning; the problem of Europe was not "recovery" but *structural readjustment*. The United States had delayed structural readjustment by maintaining its tariffs, its markets, and its productive supremacy through foreign aid programs. The report said that military expansion had an overwhelmingly beneficial effect on Europe and Third World raw materials producers; still, nondollar raw materials production fell $1.7 billion short of original estimates. Only by 1953 were the profound structural problems of Europe visible. As a result of the American military boom, exports exceeded all targets, yet the dollar gap still existed.[80]

In 1953 the Commission on Foreign Economic Policy, headed by the chairman of the board of Inland Steel, Clarence Randall, reported that if the United States did not increase its imports in light of future reductions in military expenditures, "we would face the alternatives of continued or increased discrimination against our goods and/or continued large or increased economic aid to the rest of the world."[81] The large American military expenditures more than compensated for the dollar gap and created large gold and dollar reserves in Europe. Despite these reserves, which should have allowed currency convertibility, Europeans maintained strict controls on dollar purchases; they feared the depth of the commercial disequilibrium.

The Randall Commission launched the third phase of postwar American foreign economic policy. The first phase—economic aid—lasted from 1945 to 1950; the second phase—military expenditures and economic aid—lasted from 1950 to 1954; the third phase—imports, military expenditures, and economic aid—lasted from 1955 to 1960. The final phase attempted to sell increased imports to the public with the phrase "Trade not Aid," which was coined by British Chancellor of the Exchequer R. A. Butler to make Americans open their markets. The Randall Commission warned that if corrective measures were not taken in the two years of "breathing space" afforded by long-term military contracts, "continued or intensified restrictions against American goods" would set back integration and have "serious and divisive implications for the western Community."[82]

A State Department intelligence report criticized the Randall report for treating military expenditures as economically identical to economic aid. The State Department report argued that offshore procurement orders were instead identical to American imports. Actually, military expenditures provided the benefits of both aid and imports. The State Department report claimed that if Europe did not provide military goods and services to the United States, it would have more productive resources available to provide exports to balance trade. The problem in 1953, as in 1950, however, was not productive capacity, but markets, especially dollar markets, which military expenditures guaranteed. "The problem would not be one of overall shortages," the Randall Commission reported, "such as characterized the early postwar years—but rather one of preserving domestic employment and economic activity, and of expanding sales to the dollar area to make up for the loss of income from military sales."[83]

By 1954, economists were perplexed by the dollar gap. They were unsure of how to correct it and whether or not it was permanent. They agreed, however, that continued American economic growth and dollar transfers abroad were necessary until the transition period ended. The Administration feared that the dollar gap would force a cut in world trade and American exports, or that an American recession would occur, which would "gravely weaken" the Western economy. Eisenhower vowed to maintain economic activity through

government spending: "The fear in America . . . is the fear of deflation—of going down, not up. . . . Don't let's get tagged like Mr.
Hoover did." The Administration created the Advisory Board on
Economic Growth and Stability to ensure sustained growth. Dulles
advised, moreover, that the United States had to use offshore procurement "to give some kind of economic aid" in order to avoid
forcing allies into the Soviet bloc, and to "counter-balance other
factors related to world trade in this time of crisis." Finally, Dulles
continued the Truman Administration's policy of shifting rearmament to a sustained, long-term program to put a floor under economic activity.[84]

The Randall Commission's fears proved unfounded. Beginning in
1956, American private foreign investment increased dramatically.
Military and economic expenditures abroad, moreover, did not decrease, but actually increased, as the American military network expanded and aid to underdeveloped countries increased. By 1958,
European and Japanese industry had narrowed the technology gap.
In addition, both foreign and American consumers shifted their tastes
from dollar goods to nondollar goods, particularly automobiles.[85]
Finally, the American payments deficit of $20 billion in the 1960s
increased foreign gold and dollar reserves by that amount, creating
the conditions for multilateralism which led to the Kennedy round
of GATT tariff cuts.

By 1960 the dollar gap had become a dollar glut, forcing the Kennedy Administration to appeal to Europeans to increase their contri-
butions to defense efforts in order to ease the burden on the United
States. It was no longer economically "appropriate" for the United
States to transfer dollars abroad. Military expenditures were now out
of control, however, and increased throughout the 1960s. Military
spending led to the decline in the value of the dollar as foreign reserves skyrocketed. Between 1955 and 1960 the dollars provided by
military expenditures ceased to be compensatory and became exogenous, or economically unnecessary. American priorities, indeed,
were reversed. Military needs took precedence, as the colonial world
was shaken by anti-Western liberation movements. To finance its
military adventures in the 1960s, the United States ran a huge deficit
with Europe and Japan, which inevitably led to devaluation of the
dollar.[86] The United States printed dollars to finance its payments

deficit, thus bloating foreign reserves and making Japan and Europe pay part of the cost of the Vietnam War.

The postwar transition period proved to last approximately fourteen years, twice as long as the Marshall Plan had envisaged. American transfers of dollars preserved the hope of multilateralism, supported the American economy and American overseas markets, and stimulated the recovery of European and Asian industrial allies. The strategic-economic goals of rebuilding Germany and Japan were spectacularly successful. German and Japanese shares of world production increased 5 percent and 2.5 percent, respectively, during the 1950s, and their shares of world exports increased by 5 percent and 2 percent, respectively. These gains came at the expense of Great Britain and the United States, whose shares of production fell 2 percent and 3 percent, respectively, while their shares of exports fell 4 percent each. These shifts in economic power boded a shift in the balance of political power within the Western bloc. Former State Department economist Charles Kindleberger, a founder of the ERP, concluded that military expenditures were "originally justified on balance of payments grounds," because "it was appropriate for [the United States] to have a tendency to overspend relative to the rest of the world in military and economic defense."[87]

While this chapter has only sketched the outlines of the evolution of American policy from the Marshall Plan to the mutual security system, it has I hope provided an adequate framework for understanding why the United States devoted great efforts to Japanese recovery. Multilateralism required equilibrium, which in turn required nondollar centers of production. American markets were at stake if Japan could not buy American goods, and, at a higher level of policy, Japan's failure again to dominate the Asian economy would push it to accommodation with the Soviet bloc, regardless of who ruled Japan. When we have examined Japanese trade recovery, we will be able to understand better the role of austerity, economic aid, and military expenditures in the recovery of Europe and the solution to the world dollar gap.

2. The Japanese Recovery Program, 1947–1950

In the long run a sound economic program for Japan for which adequate Congressional support can be maintained is equally if not more important to the security of the United States than the presence of United States forces in Japan, because of its bearing upon a continuing pro-Western orientation of the Japanese in times of considerable economic stress and in a situation where their strong trade ties with Communist China are likely to exert a counter influence.

—Willard Thorp, September 27, 1949

[Japanese Communism is] essentially a conspiracy from within and whether it succeeds or not depends primarily on the political, economic, and social health of Japan itself. It is these problems that are foremost in the thinking of the State Department in planning United States policy toward Japan for the present—and for the foreseeable future.

—Department of State Comment on NSC 49,
September 30, 1949

Three stages marked American Occupation policy in Japan from 1945 to 1950. From 1945 to 1947 the United States sought to destroy Japan's reactionary political, social, cultural, and economic institutions in order to limit the power of the bureaucratic elites and industrial monopolies over the Japanese public. International opinion, moreover, insisted that Japan's victims be awarded extensive reparations, and that Japanese production of strategic materials be limited. In 1947 and 1948, Americans in Washington and Tokyo hammered out a new policy to revive the economy and reestablish the economic and political elites in order to restore Japanese and Asian political and economic stability. Finally, in 1949 and early 1950, the Occupation enforced a harsh austerity program designed to strip already inadequate Japanese public consumption to minimum subsistence levels in order to promote exports and discourage imports.

By the eve of the Korean War, however, the austerity program had kept the fragile economy at levels of production inadequate to support the modernization required to make Japanese industry competitive. Indeed, the entire fabric of Asian policy was jeopardized by the failure of Occupation policy to promote the sound revival of Japanese industry. The United States faced its single greatest foreign economic policy challenge when Japan's trade-dependent economy failed to prosper in the deteriorated Asian economy in the late 1940s.

Reforming Imperial Japan

From 1945 to 1947, American Occupation policy in Japan shifted dramatically—from reforming an enemy to rebuilding an ally. In 1945 American officials vowed to eradicate the sources of militarism and thus to create a peaceful and democratic Japanese society. War bitterness and Japan's undemocratic ruling institutions made reform policies imperative, but fears of Japanese industrial competition and New Deal reform idealism also motivated American efforts to remold Japan. Washington had cogently studied the roots of Japanese aggression and concluded that the Zaibatsu monopolies and the militaristic culture had to be destroyed to prevent future aggression. The harshly repressive, semifeudalistic Japanese society was, of course, firmly in the grip of the Zaibatsu family industrial and financial monopolies. The Occupation, therefore, wrote an American-style constitution, freed labor to organize, granted civil liberties, purged advocates of militarism, and launched land reform and a far-reaching antimonopoly effort. Moreover, Japan's massive war production facilities were slated to be sent as reparations to the Asian nations overrun by Japan, both to ensure that they developed industry to prevent Japanese domination and to prevent renewed Japanese military production. With Japan's imperialistic aggression and oppressive social order fresh in mind, few doubted that Japanese bureaucrats and monopolies deserved severe punishment.

Within three years, however, the United States gutted the program for the deconcentration of economic power, restricted labor, canceled reparations, and planned to rearm Japan. This "reverse course" in Occupation policy has been attributed to the hardening of cold war tensions and the success of the Chinese revolution.[1] American officials, of course, opposed Japanese Communists and were forced to abandon hopes of an alliance with China. Global economic deterioration, however, also made Japanese revival and conservative "stability" crucial to solving the Asian and global dollar gaps. As Europe under the ERP was to provide nondollar sources of production to help balance world trade, so Japan's production was to key the revival of Asian trade.

War-induced American bitterness toward Japan was also countered by forces which tended to bind Japanese and American élites. American policymakers, bankers, and industrialists had long viewed Japan as the most advanced nation and the most reliable ally in a continent of underdevelopment and instability. Throughout the twentieth century, American business was divided about which nation, China or Japan, should be helped to ascendancy in Asia. Those with ties to Japanese industries or loans to Japan naturally opposed those seeking to compete with Japanese manufacturers in the Chinese market. Strong corporate and financial ties between Japanese and American capitalism survived the war and flourished under the subsequent alliance with Japan. The former ambassador to Japan, Joseph Grew, and his counsellor, Eugene Dooman, represented the prewar "Japan crowd" in Washington in 1945 and convinced the Administration to preserve the emperor's role to enhance social stability. Thus, in addition to cold war tensions and Japan's strategic importance, the strong prewar ties between Japan and the United States and the global dollar gap dictated the reverse course and the revival of Japanese trade and industry. At stake, ultimately, was the stability of the international economy and American access to large Asian markets and sources of raw materials. In 1946 and 1947, officials seeking to destroy the old Japanese order bowed to those who increasingly sought to preserve it. By 1948, in fact, very few officials still opposed the reverse course. Indeed, the reform era in the Occupation was the aberration in American Asian policy in the twentieth century. Although postwar reform policies had deep roots in the anti-Japanese sentiments of American officials and citizens with strong ties to Japan's enemy, China, it was the reverse course that more closely represented traditional American policy. As war bitterness ebbed, fears of economic crisis, social instability, and Asian Communism grew.

In 1945, the economic affairs division of the State Department anticipated that Japanese trade revival would help ward off an Asian and world depression. The United States' long search for multilateral trading conditions, handed down from Cordell Hull to Will Clayton, led foreign economic planners to view Japan as the key to reviving Asian trade and as an important market for American goods. State Department officials Dean Acheson and Edward Mason, two key architects of foreign economic policy, both doubted in 1945 whether the reform policies were compatible with recovery. They posed a critical question: Would or would not the United States be responsible for Japan's trade recovery? The consensus in 1945 was that Japan could trade peacefully, but should receive no American help and should have "living standards no higher than in neighboring countries."[2] The challenges of creating a functioning international economy to preserve political stability and American prosperity, however, soon eclipsed objections to helping Japan. Foreign economic policy concerns about Japan grew in tandem with strategic fears.

Initial international and American policies clearly mandated that Japan's old order be destroyed and no assistance offered to Japan's economy. The Potsdam declaration prohibited abetting Japanese recovery, and the United States Foreign Economic Administration advised that Japan should be kept from reintegrating with Asian raw-materials-producing regions to prevent future war-making capacity. The Foreign Economic Administration staff considered establishing a Western consortium to run processing industries at the source of the raw materials, or, alternatively, prohibiting Japanese business operations abroad. In September 1945, the State-War-Navy Coordinating Committee, the interdepartmental policymaking body for the Occupation, concluded that the United States would not assume responsibility for Japan's economic recovery, although the Japanese were free to recover through their own efforts. SCAP was to grant aid only to prevent "disease and unrest." The basic post-surrender directive to SCAP in 1945 listed three occupational objectives: eliminate all war industries, reduce Japan's ability to create and support arms, and establish a peaceful and democratic economy.[3]

Growing fears of an international economic crisis soon led businessmen and officials who were tied to global interests to support Japan in opposition to elites who were tied primarily to domestic interests and who feared Japanese resurgence. John F. McCloy, a Wall Street banker and later overseer of German recovery, reported to the Administration in November 1945 that profound economic dislocations—and the anarchy and economic deterioration which favored social revolution—were global and not merely European problems.[4] Edwin Pauley, however, an independent California oil baron, did not reflect Wall Street fears of international financial panic, but represented more popular views about exacting retribution from Germany and Japan and preventing their hasty revival.

Truman awarded Pauley, the leading fund raiser for the Democratic party, with an appointment as his advisor on reparations. Pauley began in Germany, where he sympathized with recovery but opposed reviving German heavy industry as the foundation for rebuilding Europe. After Herbert Hoover criticized Pauley's reluctance to help restore Germany, Pauley warned Truman that German heavy equipment exports would have to be sold on credit, which would eventually put Europe in debt to the Germans. This "would restore Germany to the same dominant position of industrial power which it held before the war," which, he feared, the Germans would use to establish political domination of Europe.[5]

Pauley applied the same thinking to Japan in November 1945. His aides, including longtime China hand Owen Lattimore (later persecuted by Senator McCarthy), proposed a daring plan to achieve a better-balanced Asian economy and to prevent future Japanese economic domination. The mission's views accurately reflected those of the Allies and other Asians, but contradicted all subsequent American policy to revive the Japanese "workshop." In light of the consequences of the rejection of Southeast Asian industrialization and the subsequent massive program to subsidize Japan's industrial domination of Asia, the Pauley report was a brilliant and perceptive example of political economy. But because it was out of step with the multilateralists who controlled American policy, it was also an impractical, naive, and doomed effort to atone for Japan's aggression. The plan expressed a legitimate concern for Asian economic imbalance, but from a historical perspective it was naive because of the "realities" of America's position as guarantor of world capitalist "stability."[6] Pauley and his staff represented a minority view of American interests, which was totally eclipsed by the cold war and the growing international economic crisis.

The Pauley staff recommended removing surplus Japanese plants as war reparations for other Asian nations, which, it claimed, would "improve the economic balance and contribute to the political stability of eastern Asia as a whole. Militaristic Japanese economic planning deliberately held back the normal industrial development of adjacent areas in Asia." Japan monopolized the processing of raw materials: "As long as the advantage lay in Japanese hands, neighboring peoples were unable to resist aggressive Japanese economic penetration": they were left with "too little industrial strength." Through industrial development, however, Asians would "trade with Japan on an equal footing, to resist Japanese control." Japan would no longer be able to control the "economic life of neighboring countries by acting as the key industrial consumer of their raw materials." The staff envisioned a Japan with living standards no higher than those of her war victims, with adequate trade, but with restricted heavy industries—especially steel, "a powerful weapon for the domination of Asia." Japan could export products (toys, cement, handicrafts, and porcelain) made from indigenous materials to reduce dependence on large imports and balance trade, and could import processed pig iron instead of raw iron ore and coking coal. Finally, they proposed limiting Japanese machine tool production to prevent giving the "Japanese an undue technological ascendancy and a dangerous ability to control the industrial and economic life of neighboring peoples."[7]

In September 1946, SCAP suggested that Pauley's restrictions might hurt the Japanese trade balance and would deny Asians Japanese consumer goods.[8] Pauley answered that, without offering credit, Japan would not export to Asia anyway. When SCAP charged that balancing Asian industry was utopian and might cause an economic vacuum, Pauley replied: "We can allow filling of this vacuum by restoring the subsidized industrial economy of Japan or by the more difficult, but more permanent relief obtainable by encouraging in all Asia industries able to live in a competitive world." For each ton of Japanese steel produced, four tons of imports were required, Pauley charged, and such inefficiency would require subsidies to make Japanese industry competitive.[9]

Reappraisal and Shifting Priorities (1946)

In 1946, Washington officials were not greatly concerned about the economic future of Japan, because of their short-sightedness about the impending dollar gap crisis and the priority they gave to European affairs. American officials in Japan, however, recognized the implications for American policy of Japan's extreme structural dependence on industry and trade. Robert Fearey, a young former protégé of Grew, wrote an important memo in April 1946 which crystallized doubts about where reform would lead. He warned Secretary of State James Byrnes that the American challenge in Japan was not demilitarization but "future Japanese economic conditions," and that allowing reforms to emasculate the corporations and cripple conservative politicians would strengthen the socialists. Harsh reforms might turn Japan toward the Soviets: "Persistently unsatisfactory economic conditions, depriving Japan of the living standards to which it believed its industry and skill entitled it, would be the likeliest cause of such a change." Even Japanese capitalists, "if impelled by acute economic distress or national insecurity," might reject the Occupation and American influence. To prevent Russia from exploiting Japanese antagonism to such harsh reforms, he advised moderating the purge of militarists and modifying the reform programs, promoting Japanese recovery, and establishing a large American military presence in Asia to bolster the confidence of Japanese corporations and conservatives. He presciently noted that Japan's "success or failure in finding adequate foreign markets [would] be the principal determinant of its future economic viability . . . and its continued peaceful disposition."[10]

Fearey's memo accurately summarized the challenges facing American policy. The combination of the strong lure of the rich resources and markets of mainland Asia for Japan, and the priority given to national security and economic growth over capitalistic cultural values by Japanese businessmen, made the American-Japanese alliance a fragile one. Henceforth, American policy would cater to the whims of Japanese corporations and conservatives, including the suppression of both labor and the left, to prevent Japanese accommodation with Soviet Russia and, after 1948, Mao's China. Within a year of surrender, even as international bodies discussed the reform programs, American officials planned to restore the old Japanese order.

Old China hand George Atcheson, the State Department's political advisor (POLAD) to MacArthur, had to concur with Fearey's dire warnings about weakening Japan's ruling structure. The fervor with which the long-suppressed Japanese public embraced reform frightened Japan's rulers and Atcheson's office, and forced the China hands who were sent to reform Japan to adopt the Grew-Dooman line. John Emmerson, in the department's Far East division, reluctantly agreed with Fearey's analysis, but regretted that cold war tensions benefited Japan so greatly. When the Moscow embassy warned that Japan would inevitably become a citadel for either the Soviets or the United States, however, Emmerson warned that "our acts should not be conditioned by a fear of communism so strong that we lean toward the very elements we set out to destroy."[11] When the global economic crisis of 1947 solidified the reverse course and the long-suppressed Japanese labor movement challenged the Occupation with a proposed general strike in 1947, the old China hands were forced to abandon their enmity toward Japan completely and to conform to the "realities" of American policy in postwar Asia.

The traditional pattern of colonial trade was so entrenched in Asia (with underdeveloped nations supplying food and raw materials in return for Japanese and Western manufactures) that only a decisive social/economic transformation, going far beyond the Pauley report, could break it. Faced with deteriorated Asian trade and a severely unbalanced world economy, American officials sought to restore and strengthen the traditional trade patterns, thus setting the course of Asian affairs for decades. Prewar Far Eastern trade totaled 15 percent of world trade, yet, in 1947, it was only 8 percent, and only 41 percent of the prewar figure. Japan's exports were a pitiful 4.3 percent and its imports 18.6 percent of prewar. Malaya, Britain's most valuable colony, had ten times Japan's exports in 1947, or $437 million. The Far Eastern economy had traditionally helped both Europe and the world balance their dollar trade by running a large dollar surplus, but with the collapse of Japanese and Asian trade it ran up a $1.2 billion deficit in 1947.[12] The attempt to revive regional trade between Japan and its Asian neighbors represented in microcosm the American attempt to revive trade between Europe and its far-flung dependencies in order to solve the world economic imbalance.

Economic deterioration led officials in 1946 to recognize the key role of Japan in the traditional Asian and world economies. In November the economic affairs office in the State Department called for most-favored-nation status for Japan and a rapid return to private trade to facilitate global recovery.[13] They viewed Japan's manufacturing capacity as the key to Asian trade, and knew that Japanese recovery would be doomed without access to neighboring raw materials and markets. An August 1946 State Department study noted that Japanese exports had doubled between 1930 and 1936, bringing about prosperity and rapid development. Export income had "dominated the stream of purchasing power and stimulated new investment in industries producing for both export and domestic markets." Export income also provided the vital foreign exchange necessary to purchase the imported food and materials to maintain Japanese domestic consumption.[14]

Japanese industrial development had historically depended on export booms, wars, and imperialistic expansion into Asia. The Russo-Japanese War of 1905 and World War I created the demand that fostered Japanese heavy industrial development. Cooperating with Britain and the United States in the "development" of China gave Japan footholds on the mainland, which it transformed into a vast empire during the 1930s and 1940s. Japan had indigenous supplies of only six of thirty-three necessary metals; she had no cotton or coking coals, little iron ore, one-tenth of her oil requirements, and only 80 percent of her food requirements. The Japanese economy closely resembled Britain's after World War II—except that Japan lacked an empire. The State Department report accurately concluded that it was "probably unrealistic to suppose that four or five years of transition will suffice to bring Japan's economy to a new equilibrium, whether at a relatively high level or at a depressed level."[15]

Washington's recognition of Japan's economic crisis was indicated when, in December 1946, Commerce Secretary Averell Harriman requested that top business executives be appointed to oversee German and Japanese recovery.[16]

To export competitively, Japan needed stable prices, but in 1946 and early 1947 Japan experienced the catastrophic inflation common to postwar economies. Wartime governments printed money to finance arms production, but the collapse of the civilian goods sector drove consumer prices skyward. Japan decontrolled prices in 1945, despite SCAP orders to reimpose strict controls on the rationing and price of foods and essential commodities, and inflation averaged 700 percent through mid-1946. In May 1946, SCAP approved the establishment of the Economic Stabilization Board to coordinate economic planning. The Japanese strategy was entitled "priority production," which followed from the board's analysis that inflation was caused by excess demand and insufficient supply. They launched emergency financial measures in early 1946, based on blocking the withdrawal of savings to reduce demand and on financing imports to increase production in the key iron-steel and coal industries.[17]

The massive war debts owed by the government to industry greatly complicated the financing of Japanese recovery in 1946. Private industry claimed 70 billion yen in war indemnities for their war production, expansion, and damages. This debt more than tripled annual government revenues; repayment would have forced the government to the printing press. The United States, however, forced the Diet (Japan's parliament) to cancel the debt to punish industry for waging war. Industry, however, had borrowed from the banks, often within their own Zaibatsu grouping. And the financial sector, panicking at the prospect of bankruptcy, forced business to repay their loans despite their canceled indemnities. Economist Dick K. Nanto, in a recent study of Occupation finance, explains how business avoided its debts and crippled the financial capability of the commercial banks:

> Japanese business, faced with these huge war debts, quickly turned from pressuring the government to pay their bills to encouraging the government to inflate prices as a convenient solution to lessen the real burden of their debts. The ensuing inflation

virtually wiped out the financial obligations of the businesses, although most had to incur new debts in order to stay alive. The vested interests of business in maintaining high rates of inflation is indisputable.[18]

The shortage of commercial loans forced the government to finance industrial reconversion itself. Tanzan Ishibashi, a staunch Keynesian who first represented business as finance minister and then as editor of the influential *Oriental Economist,* supported deficit financing. SCAP, however, discouraged this measure. The Japanese then set up a quasi-public bank, the Reconstruction (Reconversion) Finance Bank, in October 1946. The bank issued 44 billion yen in loans through 1947, which helped increase production but also fueled inflation. Inflation proceeded at 155 percent in 1947, prompting SCAP to order Social Democratic Prime Minister Tetso Katayama to stabilize the economy or risk American aid cuts. The Economic Stabilization Board responded by limiting Bank of Japan additions to the money supply in 1947. Inflation, however, was not beginning to slow, and American concern about Japan's fragile economy and the political implications of economic collapse was growing.[19]

The economic situation led George Atcheson to write to Truman on January 5, 1947, warning of the plight of Japan: "The Japanese economy is bankrupt and whether we like it or not Japan has become an economic responsibility of the United States. . . . There is no question of building up Japan to the disadvantage of any other country; the question is simply one of endeavoring to develop an economy by which Japan will be self-supporting." The elusive quest for Japanese self-sufficiency within the American orbit was pursued until it was abandoned as a failure in 1951.[20]

Planning a Self-Sufficient Japanese Economy (1947)

Edwin M. Martin, head of Japanese and Korean economic affairs for the State Department, recorded department thinking on recovery in a March 1947 memo. Noting that an economically viable Japan would reduce the global aid burden on the United States and stabilize Japan and Asia, he recommended that the department encourage barter agreements, private trade resumption, Japanese business travel abroad, Marshall Plan–type recovery aid (which the United States granted in 1948 on a limited scale), and a revolving fund to finance Japanese imports. Martin predicted that these measures would achieve balanced Japanese trade by 1950. He recognized, however, that American sponsorship of Japanese recovery might antagonize recently devastated Asian nations and create a backlash that might threaten Japanese trade expansion. To overcome this crucial flaw in recovery strategy, he suggested publicly emphasizing that Japanese recovery would "permit a substantial Japanese contribution to the economic recovery of the Far East." Moreover, he advised offering Japan's neighbors "substantial inducement," including yen credits, to enable them to purchase Japanese goods.[21]

Although recovery policy went through two years of turmoil in debate and was ultimately shaped by Under Secretary of the Army William Draper, the basic themes of Martin's memo survived. Subsequent American policy centered on stabilizing prices through reduced domestic demand to stimulate exports, and on obtaining the cooperation of Asian nations in Japanese trade recovery. The sheer magnitude of the additional exports required to balance Japanese trade at a level that would allow modernization, however, as well as Washington's opposition to an ambitious Asian aid program to "induce" cooperation with Japan, essentially doomed the recovery program. One official charged that Martin's overoptimistic 1950 target for balanced trade merely invited failure. Also, Martin's call for inducing Asian cooperation prejudged that the United States "[was] embarking on a vast loan or grant-in-aid program" to Asia, something the department feared would overextend American financial commitments and would fail because of Asia's underdevelopment.[22]

Growing concern about Japan's economy in 1947 paralleled State Department fears of European and global economic collapse. The State-War-Navy Coordinating Committee based American policy to achieve multilateralism and world trade recovery on the revival of Germany and Japan as the regional "workshops" of Europe and Asia. Dean Acheson also emphasized reviving Germany and Japan in early drafts of the Truman Doctrine, and the State-War-Navy Subcommittee on Foreign Aid emphasized the role of German production in

Europe and the revival of production in Japan to speed up Far Eastern recovery. In his May 1947 Delta Council speech in Mississippi,
the precursor of Marshall's historic Harvard address, Acheson said:
"As production and trade in critical countries were integrated into
healthy regional and world trading systems the strain concentrated
upon the United States would be relaxed." Finally, Defense Secretary James Forrestal advised Treasury Secretary John Snyder in March
1947 that he

> felt very strongly that the world could only be brought back to
> order by restoration of commerce, trade and business and that
> would have to be done by businessmen. Specifically that meant
> that in Germany and Japan people would have to recapture the
> hope of being able to make a living. That would have to be done
> by the restoration of trade between countries, which in turn meant
> the ability of Japan, Germany and other affiliates of the axis to
> get back to work.[23]

As a Wall Street banker, Forrestal recognized the importance of trade
and production for generating profits to repay loans and strengthen
the world banking system. The workshop concept was central to
both multilateralism and the balance of power struggle with the Soviet Union.

SCAP planning for Japanese self-sufficiency in 1947 paralleled
the concern in Washington. SCAP's "Possible Program for a Balanced Japanese Economy" advised a shift from textile to capital goods
exports to enable other Asian nations to produce textiles. American
efforts to revive Japanese trade in 1946 had logically centered on the
textile industry, which was relatively simple to revive, was non–war
supporting, met real human needs, and provided a market for raw
American cotton. Early in the Occupation, textiles constituted over
70 percent of Japan's exports and served as a crutch for the ailing
economy. SCAP also questioned Pauley's high reparations figures,
charging that Japan's precarious economic position made all estimates of future industrial requirements impossible.[24]

Those in Washington who sought to bolster Japanese industry made
the reparations program their first target. Secretary of War Robert

Patterson sent his assistant, Colonel R. M. Cheseldine, and Clifford Strike, president of New York's McGraw Engineering, to Japan in January 1947 to review reparations policies in light of the necessity to make Japan self-sufficient by 1951. The two had already worked together on German reparations and vehemently opposed Pauley's reform philosophy. In February, Cheseldine reported that Japan was now the primary capitalist ally in Asia, and only a "realistic approach" to self-sufficiency could spare the Administration the burden of extracting massive aid funds from a reluctant Congress. He warned that the extensive reparations program would be a disaster for the Japanese economy and the American taxpayer. He called for slashing the Pauley figures and establishing a revolving trust fund—using precious metals looted by Japan during the war as collateral—to finance Japanese imports. Herbert Hoover also joined the attack on the Pauley report, terming it too optimistic with respect to Japan's economic prospects, and charging that the threat of reforms and reparations—"industrial repressions," in his words—would lead to "industrial paralysis." Moreover, he warned that the economic imbalance could prove fatal: "The United States does not possess the strength to bear the deficient productivity which now dominates industry all over the world. We need a larger vision of the primary basis of world peace, which is productivity. Otherwise there will be disintegration of Western civilization everywhere."[25]

The growing sentiment for reviving Japan altered American plans for a peace treaty with Japan. MacArthur had envisioned an early peace treaty, believing that military occupations invariably faced unpopularity after a period of three years. State Department peace preparations had begun in October 1946 under Hugh Borton, but in August 1947 the head of the Policy Planning staff, George F. Kennan, rejected an early peace. The State Department based its Far Eastern policy on a stable, prosperous, and friendly Japan, yet, Kennan warned, Japan's economic vulnerability and its lack of Western capitalistic values posed the threat of social revolution. Japanese labor, socialism, and Communism indeed flourished in the democratic environment encouraged by the Occupation prior to 1948. Thus, until the economy was self-sufficient and conservative rule stabilized, the Occupation could not end. The planning staff recommended relaxing the purge of militarists, making economic recovery the "prime objective" of the Occupation, and using economic aid to revive Japanese trade.[26]

In 1947 the Department of Army planned Marshall Plan–type aid for Japan. As in Europe, a shortage of imported raw materials to feed Japan's idle factories remained the principal obstacle to industrial revival through 1948 and 1949. Japan lacked the foreign exchange necessary to finance industrial imports, and the American aid program—Government and Relief in Occupied Areas (GARIOA)—was limited to the prevention of disease and unrest. The Army requested from Congress a "Little Marshall Plan for Japan" to finance American exports to Japan, to parallel the $400 million sent under the ERP to Germany (which also received aid under GARIOA). Officials termed it "aid to 'crank-up' or prime the pump" of Japanese industry, to revive exports and reduce the long-term burden of supporting the Japanese economy. The Army convinced a reluctant Congress to grant $165 million for Japan under the Economic Recovery for Occupied Areas (EROA) aid program from April 1948 through July 1949. EROA financed industrial raw materials and duplicated ERP aid, but, unlike the ERP, it was limited to only one country, Japan, and was not a regional Asian aid program.[27]

Earlier studies had recommended additional mechanisms to finance Japanese imports. The United States used gold and precious metals originally slated for reparations as collateral for the $135 million Occupied Japan Export-Import Revolving Fund, run by New York banks, in October 1947. To finance American raw cotton sales to Japan, Congress created an additional $150 million fund, under PL 820, in June 1948. This Natural Fibres Revolving Fund stimulated the Japanese textile industry, helped Southern senators reduce the glut of cotton on the market, and established permanent markets in Japan for American cotton. Although securing the Japanese market for American agriculture was a secondary consideration for strategic planners concerned with sustaining Japan's economy to prevent social revolution, it was a key policy for agricultural producers, the Department of Agriculture, and many in Congress. Senator Cannon of Missouri described a rehabilitated Japan as a "magnificent market" for American raw materials and finished products in 1948. It must be kept in mind that throughout the Occupation the Japanese market contributed greatly to American exports and after the Occupation Japan became the most important market for American agriculture.[28]

Reviving imports would help production, but to promote exports SCAP had to reestablish Japanese business contacts with the world. Initial occupational directives mandated strictly controlled trade; thus, SCAP had established the Boeki Cho, or Board of Trade, in November 1945 to handle all foreign transactions. In March 1946, the United States Commercial Company, a government corporation, began to transact all Japanese trade with the United States—which amounted to almost all of Japan's foreign trade. Under British pressure to break the American monopoly in Japanese trade, SCAP established the Inter-Allied Trade Board in October 1946 and admitted four hundred foreign businessmen in August 1947. Washington's complaints about controlling trade led SCAP to allow free trade, under Boeki Cho supervision, in August 1947.[29]

SCAP also negotiated bilateral trade agreements with foreign governments to expand Japan's trade opportunities. With the chaos of postwar trade and the necessity of protecting dollar reserves, much of world trade was negotiated by governments. By far the most important of these agreements for Japan was the May 1948 Overall Payments Agreement with the sterling area, which had a limitless demand for inexpensive textiles and consumer and capital goods. Moreover, many sterling countries were located in Asia and were closer to Japan than to Britain. The British, however, pleading their own dollar shortage, refused to allow SCAP to convert Japan's sterling holdings into dollars or to allow sterling nations to pay in dollars for Japanese textiles made with American cotton.[30] Japan had to pay for the cotton in dollars, but was unable to earn sufficient dollars in America because nylon had displaced silk on the American market. Nor could Japan earn the dollars elsewhere because of the universal dollar gap. The parallel to the European trade crisis was striking.

The economic outlook at the end of 1947 was discouraging. Inflation had been halved to 150 percent, but at a cost of holding GNP growth to 8.5 percent. This was hardly a sufficient growth rate to rebuild the civilian economy and to finance the vital modernization of industry required for export success.[31]

International Repercussions of the Reverse Course

In June 1947 the State Department presented SWNCC 381, "Revival of the Japanese Economy," which followed the conventional themes of Martin's memo in March. The Army, which had to justify Japanese aid programs to Congress, called for a more dramatic "shift in emphasis" from reform to recovery policies to promote the reverse course and emphasize the gravity and complexity of the recovery task. The State Department, however, addressed a different constituency—the international community, which still viewed Japan as an imperialist aggressor. State feared that the Army's call for openly breaking from internationally mandated control and reform policies would provoke both Japan's neighbors and the eleven-nation Far Eastern Commission (FEC), which theoretically governed Occupation policies from Washington, and prejudice the international cooperation necessary to revive Japanese trade.[32]

State agreed with the Army that recovery policy wording had to be explicit. But it called for "diplomatic" wording, emphasizing the contribution of Japanese trade to Asian recovery, to minimize fears that the "shift in emphasis" implied a "reversal or repudiation of broad principles." State especially feared the policy of William Draper, a former Wall Street banker and then the under secretary of the Army in charge of German and Japanese Occupation policy. They felt that Draper's support for unilateral American action to promote Japanese revival would antagonize the Allies. Draper was the principal Washington proponent of reviving the two "workshop" economies and a key architect of Japanese policy. Charles Saltzman, head of the State Department's occupied areas division, later recalled that Draper's thinking was far ahead of that of the State Department on reviving Japan. In SWNCC 384, Draper pressed State to agree to a no-nonsense interim directive by MacArthur, bypassing the FEC entirely. State warned, however, that "many of these countries are concerned that the United States is apparently placing Japanese recovery ahead of the recovery of the rest of Asia." The State-War-Navy Coordinating Committee approved a modified SWNCC 384 in January 1948.[33]

On January 21 General Frank McCoy announced the reverse course to the FEC after a public announcement by Army Secretary Kenneth Royall on January 7. McCoy, American representative to the FEC, sent a barrage of complaints to the State Department opposing American lip service to Allied cooperation. He charged that Americans defined cooperation as Allied submission to policies formed secretly and unilaterally in Washington. He answered the State Department's charge that the FEC was obstructing recovery policies by insisting that it was the United States which had changed its policies in midstream; he argued that an interim directive was indeed uncalled for. Whereas the State Department blamed FEC obstruction on the Soviets, McCoy said that the Soviets had been cooperative in the FEC; the main opponents of American policy were Britain, Australia, Canada, and New Zealand.[34]

The State Department forced McCoy into a humiliating position in February 1948, by ordering him to withhold all expressions of American opinion or policy from the FEC indefinitely. The Allies were forced to impotently follow the newspapers to keep track of the Draper-orchestrated parade of Washington dignitaries to Tokyo in 1948 to plan Japan's resurgence. Moreover, the four-nation Allied Council for Japan, sitting in Tokyo to keep the FEC in touch with Japanese events, was ridiculed by MacArthur and reduced to a mockery by the new POLAD, William Sebald, who adjourned most meetings within seconds of convening them.[35]

The United States obstructed Allied Occupation authority because it threatened American policies to achieve a multilateral world economy. Other nations lacked the global requirements and ambitions of the United States and failed to perceive the economic necessity of reviving Japan; they had a greater fear of the resurgence of Japanese militarism and economic aggression than of Soviet aggression. Thus, the British Commonwealth conference in Canberra in 1947 called for restrictions on strategic elements of Japanese industry to prevent militarist revival; nor did it believe that "Japan should be afforded an early opportunity to become prosperous." The Australian foreign minister charged that it would be "unjust if Japan's population obtained privileges and benefits denied to the countries she devastated." The Commonwealth representative to the Allied Council, Australian W. MacMahon Ball, was the leading Allied critic of the reverse course. Echoing the Pauley report, he urged strict dissolution of the Zaibatsu and opposed reviving Japan because it would afford her undue economic influence in Asia, something he believed Japan would exploit to renew her political domination.[36]

The most directly aggrieved parties, of course, were the Asians themselves. The Nationalist Chinese reacted bitterly to recovery policies, fearing that Japan would resume her former dominating position as the hub of the Far Eastern economy. They particularly resented the United States' using Chinese gold looted by Japan to finance Japanese trade revival. Their ambassador told Sebald that China, too, had balance-of-payment difficulties, "but the United States apparently overlook[ed] this fact." General Romulo of the Philippines also "felt that the result of this policy would be to build up Japan again to a point where she dominated the Far East."[37] For Americans, Japan's supremacy in Asia was inevitable and greatly to be encouraged with lavish funding. To Asians, with the fresh memories of Japanese occupation, Japan's renewed domination was sinister and a threat to their political and economic independence.

In late 1947 and through 1948 Draper initiated a series of missions to Japan which led to the termination of reform policies. Strike and his corporation, Overseas Consultants Incorporated, returned to Japan in June 1947 to set specific levels of industry required for Japanese self-sufficiency from American aid. Strike concluded that Pauley's projected levels of industry would mean that "all chances of reaching a self-sustaining economy within a reasonable period of time would be removed." The mission recommended retaining all munitions, aircraft, and chemical plants, except for some government-owned primary war facilities. The FEC had ordered that Pauley set Japanese levels of industry at 1930–34 levels. Strike charged, however, that from 1930 to 1934 Japan had suffered from "unprecedented depression," that production had been at a "standstill," and that those economic levels were unviable. SCAP, which agreed that Pauley's figures were too low, defended the FEC policy, noting that Japan had benefited from an arms boom and other preparations for Asian expansion and had achieved the world's most rapid recovery from the depression in 1932.[38] Using post-1934 figures allowed Japan to retain military plants built to arm Japanese armies in the war with China.

Strike and his colleagues were not in Japan to debate economic history but, instead, to justify Japanese revival. Their philosophy of Far Eastern recovery was simple—to help Japan recover its economic superiority and allow it to shape the Asian economy around its need for raw materials and markets:

We realize that other Far Eastern countries are in need of industrial equipment and the ultimate decision with respect to reparations should be based on a balancing of needs to obtain maximum benefits for the region as a whole. It is our opinion that this can be achieved most surely by leaving Japan free to reconstruct and use as quickly as possible the bulk of her industrial capacity.[39]

Foreign governments, as well as some Americans, opposed the brazen American gutting of the reparations program. A former member of the Pauley mission reacted bitterly to Secretary of War Patterson's "rather startling administrative antics . . . in appointing a mission of his own and apparently allowing it to ride roughshod over policy which had been developed by federal and international agencies." The FEC also blasted the Overseas Consultants report for using 1937 wartime levels of industry. Draper noted colorfully in the margins of the FEC critique of Strike's work that the proposed FEC limits on Japanese industry were as realistic as "Alice in Wonderland." When the FEC wrote that the Strike report "appear[ed]" to contradict Allied Occupation policy, Draper unashamedly noted that it was, indeed, a clear contradiction.[40]

While the FEC was held at bay by McCoy's orders to stall, Draper and Kennan went to Japan in the spring of 1948 to review and confirm the reverse course policies. With MacArthur, they agreed that reparations shipments would take twenty years to complete, and that the equipment would rust and become unusable outside its original factory setting. These claims, though self-serving, were probably correct. Without a much more ambitious program of financing Asian industrial redistribution, the aborted reparations program would likely have had no significant impact on Asian development.[41]

Draper had gathered a distinguished group of his banking and industrial peers to accompany him to Japan: Wall Street colleagues Percy H. Johnston, chairman of Chemical Bank (who was nominal head of the mission); Robert F. Loree, former vice-president of Morgan Guaranty Trust, and chairman of the National Foreign Trade Council; and former president of Studebaker Paul Hoffman, who was appointed the head of the ECA during the mission. After a two-week whirlwind tour, their May 19 report, not surprisingly, confirmed Draper's policies. They called for expanded Japanese raw materials imports and export outlets to reduce the aid burden, a national austerity program to cut inflation by balancing budgets and reducing social services, a shift in trade from the dollar area to both Southeast Asia and the sterling area, and an 800 to 900 percent increase in exports. Finally, the Draper-Johnston mission recommended slashing the already low Overseas Consultants' reparations figures by another 60 percent, thereby flouting State Department warnings against unilateral and heavy-handed American decisions which would antagonize the FEC.[42]

Secretary of State Marshall cautioned Kenneth Royall in September 1948 that unless primary war facilities were removed, Japan's hopes for international acceptance, crucial to trade recovery, UN membership, and most-favored-nation trading privileges, would be lost. The Allies vociferously complained to the State Department that scrapping the reparations program and levels-of-industry limits was flouting world opinion. Indeed, State counted on the Draper and Strike reports to prepare the international community for the "shock" of the official termination of the reparations program in 1949.[43]

There were two remaining State Department dissenters in 1949: the legal division, offended by the illegality of American policy, and, surprisingly, Paul Nitze, who became a key architect of world rearmament in late 1949. In January 1949, the legal division advised that FEC provisions clearly mandated that all "industrial machinery and equipment in primary war facilities" be made available as reparations. It was "unthinkable that the United States government, in view of the commitments entered into as above stated, should now propose to leave primary war facilities in Japan," the legal experts advised Acheson. Using the aid burden on the United States as a rationale, as proposed by the State Department, was especially "unfortunate" and "demeaning," it continued, and would open American policy to the charge of "intent to thwart the basic tenet of the Potsdam Agreement."[44]

Nitze agreed with the majority that Japan no longer constituted a military menace, but disliked "having in Japan a large volume of industrial facilities heretofore used exclusively for military production, now idle and unlikely to be put into economic operation." Perhaps fearing that the Japanese would accommodate China or the Soviets, he warned: "The possibility cannot be ruled out that they could become an embarrassment if not a security threat to the United States interests in Asia." Nitze said reparations were primarily a political, not an economic, problem; from a political point of view the United States should offer reparations to overcome Asian hostility toward Japan. In response to Nitze's plea, SCAP and the Army argued that although the arms plants would not be used, their removal would absorb Japanese energies, money, and shipping, and thus delay recovery.[45]

POLAD William Sebald and other State Department officials expressed American impatience with moralizing allies when the revival of industrial anti-Communist nations such as Japan had become the key to American policy. International cooperation and the FEC had become a "straitjacket" from which the United States had to "disengage itself" to assert its power unilaterally: "We are, it seems, caught in our net of immediate postwar internationalism."[46] General McCoy and his assistant, Charles Saltzman, however, argued that international cooperation was vital to Japan's future trade. Saltzman charged that MacArthur, who refused to carry out Washington's recovery policies without first securing an end to reparations to please Japanese business, had exaggerated the burden of plant removals on the Japanese economy. The Japan-oriented Far Eastern division countered that ending reparations would not harm Japanese trade, because Asians would trade according to their commercial needs, not their political convictions. This proved overoptimistic, as anti-Japanese sentiment and the failure to address legitimate reparations claims handicapped Japan's economic expansion into Asia in the 1950s.[47]

Dean Acheson, characteristically, was unmoved by American legal commitments to reparations. He reasoned that since Japan was disarmed and plant removals would have to be financed eventually by the United States, reparations should cease. General McCoy pleaded with Acheson not to submit to the "localitis" of SCAP, which catered to the viewpoints of Japanese leaders and not to those of the world community. Finally, NSC 13/3, approved by Truman in May 1949, stated that "regardless of the likely unfavorable reception" by its allies, the United States would advance an interim directive by SCAP to halt the reparations program.[48]

Naturally, Japanese business was "elated" about the end to reparations and "surprised" that they could retain their primary war facilities. Other nations, however, protested the unilateral American action after McCoy announced the new policy to the FEC on May 12. Australia, New Zealand, and Canada all filed complaints, and Ambassador Romulo of the Philippines launched a strong attack on American arrogance.[49] The FEC thereafter ceased to concern American officials; the Allied Occupation had become an American protectorate in Japan. American officials had planned during the war for unhindered American control of the Occupation. Impatient American officials agreed that American power and global interests were best served when "allies" left serious decision making to the Americans.

The Politics of the Reverse Course

Two primary advocates of reform in Japan were Courtney Whitney, head of the Government Section of SCAP, and Edward Welsh, head of decartelization in the Economic and Scientific Section (ESS). The Government Section battled over Japanese politics with G-2, the intelligence arm of the Far East Command, headed by the notorious General Charles Willoughby. Willoughby (whom MacArthur termed "my lovable fascist") became General Francisco Franco's intelligence advisor when the Occupation ended. Whitney's Government Section liberals, fearing that G-2 and other reactionary elements would sabotage the reform program, encouraged the Social Democrats to form a cabinet under Tetsu Katayama in late 1947. The government had little power in the Diet and proved incompetent to carry out an effective antiinflation program. G-2, which viewed Japan as an anti-Communist American military base, helped bring down the cabinet by tipping off the conservative Liberal party (under Shigeru Yoshida) about Social-Democratic involvement in the massive Showa Denko political bribery scandal.

MacArthur issued lofty statements about the complete democratic transformation of Japanese society inspired by his rule. In reality, the corporate monopolies and their conservative bureaucratic allies defeated the intent of much reform legislation by not implementing the laws. SCAP "liberals," led by Whitney and Welsh, battled alongside Japanese socialists, reformers, and labor groups against the old Japanese order and its conservative SCAP allies. Readers must go elsewhere for the fascinating and revealing history of the domestic side of the Occupation. Suffice it to say that the domestic reforms designed to create independent unions and reduce the power of the militarist clique and the control of the economy by the monopolies were either abandoned or rendered ineffective.[50]

The "Japan lobby," a group of pro-Zaibatsu American business and conservative leaders, spurred the reverse course by exerting pressure on the Administration to abandon the reform program in 1947. Led by Tokyo lawyer James Lee Kauffman and *Newsweek* editor Harry Kern, the lobby argued publicly that American deconcentration policy was socialistic because it sought to redistribute the ownership of Japanese monopolies. At SCAP headquarters in 1947, Kauffman had stolen a copy of FEC-230, the American-drafted and comprehensive plan to "democratize" the ownership of Japanese business. Kauffman drafted a highly critical report to the State Department, Kern blasted the plan in *Newsweek,* and Senator William Knowland, a Republican from California, attacked it on the Senate floor. To promote Japanese interests, the lobby founded the American Council on Japan, composed of financiers and industrialists who sought to revive Japanese business.[51]

Direct requests by corporations to protect their interests and business associates in Japan complemented Japanese lobby pressure. These requests helped reinforce the belief of many officials that economic controls inhibited investors' confidence in Japan. The National Foreign Trade Council, representing the largest American corporations, sent the heads of General Electric, International Telephone and Telegraph, and Standard Oil to advise Draper and Walton Butterworth, head of the Far East division of the State Department, on July 26 and 27, 1948. The president of General Electric, which had significant investments in the prewar Japanese electronics industry, said that American corporations were anxious to reinvest in Japan, but that SCAP's deconcentration policy, the purge, and the economic controls created an unfavorable business climate. Under these conditions, the corporations feared for the profitability of their affiliates; they also complained that Japanese companies had not yet learned "how to deal with organized labor." The group told Butterworth to urge Truman to assure Japanese business publicly that the United States was committed to recovery and decontrol. Butterworth answered that Royall and Draper had already made such statements but that "each time one had been issued there had been very adverse reactions from other Far Eastern countries."[52]

The Japan lobby influenced such officials as Kennan and Forrestal, who became convinced that MacArthur was unwittingly turning Japan socialistic with New Deal antimonopoly policies. Kennan's visit to Japan in March 1948 was intended to convince MacArthur that reforms had gone far enough. The supreme commander, surprisingly because of his anti-Communism and empathy toward Japanese business, vehemently defended the purge and deconcentration programs: he had taken Kauffman's assault personally and banned him from Japan. He had never been a businessman and had spent years outside the United States; he thus held an anachronistic, laissez-faire idea of American corporate organization, which, of course, had steadily evolved toward the Japanese oligopolistic model. The Japan lobby argued that the reform legislation would never have been tolerated in the United States. MacArthur defended those on his staff who advocated easing the monopolies' grip on society and charged that the Zaibatsu record was one of "economic oppression and exploitation at home, aggression and spoilation abroad." The monopolies had geared Japan for war, he said, and the only opponents of deconcentration in Japan were the hated reactionaries and Communists, the latter of which knew that monopolies were inherently socialistic.[53]

Ultimately, the program was dropped before any measures were taken, other than abolishing the Zaibatsu holding companies. Edward Welsh angrily charged that conservative Japanese politicians and American friends of the Zaibatsu had reinforced the "undemocratic" nature of Japanese capitalism, suppressed freedom of enterprise, and yet had made it appear that "Japan has practically overnight become free of cartels and combines and Zaibatsu influences." The Japan lobby had also charged that the purge had left the economy in the hands of clerks, an obvious exaggeration that angered MacArthur. He argued that those who were purged, who had led Japan in the 1930s and early 1940s, were old and incompetent and only kept younger and more active men from advancement. Although he defended the purge, MacArthur did agree with Kennan and Draper that reparations had to end, and that American policy had to concentrate on industrial and trade revival.[54]

Kennan was convinced that ESS controls on the economy slowed recovery. The issue of SCAP's economic competence became the focal point of a bureaucratic struggle between the State and Army departments over the most effective way to promote recovery. All American officials agreed by 1948 that recovery could come only by trade with Asia, internal financial stability for export competitiveness, and strong conservative leadership. Beyond those were two contrary measures often supported by different factions—weakening ESS power and promoting active American intervention in Japan's economy. State Department officials in the Far East division, Sebald, and business interests advocated greatly reducing SCAP's role in the economy—a generally laissez-faire approach. Butterworth, head of the Far East division, said that "merchant greed will motivate recovery" if Japanese business were freed from controls. The department, moreover, felt that the ESS was indeed incompetent. The ESS head, General William F. Marquat—one of MacArthur's inner circle— was not an economist. William Draper recalled that when he visited Tokyo in May 1948, MacArthur asked him to "find me somebody who knows something about running the economy of Japan, because I don't. And my military officers who are responsible for it don't either."[55]

The laissez-faire advocates believed that stifling Japanese business with controls would drive Japan toward accommodation with the Soviets if the economy failed to recover. The occupied areas division was even more pessimistic and believed that world trading conditions were so unfavorable that merely freeing Japanese business would not bring self-sufficiency. They argued that unless the United States launched "positive" programs to guarantee Japan markets and aid, Japanese business would become frustrated and insecure and seek accommodation with the Asian mainland. Their pessimism was well founded, and, though the laissez-faire approach dominated American policy in 1949, "positive" measures proliferated in the 1950s.[56]

In late 1948 and early 1949 the State Department sought to reduce, if not eliminate, SCAP economic influence. Charles Saltzman told Draper that the parallels between German and Japanese recovery policies should be reflected in occupational organization. The State Department and the ECA had largely replaced the Army in the political and economic administration of Germany and sought to do the same in Japan. The State Department's Walton Butterworth, head of Far Eastern affairs, and Willard Thorp, head of economic affairs and a key architect of multilateralism, wrote in September 1949 that the "experience, organization and personnel" of the ECA would be best suited to run the Japanese economy; the ECA's "greater competence and prestige" would attract more capable business leaders. The Army, however, had advised the State Department that Mac-Arthur, because he believed the Japanese were loyal to the Occupation only because of his emperorlike aura of authority, would never step down before the Occupation ended. To circumvent SCAP authority, Thorp and Butterworth proposed that Hoffman appoint MacArthur as ECA representative to Japan and then appoint an ECA official to run the economy as MacArthur's deputy. They also suggested putting the Occupation on a "pay-as-you-go" basis in Japan, meaning that the Japanese would receive dollars for their expenses incurred on behalf of the Occupation, which would reduce the need for economic aid. The Army replied that its policies in Japan were mandated by Congress and the FEC and could not be changed.[57] State also considered using the "Standby SCAP" idea circulated by the military in 1949 to assure the continuing legality of military base rights in Japan. The Joint Chiefs of Staff feared that the rights of an occupier would be denied if the United States ratified a peace treaty. The Russians, however, not having made peace with Japan, would retain occupier status and could legally land occupying troops. The Joint Chiefs held up peace treaty plans through 1950 over this bizarre theory. They planned to leave only a token SCAP presence to preserve the Occupation. State saw in this plan a means of wrenching economic control from the Army. Ultimately, the Army insisted that MacArthur would never agree to stripping the power of his clique of generals, and the Far East division concluded that the interdepartmental bloodletting that would be necessary to overrule the Army would cancel any benefits of an ECA takeover. When Joseph Dodge went to Japan in 1949, State realized its goal of imposing an ERP-like austerity program in Japan under non-ESS leadership.[58]

Concerned primarily with creating a self-sustaining alliance be-

Kennan word 1948 *NSC 13/1*

tween Japan and the United States, Kennan drafted PPS 28, "Policy with Respect to Japan," in March 1948. He listed seven measures to promote trade recovery and self-sufficiency: establishing a single foreign exchange rate; promoting Japanese business travel abroad; expanding foreign business in Japan; granting additional cotton credits; simplifying trade procedures; granting private loans to Japanese business; and instituting a policy of transferring technology to Japan. He urged returning initiative to Japanese business and strengthening the Japanese police force to prevent the social instability that, he feared, would lead to revolution. Kennan's report, which essentially reflected Draper's thinking, became NSC 13/1 in June 1948. The American strategy to decontrol the Japanese economy, to "radically" cut Occupation personnel, and to give Japan a carte blanche to abolish reforms was designed in part to bypass the FEC. The Allies would be helpless to impose reforms, and the United States could "obtain general international de jure recognition of a de facto situation." NSC 13/3 mandated continued financing of Japanese imports and "vigorous and concerted effort by all interested agencies and departments of the United States government to cut away existing obstacles to the revival of Japanese foreign trade . . . and to facilitate restoration and development of Japan's exports."[59]

State Department concern over the effect of the continuing American control over Japan on Japanese attitudes toward the United States emerged in 1949. Acheson wrote that a critical weapon against Japanese and Allied resentment at the drawn-out Occupation was to blame the Soviets for any delay in a peace treaty. The Joint Chiefs of Staff's opposition to a treaty and State's own refusal to disband the Occupation until Japan's conservative rule was stabilized prevented a peace conference. Acheson, however, explained to American officials that a policy of concealing American obstruction of peace plans and instead blaming the Soviets was "psychologically of great importance" to American prestige in Japan and the world.[60]

Toward Economic Stabilization

Ironically, the drive to decontrol the economy and to unleash business was countered by American desires to enforce classic deflationary policies on Japan to balance her dollar accounts. Under the ERP, ECA officials were empowered to review Europe's internal financial policies to control budget deficits, limit public works, and restrain prices. For international bankers such as Draper, deflation was the only "sound" remedy for payments deficits. MacArthur's plea for economic advice, the suggestion by a conservative Japanese leader that Americans could enforce a tough deflationary policy better than Japan's rulers—who had lost credibility with the public—and Washington's concern over the quality and authoritativeness of American economic leadership in Japan led Draper to seek a tough financial advisor for SCAP. He naturally turned to Joseph Dodge, who had helped him with the German currency reform. Dodge, president of the Detroit Bank, had recently been elected president of the American Bankers' Association, however, and turned down Draper's request.[61]

Draper then sent a mission to Tokyo, led by the Federal Reserve's Ralph Young, to study the feasibility of establishing a single foreign exchange rate. The sheltered Japanese economy had thousands of different exchange rates to subsidize business. Importers paid low rates for foreign exchange, and exporters received higher rates for their goods. Even before the mission left, however, the National Advisory Council on International Financial and Monetary Affairs (NAC) decided that economic stabilization to cut inflation must precede a single exchange rate.[62]

The chief advocates of deflationary policies were the Treasury Department and the NAC. The NAC, financial counterpart to the National Security Council, was chaired by Secretary of the Treasury John Snyder, a St. Louis investment banker. Treasury and the NAC generally opposed the policy of relying on foreign aid to keep foreign living standards high enough to ward off social conflict. Their thinking reflected the financial view of bankers interested primarily in imposing conservative financial policies and austerity on weak foreign economies, whereas the State Department and SCAP worried about driving Japan into the arms of the Soviets or precipitating internal social revolt. Treasury officials were extremely cautious in their foreign policy input, however, because Secretary Morgenthau's disastrous involvement in political policy in Germany had greatly reduced Treasury influence. To regain its credibility, Treasury limited its advice to financial considerations.[63]

On April 21, 1948, the NAC resolved to impose financial controls on Japan in order to curb inflation. Treasury told Young that the principles of the bilateral agreements forced on European aid recipients, which gave the ECA control over price stabilization and budgetary and credit policy, were also applicable to the Japanese aid program. The Young report of June 12 said recovery aid would fail to achieve balanced trade unless prices were first stabilized to make exports competitive. Domestic purchasing power, already at precariously low levels, had to be further suppressed to prevent exportable goods from being diverted to the domestic market. Young warned, however, that Japanese officials would not enforce politically unpopular austerity policies.[64]

When SCAP complained that further impoverishing Japanese workers would cause social conflict, Treasury disagreed: "Washington does not fully accept SCAP's view that the Japanese people have submitted to a *severe* degree of austerity and have accepted *drastic* economic deprivations." Treasury felt that heavier taxes were not "beyond realization under the existing conditions of poverty in Japan." The NAC staff advised that economic controls to stimulate exports were required.[65]

In early December, the NAC drafted a stabilization program to promote recovery. The Army, with some support from the State Department, echoed SCAP's warning that if pushed too far, austerity could cause social unrest in Japan. They also argued that if SCAP enforced an austerity program to reduce living standards in Japan, the Japanese would think that the United States was promising them economic success, something the ESS was neither competent nor powerful enough to guarantee. SCAP had also noted that NSC 13, calling for ESS decontrol, contradicted the policy to implement stabilization controls. Yet the NAC, more concerned with enforcing austerity than preserving social stability, advised Truman that stabilization had to precede all other efforts, or the recovery effort would fail.[66]

The ESS reacted to Japan's economic crisis with its first comprehensive economic program, popularly termed the "Green Book," in October 1947. Written by Emmerson Ross, on loan from the Army, it emphasized that Japan had to maximize exports and shift from dollar trade to trade with Southeast Asia and the sterling area to ease the dollar gap. The ESS reflected those priorities when it rejected the Economic Stabilization Board's Five-Year Plan in early 1948. The board had not yet sufficiently adopted Draper's policy to maximize exports to balance trade, and still pursued the Japanese business strategy of raising production to ease inflation through better-balanced supply and demand. The significant difference between American and Japanese strategy was that the Americans insisted on suppressing domestic consumption to promote exports, whereas the Japanese felt that moderate inflation was preferable to a recession. Thus, SCAP made the Economic Stabilization Board rewrite the plan to emphasize production for exports and limited domestic consumption.[67]

SCAP's desire for stabilization was also reflected in the November 1948 "Program for a Self-Supporting Japanese Economy"—also called the "Blue Book." Written by the ESS director of economics and planning, Sherwood Fine, the plan listed nine measures for recovery, including price stabilization and coordinated aid programs to expand Japan's opportunities to earn dollars through Asian trade. The Blue Book was the first American plan to abandon the goal of a Japanese standard of living equivalent to that of 1934 to 1936, which had been set as the Occupation goal. Fine wrote that a lower living standard, reflecting suppressed domestic consumption, would promote export competitiveness.[68]

Truman adopted the NAC's advice on December 10, 1948, and approved the revised Blue Book plan as a nine-point stabilization directive to SCAP. Fearing that MacArthur would cooperate with the Japanese to sabotage the harsh austerity program, Washington ordered him to implement a balanced budget, limits on wages, free trade, and a single exchange rate. MacArthur immediately wired a request to end reparations in order to reassure Japanese business, and complained of the contradictory pressures SCAP faced—on the one hand, he was to *force* the Japanese to stabilize, and yet at the same time he was to do no more than *mildly suggest* that recovery policies be enacted for fear of offending them. Concerned about strict enforcement of stabilization, the Administration resumed its search for an economic czar for Japan. The Army had considered the presidents of General Electric and Bankers Trust as substitutes for Dodge. Truman, however, summoned Dodge on December 10 with a plea to go to Japan. Dodge balked, but when Truman assured him that the

National Security Council had ordered tough stabilization policies and warned that Japan would otherwise become an economic disaster, Dodge accepted the task. The period of policy development had finally ended, the FEC was stilled, and the drama shifted to Japan.[69]

Capital Accumulation and Export Competitiveness: The Dodge Plan

Dodge sought to balance Japanese trade as quickly as possible in order to end the dollar gap funding that was increasingly threatened by congressional budget cuts. The son of a poster painter and a self-made banking magnate, Dodge brought old and simple theories to Japan, not new, complex, Keynesian ideas. He reflected the classic banker's view of the world: wealth is created by profitable capital investment and is dissipated by nonprofit social welfare and public improvement expenditures. The Japanese people had to consume less than they could afford, Dodge insisted, to accumulate the capital to enable the private banking system to finance industrial recovery. In the eyes of SCAP and the Japanese, and even in his own eyes, Dodge became a symbol of the harsh austerity policies he ordered: balancing the budget, trimming industrial and government payrolls, and slashing wage gains and business costs.[70] In this respect Dodge shared the spotlight with MacArthur, who also deliberately sought to be more of a grand symbol of Occupation authority to the Japanese than a flesh-and-blood administrator.

Without trade with China and Manchuria, Japan had to survive by competing with Europe and North America in world markets. Dodge explained that Japan's large population and shortage of arable land and industrial raw materials dictated that she trade extensively in order to prosper. Japanese exports carried a double load: they had to earn the foreign exchange to purchase the imports Japan consumed domestically, and they had to pay for the imports used in export manufacture.[71] By restricting the purchasing power of the Japanese people, Dodge sought to force producers to seek foreign outlets for their goods. The domestic economic, social, and political ramifications of suppressing labor demands and reviving the huge Japanese banks and industrial combines set Japan firmly back on the path of monopolistic capitalism that Draper, the State Department, and Japanese business desired. Austerity policies also contained an antilabor bias that neatly complemented the political "red purge" of early 1950, when Japan witnessed the rejailing of Communists interned under the militarists and the simultaneous depurging of the wartime leaders. American policy in 1949 simply reflected the multilateral thinking that underlay foreign policy. Japan would recover as a "workshop," the linchpin of Asian capitalism; it would export its production rather than develop large internal markets.

Here our concern is mainly with the Dodge Plan's role in Japanese trade recovery. Two themes emerge: the promotion of Japanese exports, and increased emphasis on trade with Southeast Asia (Chapter 3 will explore the latter subject in depth). The Dodge Plan must be judged by its success in stimulating investment sufficiently to start Japan on a path of sustained industrial modernization before the plan was eclipsed by the outbreak of the Korean War in June 1950.

Dodge began by implementing the nine-point stabilization directive. He balanced the budget, increased the efficiency of tax collection, tightened credit, reduced wage and price increases, controlled trade, and allocated supplies to favor exporters over those manufacturers producing solely for the domestic market. He well understood Japan's structural trading problems: Japan was a marginal supplier in world markets—other nations' marginal propensity to import Japanese goods was low, and the markets in her Asian empire and raw silk sales to the United States that she had formerly relied on to balance her trade were no longer available. Japan had to gain a foothold in world markets before other suppliers normalized their trade: "Japan must establish her position in existing markets now when resistance to Japanese goods will be lower because of the mobility of normal sources of supply to furnish the goods demanded by the markets of the world." Just as in Europe, so in Japan the world dollar gap was the principal obstacle to balancing trade, because Asia had few dollars for Japan to earn to balance its deficit with North America. Dodge suggested that an Asiatic payments union—a repeated request of the Japanese in the 1950s—would facilitate Asian trade. He later rejected the idea, however (as the United States would do in the 1950s), both because Asia lacked sufficient banking expertise, economic integration, and communications systems, and to prevent the formation of an Asian soft-currency bloc that would discriminate against American products.[72]

Dodge said that the principal task for Japan was not merely to increase production, but to adjust increased output to the demands of foreign competition. Increased output would not automatically increase exports. Indeed, increased production and consumption would only increase Japan's import bill and worsen the payments deficits. Dodge warned that the world recession and the buyer's market of late 1949 meant a "period of the most intense competition in international commerce. Japan's problem is to prepare itself now to engage in this intense world competition on an effective and self-sustaining basis. Japan cannot provide for itself as a high cost, low quality producer. Fundamentally the stabilization program is aimed at ensuring Japan an opportunity to meet this world trade problem." Noting the parallel to the ERP, Dodge said, "Japan's problems do not differ a great deal from those of other nations."[73]

He turned his attack on the lending activities of the Reconstruction Finance Bank. Its loans in the beginning of the recovery process in 1946 had spurred increased output and helped ease supply problems, but Dodge felt that the loans were inflationary. Following the example of the ERP, in April 1949 Dodge replaced the bank's lending function with yen counterpart funds from the sale of GARIOA goods. In eight months he disbursed 62 billion yen of counterpart funds to retire the bank's debentures, an extremely deflationary policy since it removed the funds from circulation. He offset this somewhat by investing 55 billion yen of counterpart funds in public and private basic industry—coal mining, ship building, and electric power production.[74]

Dodge balanced the budget and established a single exchange rate in April 1949. Observers of Japanese finance have since debated whether the budget was merely balanced, or whether it was "superbalanced" and deflationary. The Young mission had recommended an exchange rate in the range of 270 to 330 yen per dollar. Dodge, however, set a devalued rate of 360 yen to encourage exports and discourage imports. The NAC had advised that Britain would soon submit to American pressure to devalue the pound, and suggested that the 360 rate would anticipate the general devaluation that took place in the fall.[75]

Dodge served as the focus of Japanese public discontent over the massive layoffs in government and private industry caused by the deflationary program. To avoid defeat at the polls, even sympathetic Japanese leaders publicly opposed Dodge's efforts. As a State Department official noted: "Recovery of a deficit economy requires such harsh and necessarily unpopular measures as could be supported only by bold and able political leaders without resulting in their own political suicide." MacArthur and SCAP officials also sought to shift the onus of deflation onto Dodge to preserve the public's goodwill toward the Occupation. Dodge consciously acted as a magnet to attract the resentment against American policies and sought to project a stern and formidable image, because he believed that only by making the program seem as tough and extreme as possible could he stabilize the economy.[76] Dodge left a legacy of austerity in Japan that is still associated with his name, whenever the Japanese government has enforced austerity policies to prevent payments deficits from threatening foreign exchange holdings.

Export Promotion under the Dodge Plan

Despite its increased controls on Japanese prices and allocations in 1949, SCAP also moved to free Japan's foreign trade. The strictly supervisory Foreign Exchange Control Board replaced the Boeki Cho in February 1949. The board allocated foreign exchange to importers of machinery and raw materials to encourage industrial production for export. The central institution for promoting Japan's exports was established in April, the powerful Ministry of International Trade and Industry (MITI).[77] Driven by Japan's extreme dependence on foreign trade, which made the entire economy vulnerable, MITI has to this day worked closely with industrial combines and their export associations to increase Japan's foreign markets. The obvious success of this government-led trade system has prompted Japan's competitors to label the economy "Japan Incorporated." Japan's long-standing obsession with exports matured during Japan's postwar economic crisis.

Three American missions visited Japan in late 1949 and offered contradictory advice on decontrolling foreign trade. The first, the

Foreign Trade Advisory Commission led by Ormond Freile from the office of the assistant secretary of the Army, consisted mainly of Commerce Department personnel. It recommended abolishing the seventy thousand Japanese export floor prices established to prevent the reoccurrence of the Japanese dumping of the 1930s; abandoning all trade controls; and giving banks control over export financing and exchange. British interests greatly feared Japanese "social dumping"—that is, ultracompetitive export pricing made possible by exploiting labor and enfeebling unions. Britain's powerful unions and social welfare system prevented her from competing with the more aggressive and exploitative capitalistic economies. The British response was to defend the rights of Japanese workers and to promote China as the logical outlet for Japan's exports.[78]

In September 1949, the director general of the Joint Export-Import Agency for Germany, William J. Logan, led a mission to Japan and concurred with Freile on trade decontrol. Logan believed that increasing imports would stimulate Japanese production and eventually increase exports. Both the EROA program and the ERP, designed to finance increased European imports to stimulate industrial recovery, reflected this approach. The Logan Plan was an import-first policy, which made the approval of import licenses semiautomatic. This policy was followed in 1950 and early 1951, until strict controls on imports were required by the large 1951 import surplus. The third mission, led by Jan V. Mladek and Ernest A. Wichin of the International Monetary Fund, compiled a "Report on Exchange and Trade Controls in Japan" in November 1949. They contradicted Logan and Freile by emphasizing the necessity of controls both to prevent the leakage of foreign exchange through unnecessary imports and to compensate for the absence of currency convertibility. Moreover, they advised, controls could be retained after the peace treaty to

> assure that the economic situation does not seriously deteriorate and that American aid funds are not misused. The controls which remain should assume indirect forms to become less conspicuous and obvious. In view of the tremendous importance of trade for the Japanese economy, it would appear that the direction of the exchange and trade controls would offer a very powerful instrument to control the main development of economic life in Japan.

The contradictory advice on import controls reflected the problem of how both to allow essential imports without bureaucratic red tape and at the same time to limit nonessential imports.[79]

Congressional fiscal conservatism and distaste for foreign aid imperiled the Japanese recovery program, as it did the ERP. MacArthur complained to the Army in December 1949 about the proposed 70 percent slash in GARIOA appropriations (which had yet to be approved by Truman). Marquat warned that the cut would have a "devastating impact," because all programs, especially stabilization and trade with Asia, depended on American aid financing. The ultraconservative NAC, however, concluded from "Blue Book" figures that, by squeezing the Japanese as much as possible, aid could be cut by 50 percent and that slashing aid would be a good incentive for Japanese austerity. Army pressure ultimately forced Congress to grant the full appropriation.[80]

The expiration of the Overall Payments Agreement with the sterling area crippled Japan's meager trade recovery in July 1949. The original agreement with Japan's largest export market had been signed in 1948, but the sterling area had not been able to provide food and raw materials, at competitive prices, to match its imports from Japan. Japan thus ran a surplus with the sterling bloc and was unable to convert her 8 million pound reserve into dollars. This only increased Japan's dependence on dollar supplies and aggravated the dollar gap. Through the summer and fall, SCAP and British negotiators battled over the new terms, with SCAP threatening to cut off all trade unless Britain allowed Japan to convert her sterling into dollars. The British answered that Japan would gain export markets only if she were a soft-currency nation without the right to convert. Only then could sterling-area importers buy in Japan without fearing that the resulting deficit would drain their meager dollar reserves. The British could afford to be stubborn. They knew that Japanese exporters were concerned primarily with their own companies' markets and not with Japan's overall dollar gap, and would pressure the government to resume trade.[81]

SCAP finally relented, and the 1949 Overall Payments Agreement, denying convertibility, was signed on November 22. The agreement caused a flood of exports to the sterling area—especially textiles, which had been affected very little by the sterling devaluation of 1949. Machinery exports, however, upon which long-term

Japanese hopes for industrial export recovery lay, "registered a remarkable decrease" as devaluation of sterling raised Japanese prices above the world average.[82] Japan could not, of course, rely solely on textile exports; only when machinery production was modernized through technological improvements—a long and costly process—could Japan overcome the dollar gap.

In addition to blocking Japanese conversion of sterling, the British blocked Japan's access to the General Agreement on Trade and Tariffs (GATT) and the International Wheat Agreement. American wheat exports created a significant portion of the global dollar gap, and other nations naturally sought to buy nondollar wheat from Canada and Australia to conserve their scarce dollars. The International Wheat Agreement rationed nondollar wheat at controlled prices, and Japan wanted to share in this system. The British, however, feared that Japanese purchases would create a shortage of sterling wheat and would force Britain into buying dollar wheat, which, of course, would transfer part of Japan's dollar gap to Britain. Britain's interest in blocking Japanese access to the agreement helps illustrate how and why the global dollar gap frustrated the Japanese recovery program.[83]

Whither Japan? The Crisis of the Dodge Plan

International economic conditions doomed the Dodge Plan from its inception. Foreign demand failed to absorb the surplus production created by the suppression of domestic demand. The balanced budget had prompted massive layoffs and slashed welfare and public works expenditures. Inventories mounted, production dropped, and, most important, modernization of Japanese industry through capital investment stagnated. Investment had been financed by Reconstruction Finance Bank loans, but now depended on counterpart fund disbursements. Japanese business, however, complained incessantly that the funds were not being released rapidly enough to support investment and to prevent deflation. The Japan Management Association, the Economic Stabilization Board, the Bank of Japan, and, especially, the *Oriental Economist* complained that Dodge's "severe deflationary policies" stifled investment and sales. The Economic Stabilization Board pleaded for looser credit policies in early 1950 to prevent a "vicious spiral of contraction," and warned that Japan's industrial base would erode and social and economic stability would be threatened. Japan faced a herculean challenge: to increase exports by $1 billion to balance trade in spite of the global dollar gap, sterling Imperial Preferences, inconvertibility, tariffs, discrimination, and Asian nationalism.[84]

These problems justified Japanese insecurity about export recovery. In February, the *Asahi* newspaper warned: "Japan's foreign trade is now faced with a very grave situation by causes that are beyond control." Japan was locked in a structural trap. High shipping costs—caused by dependence on North American imports—increased Japan's inflation and aggravated her balance-of-payments and export competitiveness problems.[85]

The Army's fears of social deterioration were confirmed. By April 1950, unemployment had reached 500,000, double that of 1948 and 70 percent higher than 1949. The stock market plunged, and small-business bankruptcies spread. Tight money and insufficient domestic and international demand plagued business. The social problems were reflected in political pressures when the restless public and the Diet forced Yoshida and Finance Minister Hayato Ikeda to disavow their support for the Dodge Plan. Ikeda had drawn anger in the Diet for stating that small-business bankruptcies were inevitable and for permitting the Dodge Plan despite the people's suffering. Despite MacArthur's warning that going over SCAP's head would not be tolerated, Yoshida sent Ikeda to the United States in April 1950, to appeal personally to Dodge to ease his policies. Assuring Dodge that labor was docile—more worried about their employment and wages than their organization after 250,000 government workers were fired—Ikeda requested a wage increase for the beleaguered government workers and export credits to stimulate demand. He complained of the mounting inventories, bankruptcies, and the failure of exports. Dodge, who had been warned of the purpose of Ikeda's mission by the Army, sympathized, but maintained that only SCAP had the authority to revise policy.[86]

The possible consequences of economic collapse in Japan for Japanese political stability and the Pacific alliance alarmed American observers in early 1950. *U.S. News and World Report* reported on

April 28 that Japan was on the "verge of an economic depression," and that deflation amounted to "economic suicide." Elements of the ESS staff also opposed such extreme austerity. In early 1949 they charged that the Dodge Plan implied "such drastic measures [that they would] seriously threaten the objectives of the nine-point program." In January 1950, Kenneth Morrow, the head of the programs and statistics division, warned Marquat that "Japan ha[d] entered a deflationary economic crisis threatening progress toward self-support." He said that using counterpart funds for debt retirement was overly deflationary: "Unless a shift is made and made quickly, there may well be a serious relapse in Japan's progress toward recovery and an intensification of the present credit crisis." He noted that the production index had stagnated from April 1949 to January 1950, despite increased aid-financed imports.[87]

Another circle within SCAP, however, treated Dodge as a financial god and believed that the economy *was* becoming more efficient. Obviously, laying off workers raised business productivity in one sense, but increased production and the consequent benefits of greater economies of scale were the only long-term means to achieve greater efficiency and finance plant modernization. Marquat, Fine, and Dick Diehl, the Treasury attaché who worked closely with Dodge, all blamed the alarmism on a Japanese conspiracy to force SCAP to relax its policies. They especially despised the *Oriental Economist,* a key forum for Japanese business opposition to deflation. Dodge and Fine urged an investigation of the facts behind the "propaganda" about the mushrooming small-business failures. Dodge suggested that many of the victims were only inefficient businesses that had profited from inflation but could not operate under less favorable conditions.[88] SCAP's official statements painted a rosy picture of stable prices and gradually increasing production and export figures in the spring of 1950. Spurred by the end of the American recession, the consequent easing of the world dollar crisis, and the spurt of sterling exports, the indices crept up through June, but Japan's position was so grave that far more dramatic improvements were necessary to set the economy on the path of modernization and recovery.

It is prudent to discount some of the fears of imminent collapse. Japanese business had traditionally been alarmist. Caution and pessimism were sound approaches given Japan's extreme economic vulnerability. Business, moreover, had an interest in exaggerating its plight to avoid painful economic adjustments. The Dodge Plan, however, clearly did not set Japan on a self-sustaining path of industrial modernization. Owing primarily to the harsh international climate in 1950, Japan was treading water, not modernizing. Massive investment, requiring the stimulation of industrial demand, was the only answer to Japan's competitive problem. Classic austerity was not, therefore, entirely appropriate to put Japan's industries to work. It did consolidate conservative-corporate rule in Japan by giving teeth to the antilabor red purge.

A recent econometric study casts doubt on many of the commonplace assumptions about the Dodge Plan. Economist Dick K. Nanto discovered that the plan was not as deflationary as has been assumed, because Japanese financial officials offset austerity measures by lowering taxes and using liberal credit policies. Dodge criticized but tolerated these violations of his principles, because he did not want to cripple the economy totally and sought mainly to impose an *atmosphere* of austerity. He explained that he had initially acted with such harshness in order to end the dollar gap in time for a 1950 peace treaty. When the treaty was delayed, Dodge said he could then "spread it out." Thus, Marquat's assurance to the Army on June 13, 1950, was true: "Neither in conception nor execution has the 'Dodge line' been as rigorous as assumed." Nanto also discovered that, contrary to SCAP's belief, inflation was largely curbed by the time Dodge arrived in Japan. Thus, the attack against inflation was neither as deflationary nor as successful as has been thought.[89]

This study cannot render a definitive judgment on the Dodge Plan. Yet the likelihood is that its significance has been exaggerated. Japan's position required massive industrial stimulation, which the Dodge Plan and international conditions prevented. Since the plan had little impact on prices, it served primarily to reduce the power of labor, provide the private banking system with a renewed grip on the economy, add to the considerable economic deprivations of the Japanese people, and delay industrial recovery. Historian Chalmers Johnson, agreeing with virtually all observers, concludes that the plan did cut inflation, "but it did so at the cost of a recession in Japan, a sharp rise in unemployment, and some of the harshest working conditions during 1949 and 1950 since the end of the war five years earlier. Thousands of workers were fired to lower unit costs (over 100,000 in the National Railroads alone). . . . Stabilization rather than economic growth was what SCAP had managed to achieve."[90] Classic bankers' austerity, at great social cost, did little to advance Japan from its position in world trade in 1947. Despite the efforts of Japanese business to subsidize industrial recovery, Japan had yet to reap the harvest of the Keynesian revolution.

3. The United States and Japan in Southeast Asia, 1947–1950

The crux of Japan's recovery problem is her foreign trade, and this in turn is dependent upon three factors over the next five years, currency convertibility, U.S. appropriations, and recovery in the Far East. The first is unlikely on a sufficient scale to help Japan. The second is, even if forthcoming, a temporary palliative. The third holds the key to Japan's recovery. With colonies lost, and with conditions chaotic in northeastern Asia, Japan's principal alternative to dollar areas as a source of imports, Japan is presently dependent upon dollar areas while looking to unsettled southeast Asia as a supplementary source of food and other imports and a probable major market for fabricated products.

—*Jerome Cohen*, Japan's Economy in
War and Reconstruction

Is there any reason why the Philippine Republic, with all its just and rightful sympathy for the American taxpayer, should agree to a deal under which the Japanese will profit and prosper and the Philippines will remain on the old colonial basis of providing basic and strategic materials to a former enemy in exchange for the modern equivalent of glass beads, brass rings and hand mirrors? Especially when the Philippines can make its own glass beads, brass rings and hand mirrors.

—Manila Times *Editorial, May 7, 1948*

103

Preserving the East Asian Status Quo

Since the 1880s the Western imperialist powers had viewed Japan as a junior partner in the development of Asian resources and markets. The United States and Britain had historically cooperated with Japan over the control of China, but after 1929 the Japanese vowed to match the economic might of the West by carving out their own Asian sphere to feed their industries. Japan used government subsidies for heavy industry, and exploited markets created by World War I to develop an economic base. Prompted by the collapse of world markets in the 1930s and by the failure of classic deflationary policies, Japan challenged the Western imperialists by invading China. The West had historically justified its military expansion in Asia as "spreading civilization and stability," and Japan believed that it could advance these same noble causes while freeing Asia from Western domination, and also securing badly needed markets and sources of raw materials. The invasion of China, however, defied American multilateral/open-door aims, handed down from Hay to Wilson to Hull.

Many Americans with influence over Asian policy respected Japan's economic stake in the Asian mainland in the 1930s, but they argued that Japan would realize extremely valuable advantages by cooperating more fully with the West. Joseph Grew, ambassador to Japan, believed that Japan was "entirely justified in taking all legitimate and reasonable safeguards to enhance and conserve its own security and safety." Americans, too, were interested in the "commerce and economic development of Far Eastern countries" and "would not view favorably the infiltration or the growth in those countries of subversive influences"—that is, Communism.[1] Americans explained that Japan had more to gain from free trade and more to lose from exclusive colonialism than did other powers, since she depended heavily on foreign trade. The Japanese said that multilateralism was a fine theory, but argued that, in reality, Japan was surrounded by exclusive colonial powers which denied her access to her geographical neighbors; they cited British invasions of Syria and the American sphere in Latin America, protected by the Monroe Doctrine, as examples of Western aggression to gain commercial advantages.[2] They claimed that the only difference between Japanese and American imperialism was Japan's more primitive methods.

Hull countered that the United States had turned a "new leaf" in its Latin American policy. He said that Latin America was open for cooperative development by *all* powers, and that the United States had indeed profited by "renouncing its previous policies of stationing armed forces in Latin American countries." He mentioned "the great increase that had taken place in United States trade with those countries." If Japan adopted an open policy in China and dropped the symbolic term "Greater East Asia," he continued, she could "derive an incalculable advantage in the way of trade." Hull explained that formal colonialism was too expensive and confining; Japan could indeed trade with Indochina without the burden of military occupation. Sumner Welles, moreover, pleaded for the Japanese to realize "how much Japan would profit if, for example, British Imperial Preferences were abolished and Japan could trade with all the Pacific nations, including Canada, Australia, and New Zealand, on the same terms on which England could trade."[3] Japan, however, could not prejudice its economic security by waiting for Western imperialistic powers to reform and grant equal trading privileges to Japan.

American businesses with interests in Japan pressed the Roosevelt Administration to recognize a modus vivendi in Asia based on Japanese domination. The Administration agreed that pro-American forces in Japan would triumph only if the United States could assure Japanese access to critical Asian markets.[4] On November 15, 1941, only three weeks before Pearl Harbor, Hull presented an economic cooperation plan to the Japanese. In return for peace and equal rights in China, the United States would join with Japan to "suggest to China the inauguration of a comprehensive program of economic development with most-favored-nation treatment to be given" Japan and the United States. The cooperation scheme would apply to all Asian countries and would constitute "a long forward step" in obtaining Japan's objectives.[5] The State Department believed that by cultivating the goodwill of dependent territories with appeals to political nationalism it could elicit cooperation in multilateral development programs. Americans sought to end formal and exclusive colonialism in order to unshackle world trade and to enable "important nations to join in a liberal commercial program for vastly increased production and healthy trade in all parts of the world."[6] Japan could secure her economic requirements under American plans because the existing division of labor between primary producing areas and manufacturing nations would continue.

The American plan promised something for everybody, except the European colonial powers. Asians would gain political independence, albeit under Western and Japanese economic control, and Japan and the United States would gain long-sought access to Asian resources and markets. This scheme derived from American policy toward settlement of the Boxer Rebellion in 1900, when the United States sought free trade and commercial advantages for the West while preserving Chinese territorial integrity.[7] In 1941 Japan's favorable strategic position dictated that it reject the American offer; to retreat in expectation of sudden changes in Western colonial policies made no sense. After World War II, however, Japan's economy more than ever required access to Asia, and the United States gradually came to offer Japan the same terms of cooperation in Asia that Hull had proposed in 1941. American policy required reviving Japanese industry and trade to stimulate the Asian economy and to help create international economic equilibrium. Thus, the reverse course in 1947 and 1948 represented continuity in American policy toward Asia from the 1930s.

Before the Japanese surrender, the United States was caught between the forces of emerging Asian nationalism and declining European colonialism. In November 1944, American multilateral principles led Max Bishop, State Department representative to the British-dominated Southeast Asian Command, to oppose European plans to reconquer Southeast Asia. Bishop advised that if the United States could not win Europeans over to multilateral cooperation in Southeast Asia or form a third force to seize local nationalist sentiment, Asians would turn to Russia for anticolonial support.[8] Another American official in Southeast Asia warned in 1947 that even if the French won a military victory in its struggle in Indochina, the "hatreds engendered will defeat French civil and economic objectives and threaten all Western interests in Southeast Asia. [The] Soviet [Union is] . . . not directly active [in] Southeast Asia and need not be as [the] democracies [are] performing most effectively [on] their behalf," by repressing nationalism.[9] Other Americans in Asia protested the "criminal and bestial" French military oppression of the popular Indochinese nationalist movement.[10] European imperial reconquest of Southeast Asia violated American multilateral principles and threatened American plans to turn Southeast Asia into another Latin America, where political nationalism was tolerated as long as it did not interfere with traditional colonial trade patterns. Yet, in Washington, State Department officials were reluctant to oppose European recolonization of Southeast Asia for fear of weakening and antagonizing their industrial allies and of provoking chaos and revolution in the wake of independence.

European reconquest was intolerable for Southeast Asians, bitter after decades of European domination and Japanese occupation. Japan had fostered Asian pride in the hopes that other Asians would drive out the Europeans; by 1945 nationalism dominated Southeast Asian politics. Southeast Asians sought independence and economic diversification to free themselves from their dependent position as a primary producing backwater of the industrial West. They eagerly embraced the UN's Economic Commission for Asia and the Far East (ECAFE) to foster their economic development; they rejoiced that their dominating neighbor, Japan, was controlled and demilitarized; and they marveled at the Marshall Plan, looking to the United States for both help in their struggle for independence and economic aid to develop their productive capacities. Although economic diversification was the only route to true national independence, their primary task was to develop national maturity, cohesion, and organizational strength. Colonialism, although it introduced modern thought to élites, stifled Southeast Asian evolutionary growth and retarded its initiative and self-confidence.

Above all, the degree of national economic integration they achieved would determine their hopes for self-generating economic growth. Southeast Asian economic integration with Japan and the West, developed under colonialism and a goal of U.S. multilateral plans in 1947, would, in the main, retard domestic economic linkages. "Strong domestic linkages" means that increased demand by one sector of the economy stimulates many other sectors; spin-off effects of the development of the American automobile industry are good examples. If these linkages are poorly formed, however, increased demand by one sector merely increases imports, which can lead to balance-of-payments problems. Payments deficits provoke the imposition of deflationary policies by Western financial bodies, especially the International Monetary Fund and the World Bank, leading to slower growth and lower living standards.[11]

American political diplomacy in Asia sought a "third force" between colonialism and militant, anti-Western nationalism. Hull's multilateral policies were the foundation of the postwar planning of the State Department's Office of Economic Affairs, led by Will Clayton. In 1945 it sought free and expanding Asian trade to increase world markets,[12] since American business needed free access to expanding foreign markets (see Chapter 1). This multilateral policy contradicted the more temporary and war-induced recommendations of the Pauley report, which sought to reduce Japan's domination of the Asian economy, and implied freedom for Southeast Asia to protect its infant industries through nationalistic economic policies. Japanese business, which greatly influenced SCAP's Economic and Scientific Section, agreed in 1946 that the Japanese economy required extensive Asian trade. In order to facilitate such trade, SCAP promptly sent a trade mission to Southeast Asia to explore the "important and traditional" market for Japanese exports and the "normal" source for Japanese raw material imports.[13] In November 1946, State Department officers first discussed an "East Asian Regional Economic Plan," including most-favored-nation tariff status for Japan. Such ideas, however, though consistent with multilateralism, were too controversial in the aftermath of war; if they leaked they could destroy U.S. prestige in Asia.[14]

In 1947, the State and Army departments emphasized the necessity of Japanese trade with Southeast Asia in their policy deliberations. Substituting Southeast Asian materials for American primary products would be one step toward solving the dollar gap puzzle. The March 1947 Martin memo suggested offering reparations to soothe Southeast Asian resentment toward Japan and to stimulate regional trade. Martin thus neatly tied Japanese recovery and Southeast Asian development together into a combined program, in an effort to convince Asians that Japanese recovery would be crucial to their own development. SWNCC 381, the State Department recovery plan, said that Southeast Asia required foreign capital because of inadequate local capital development. Proclaiming the ultimate trickledown theory, State claimed that the United States had to build up Japan so that Japan could eventually export capital to develop Southeast Asia. It inaccurately equated the financial position of Asian nations with that of the United States in the nineteenth century when America used British capital to develop its economy. George Kennan summarized department thinking: without Asian trade, "Japan face[s], even [in] the best of circumstances, an economic problem of extremely serious dimension," which, he felt, would threaten the stability of Japan and her loyalty to the United States.[15]

Doubts about the prospects for Japanese–Southeast Asian trade created pessimism about the success of recovery plans. John Allison (later, ambassador to Japan) told Butterworth in December 1947 that SWNCC 381 insufficiently emphasized Japan's need for Far Eastern trade. The recovery of Japan depended on regional cooperation and the return to triangular trade, he said, to enable Japan to balance its dollar deficit through dollar earnings in Southeast Asia. Allison suggested using "imagination" to overcome the contradiction between Southeast Asian political nationalism and the economic realities of Japanese trade needs. While the United States could plead the burden of supporting Japan to fellow industrial powers to justify the "reverse course" in Japan, he warned, such parsimony would not impress the impoverished Southeast Asians. A Marshall Plan for Asia was impractical from the standpoint of the United States, he warned, but a single-nation trade program for Japan would certainly be doomed to fail. With the probable "loss" of China, he said that the "cooperation of these Southeast Asian nations may become absolutely essential if Japan is to be kept from falling into Soviet arms as a result of economic opportunities in Northern Asia."[16] American policy during the following decade indeed centered on helping Japan integrate with Southeast Asia to avoid forcing Japan into economic accommodation with the Communist mainland.

The United States and ECAFE

In 1947, SCAP officials also emphasized the necessity of Japanese trade with Southeast Asia. In October, the ESS made progress in trade with Southeast Asia the critical variable in its timetable for Japanese self-support. Given "progress" in the Far East, Japan's trade would balance by 1951; otherwise, SCAP projected, it would take until 1953.[17] SCAP invited Dr. P. S. Lokanathan, secretary general of the United Nations Economic Commission for Asia and the Far East (ECAFE), to Japan and explained the plan to integrate the region with the Japanese economy. He was told that, since Japan seemed unlikely ever to balance her trade with the dollar area, SCAP had decided to "focus upon eventual integration of the economy of Japan with the economies of Asia and the Far East rather than with the economy of the United States."[18]

American relations with ECAFE illustrated the problem of encouraging political nationalism while at the same time discouraging economic nationalism. At the 1947 conference, the American representative, Monnet Davis, urged Southeast Asian nations to pull themselves up by their bootstraps and assured them that the United States would help. The Southeast Asian press, not eager for a Horatio Alger lecture but anxious for economic aid, interpreted Davis's speech as possibly signaling a large American aid program for Asia. Under Secretary of State Robert Lovett, however, immediately ordered Davis to disavow that possibility, which, not surprisingly, disappointed the Asians. The Philippine press reported that the United States sided with the British against the Philippines and was supporting the "virtual subordination of ECAFE to the British controlled Southeast Asian Commission,"[19] the Western military alliance in Southeast Asia.

When it denied aid funds, the United States eliminated its most potent diplomatic weapon to elicit Southeast Asian cooperation in Japanese recovery. The decision was, however, consistent with American interests; since limited funds were available, an aid commitment might threaten vital dollar funding of industrial allies in Europe and Japan, and it would inflate Southeast Asia's expectations about the benefits of aid and the depth of the American commitment. There was a sharp difference between European recovery (based solidly on established infrastructure, organization, and skilled labor) and development in Southeast Asian nations (based on fragile monocultural economies, with their cohesion, organization, and maturity stunted by decades of colonial domination).

Nationalist China and some of its American friends reacted bitterly to the Japan-centric Asian policy of the United States. But by 1947 the Nationalists' rampant corruption and incompetence led the

State Department to cogently discount the Chinese revolution on the strategic balance sheet. Even a victorious Nationalist regime would be a weak and unreliable ally compared with a socially stable and economically powerful Japan. This fact weakens the arguments of many who cite the final collapse of Chiang's forces in 1949 as the critical factor in U.S. intervention in Asia in early 1950. As early as 1947, China hands had to admit that Chinese chaos would preclude an effective American influence. One wrote to a friend in Shanghai that the United States, regrettably, had to focus on Japan; China's instability would prevent it from guaranteeing export deliveries to fulfill its role in a regional economic plan "that will work." Only Japan could anchor economic recovery, he continued: "We are working on some ways of tying the interest of other countries more directly into revival of Japan's economy . . . but by something short of complete regionalism."[20]

The Chinese press criticized the "idea that the Far Eastern recovery program be built around Japan's industrial capacity." They feared Japanese domination and knew that it would jeopardize the industrial plans of other Asian countries. Carlos Romulo of the Philippines agreed, warning in late 1945 that the Japanese were acting meek only to fool the Allies and that Japan should be occupied by the Chinese: "Our fight against Japan has just begun." China hand Robert Barnett agreed with Martin that circumstances dictated that Japan was the best option for the United States, but felt that "of course there [would] be political problems. . . . Some will say making Japan the fabricator of Asia's raw materials will retard industrial development of Southeast Asia." If the United States "switched sides," he continued, and cooperated with Japan's economic ambitions, and if Japanese textiles again dominated Asian markets, Southeast Asian, Indian, Chinese, and European exporters might blame the United States, not necessarily Japan. He warned that "the cranking up operation undertaken on sole or dominantly American responsibility opens the door to charges of American economic colonialism which would be hard to refute," and which might prejudice the entire recovery program. Barnett believed that the Japanese recovery policy conflicted in spirit with the "open door," Hull's nonrecognition note, and the American defense of China and the Philippines from Japanese imperialism.[21] He misread the essence of open-door policy and

Hullian multilateralism when he claimed that the United States reversed its Asian policies after World War II. Hull had proposed to powerful prewar Japan a plan for the cooperative "development" of Asia. This offer was even more necessary after the war as the United States sought to prevent a prostrate Japan from succumbing to the lure of economic opportunities in Communist north Asia.

The Ideology of Neocolonialism

State Department Southeast Asian officers had little sympathy for the nationalistic economic aspirations of Southeast Asian nations. They sought to free American Asian diplomacy from the confines of ECAFE, which harbored the anticolonial ideology of the Soviet Union and which emphasized the desirability of generous American aid. ECAFE, moreover, strongly supported the nationalist forces in Indochina and Indonesia. Before the 1948 conference, two Southeast Asian officers warned their superior about U.S. participation in ECAFE:

> It is not difficult to imagine the sorry figure which the United States is going to present at the conference. The only reason we are welcome is because we have money. Accordingly, as we have no intention of establishing an ECA for the Far East, our position will be that of a fat cow which is going to play coy with the milkmaid and not produce. It is hard to see what advantages will accrue to us from this role or from encouraging our poor relations to form a combined front against us.

The Soviets, they continued, would put the United States and the European colonial powers on the defensive with respect to Indonesia and Indochina. The United States would "then oppose these applications, and in so doing be reduced to what Churchill calls 'frothing pious platitudes' on our abiding sympathy for the nationalist aspirations of dependent peoples. It can hardly be maintained that we are going to win friends in the Far East by this kind of performance." Yet, the department did rely on such diplomacy, despite the belief of Southeast Asian experts that the United States was above stooping to plead with the backward Asians. The Soviets, they argued, would raise anticolonial issues which would be "false, misleading and quite unworthy of our notice." These would force the United States to be "negative and apologetic. If ECAFE had ever accomplished anything or appeared likely to accomplish anything, there might be some compensation for the indignity and absurdity of our position. No tangible gains which might accrue to us are, however, discernible."[22]

These officials believed that American diplomacy was at a disadvantage when confronted at ECAFE by a unified and ambitious Asia. The United States could be more persuasive if it confronted each of the weak nations individually and made bilateral agreements. They argued that the United States cheapened its position by pleading for cooperation. If the United States "set a higher value upon itself," adopted a "more realistic attitude," and dropped "its air of eager prostitution," the pressure would shift to the Soviets to show what contribution they could make to Far Eastern development. State Department officials, however, ultimately chose military intervention over withdrawal from Asia. Southeast Asian officers urged the United States to fragment Asian nationalists and undermine ECAFE, which "serve[d] merely as a sounding board for those who [were] in ideological opposition to the United States," or were disappointed by the lack of American aid.[23] Another official warned that Southeast Asians "show[ed] little or no interest in merely expanding their production of foodstuffs and raw materials." They would not accept conditional aid designed to channel their development along lines desired by the West, nor would they grant concessions to private capital investment from abroad. They knew, he advised, that expanding their production would threaten their raw materials prices and market position, and would deplete their resources. Raw materials were uniform and irreplaceable, and increased production would only help the terms of trade of industrial nations and hurt the terms of trade of nonindustrial nations.[24]

When Myron Cowen, ambassador to the Philippines, told the 1948 ECAFE conference that a large U.S. aid program would not be forthcoming, the Asians were forced to look in new directions. Secretary Marshall had ordered Cowen to vote against continuing ECAFE if any sentiment could be found to disband the organization. He also ordered Cowen to delete from his speech the argument that "heavy industry is not a *sine qua non* for improved standards of living . . . [in order to] forestall any unfriendly questions about America's plans for industrial rehabilitation of Japan."[25] Instead, Cowen lauded the experience of the United States as a debtor nation, which had "neither feared nor experienced any domination by its creditors." He overlooked the historical reality of vehement U.S. economic nationalism in the nineteenth century, especially the significant role of tariff protection, and the resentment of European financial influence. Marshall reminded him that the "major objective" of U.S. economic policy in Southeast Asia was "to increase production of food and needed exports for Europe and Japan."[26] Economic pressures to revive its industrial allies and stimulate colonial trade patterns clearly cast the United States with the metropolitan powers and alienated the nationalistic intelligentsia of Asia, from which the United States hoped to cultivate its "third force."

Asian nations placed their development hopes on ECAFE's Committee on Industry and Trade and its subcommittee on iron and steel. Americans, however, argued that the committee was unnecessary and its goals unrealistic, because European studies showed that there would "probably be excess world steel capacity . . . by 1953 if all presently planned steel investment programs are complete. . . . The programs of the European steel producers particularly are predicated on the existence of large overseas export markets. It is likely that there will be strong competition among European and Western Hemisphere producers for the markets of the Far East and Asia." The American policy paper on ECAFE warned, however, that this was "unfortunately . . . a point that cannot be strongly stressed in ECAFE meetings, since it would provide an opening for Soviet representatives to charge that the United States intends to keep the Far East industrially undeveloped to protect its access to the raw materials of the area."[27]

In the FEC, the Soviets had suggested that "the Asian countries . . . be encouraged to develop their industries with the aid of tariffs so as to avoid being crushed by imports from the Western countries." From the perspectives of Europe, Japan, the ECA, SCAP, and the State Department, world economic recovery had to occur along pre–World War II lines; contrarily, the colonies and ex-colonies sought to diversify and shatter the monopoly on industry held by the West and Japan. The American position paper on ECAFE claimed: "It is, of course, a fallacy that industrial development must be based on an indigenous steel industry." In 1949, the United States again preached the benefits of importing capital and exporting raw materials, and it again cited its own economic history and its lack of fear of foreign domination.[28]

American antagonism toward economic nationalism and industrial development also surfaced at the Institute for Pacific Relations conference in London in 1947. A British member noted that the 1930s depression had cut the flow of supplies from Europe to Southeast Asia. Thus, "some local development of industry took place . . . before the war and, under a psychological urge for more diversified economies, is certain to continue." An American member drew attention to the danger that local development might degenerate into a policy of autarky, which could, if adopted widely, "strangle world trade and harm both the Far Eastern countries and the world at large." The American suggested that Southeast Asians rely on workshop economies such as Japan for manufactured goods.[29]

The Quest for Integration

Through 1948 and 1949, Japanese business and government representatives, the Army, SCAP, and others pressed for rapidly expanding Japanese–Southeast Asian trade as a key to recovery. Sebald reported to Washington that Japanese businessmen "were anxiously looking forward to the time when they may return to Indonesia." Hisato Ichimada, governor of the Bank of Japan, requested a "Marshall Plan for Asia" to promote Japanese recovery by increasing Southeast Asian purchasing power. The Japanese Economic Stabilization Board based its 1948 Five-Year Plan on triangular trade, through which Japan could cover its deficit with North America by earning dollars in Southeast Asia—a plan identical to the solution to Europe's dollar gap.[30]

Although it assumed that Japan's trade with Southeast Asia would grow, the Army expected Japan to have a dollar deficit through 1955. In its 1948 EROA aid proposal to Congress, the Army pleaded that "unless raw materials become available and trade can be resumed, Japan will not reach the levels of production necessary to its own solvency."[31] In the "Blue Book," Sherwood Fine wrote that Japanese trade with Asia "represents the natural and necessary course for Japan and the highly inter-related economies of the Far East." The SCAP plan assumed that political and economic conditions in Asia would permit the necessary expansion of Japanese trade, and that the United States would create an integrated and expanding aid program for Asia. In addition, the National Security Resources Board advised the National Security Council that while many Asians "were most reluctant to see Japan establish her erstwhile trading position . . . we must either help them in re-establishment of their markets, or we must be prepared to bear the cost as a continuing drain against the United States and its resources." It suggested that the Army, the State Department, and the ECA act in "close concert" to devise methods to guarantee Japanese markets and sources in Asia. When Draper appealed to the State Department for such a program, Lovett replied that it was only being discussed, that the real objective in Southeast Asia was to increase raw materials production and exports, and that aid was only a means to this end.[32] The American perspective, for budgetary, political, strategic, and multilateral reasons, became so Japan-centric that MacArthur, who certainly was intimately aware of Japanese brutality in Asia, complained to Kennan that "Far Eastern countries were shamelessly selfish and negative toward Japan." He did admit that this was "understandable," but said that it was no reason for them not to cooperate wholeheartedly in promoting Japanese recovery.[33]

In December 1948, the State Department invited noted international economists to discuss the possibility of a coordinated American economic program for the Far East. The "basic question," stated John A. Loftus, "[was] can we find a focus of integration like the one we have in Western Europe?" Apart from Japan, Asian nations had competitive primary producing economies with links to Europe, not to each other. ECAFE pushed regional industrialization, which would stimulate regional integration, but was not in American interests, Loftus continued, because "it would reduce our raw materials sources, and we don't need to export capital goods" (suggesting that in the early postwar period the United States had adequate capital goods markets). To cover the Asian dollar gap, the economists recommended that the United States increase its rubber, tin, and strategic materials imports from Southeast Asia. The American goal in Japan, they agreed, was "to get off the hook as quickly as we can [and] the most obvious way is to re-establish the Japanese economy in its pre-war position."[34]

Coordinated aid meant combining two aid programs into one, or using one aid program to supply two foreign nations. Under the ERP's Aid to Dependent Territories Program (the European parallel to the effort to integrate Japan and Southeast Asia), the ECA sent dollars or counterpart funds to increase raw materials production in European colonies. This was designed to increase Europe's dollar earnings in two ways: it would increase primary production in nondollar areas to reduce European dependence on American supplies, and it would increase the capacity of the colonies to import from Europe, which would ultimately help finance European industrial modernization. Martin's March 1947 memo was the first of several to suggest aiding Southeast Asian countries to induce them to trade with Japan.[35]

In October 1948, Butterworth advised Lovett that broad proposals for coordinated aid to Asia were "being made rather frequently of late." Draper had told the National Security Council, and the State Department agreed, that the United States must ensure "that the markets of Asia provide an effective demand for Japanese exports in order that Japan may become self-supporting." With political and military stability and coordinated aid, Butterworth said, it would be possible to resume the "flow of normal exports to the rest of the world" at little cost to the United States. He warned that the Asians had an "overriding ambition" for development, but that the United States must dispel all thought of a Marshall Plan for Asia because of the region's instability and structural backwardness, and because private capital was better suited to develop its resources.[36]

Butterworth cogently warned that American aid would not increase the standard of living in Asia. (He cited, for example, the problem of a high birthrate, which would negate productivity gains.) He correctly anticipated that American aid programs would have little to offer many underdeveloped areas and prophetically argued the greater practicality of investing in "stable" areas, especially police states such as Taiwan and South Korea. These states have established a highly favorable climate for private investment and profit; they have attracted capital, and achieved a form of "development," albeit very uneven development. But, he added, in reference to primary production and the workshop concept, "this is not to say that the gradual development of Asia's resources at a realistic rate would not contribute to the eventual expansion of world trade." Small aid programs, possibly using IBRD funds, and focusing on stable primary producing areas such as the Philippines, might indeed serve American interests. He warned against pushing integration so hard that it would incite a nationalistic backlash, and he advised Lovett not to create elaborate bureaucratic machinery, but to use single-nation, bilateral aid programs. Lovett agreed that the problem merited intensive consideration, but the studies which followed in 1949 were considered still too sensitive to discuss openly.[37]

While the department was wary of provoking anti-Japanese sentiments by publicly discussing integration, there was much public discussion in the United States in 1948 and 1949 concerning Japan's grave trade problem. Jerome Cohen wrote in *Pacific Affairs* that "basic solutions [to Japan's problems] can come only with a complete integration of the Japanese economy with those of all other Far Eastern countries." Unless the United States developed a "comprehensive and coordinated program for the revival of all Far Eastern countries," the Japanese program would fail. Robert Barnett echoed this pessimism in *Far Eastern Survey,* and it was also shared by SCAP officials, who felt helpless when confronted with the massive economic problems of Asia. The *Nation* printed two opposing views on Japanese recovery policy. Yole Granada, a former SCAP historian, pleaded for support of Japanese expansion in Asia. Her adversary, Harold Strauss, admitted that her economic logic was correct but charged that her moral principles were askew. He said that the program was similar to that of Japanese expansionists in 1941: "I have heard more than one Japanese predict that the American army would win for Japan what its own army failed to win." He warned that without limits on its expansion, Japan would inevitably dominate the Asian economy. Concurring with the Pauley report and with McMahon Ball, Strauss said Japan would abuse her economic power to take political advantage of other Asians.[38]

Another former SCAP official, Joseph Z. Reday, blasted the Pauley report in *Far Eastern Survey* in June 1949. He charged that "to end Japan's industrial supremacy among the nations of the Far East" was "largely economic nonsense, since Japan's economic position vis-à-vis Asia cannot be significantly altered by a political operation, except at the expense of great economic dislocation throughout the area." He insisted that Japan was the key consumer of Asian raw materials because she naturally industrialized more quickly, and that her dollar deficit could be solved only by "adequate or realistic consideration of the problem of reintegrating an industrial Japan into the largely unindustrialized Far Eastern milieu where she belongs."[39]

Joseph Dodge was perhaps the most influential advocate of coordinated aid to further integration. He told the National Advisory Council that under the ERP, which provided ample dollars to stimulate intra-European trade, a "growing market was created for German production while Japan continues to exist in an area of political and economic disturbance having production, trade and income levels still below pre-war." Because Japan was the only country under direct American control and the only economic power in Asia, Dodge said, "It is probable that the development of our future Far Eastern policy will require the use of Japan as a springboard and source of supply for the extension of further aid to the Far Eastern Areas." Soon after arriving in Japan in February 1949, he cabled Draper to advise ECA administrator Hoffman that "one of the principal aims of the United States foreign policy in the Far East must be the greatest possible integration of United States aid programs to the end that United States appropriated dollars may be used several times over" to stimulate Far Eastern trade. He recommended coordinating Army and ECA aid programs to finance development projects that would enable Japan to buy more raw materials in Asia instead of importing them from the dollar area.[40]

To facilitate Japanese trade recovery, Acheson directed American officials in Asia in July 1949 to cooperate with SCAP. They were to encourage increased food and raw materials production for all industrial nations, but especially for Japan. He explained that Japan would thus gain dollars to reduce both her deficit and the necessity of American aid; Acheson wrote that although this constituted a regional aid program, it was not similar to the ERP. All aid agreements would be bilateral; there would be no American commitment, no regional organization, and only $400 million would be spent from 1949 through 1952, including IBRD funds.[41]

By dealing with weak Southeast Asian nations individually the United States could dominate the discussions and channel development efforts toward primary production. Acheson recognized, however, that development was seen by Southeast Asian nationalists as a means of achieving independence: "The Asian country's desire for economic development has an emotional, and therefore a political significance which is quite independent of the question of whether development would contribute to the eventual improvement of balance of payments and living conditions." The United States would not support "unsound" nationalistic policies, he said, but must attempt to convince Asians that the American program would advance their development and satisfy their nationalistic aspirations. Moreover, the United States had to focus Japanese economic ambitions on Southeast Asia to "avoid preponderant [Japanese] dependence on Chinese sources" of critical imports, which would expose Japan to Chinese blackmail. Since the United States and Europe tended to monopolize trade with Latin America and Africa respectively, he explained, Japan would have to compete successfully in Southeast Asia in order to prosper.[42]

The China Equation

American economic and strategic policy in Asia can be reduced to a simple equation: Japan's dependence on trade would force her into accommodation with China unless she achieved a large stable trade with Southeast Asia. American officials, from Fearey and Kennan through Dulles, argued that Japan lacked the capitalistic and individualistic heritage of Europe, and could thus quickly adapt to socialistic organization and policies. If Japanese business decided it required significant trade with China, it would not hesitate to make diplomatic concessions to the revolutionary government. Through 1949, U.S. officials presumed that Japan could rely on limited trade with China to ease the dollar gap and shipping costs. But the danger of Japanese-Chinese collaboration left the United States with a difficult decision. Even the foreign trade and commerce division of

SCAP, which would see its trade recovery policies advanced by increased Chinese trade, could not decide how much should be allowed. The State Department and the Army agreed in 1949 that China trade was a "grey" issue, with no clear path to choose.[43]

Despite the economic logic of permitting Japanese trade with China, American officials feared its effect on Japan. In May 1949, Acheson warned that the "whole Far East [was] feeling [the] impact [of] Commie advances in China." He reported that the Japanese were both impressed and uneasy about the Communists' gains: "Japan will either move toward sound friendly relations with non-Commie countries or into association with the Commie system in Asia."[44] If the United States recognized China, it might thus encourage Chinese Titoism. Close Russian-Chinese ties and the cold war psychology of NSC 68, however, dictated preventing other industrial allies from selling modern equipment and food to China, in hopes of causing economic collapse. In March 1949 Truman approved NSC 41, which concluded that SCAP should pursue trade with China to the extent that it would help Japan's trade, but "every effort should be made to develop alternative sources on an economic basis, particularly in areas such as South Asia where a need exists for Japanese exports." Despite this approval, implementation of such a sensitive policy proved difficult, although the United States did lift some restrictions on Sino-Japanese trade in early 1950.[45]

The British pressured the United States to recognize China in order to preserve their entrepôt in Hong Kong, their commercial ties to the mainland, and a Chinese outlet for Japanese trade to reduce Japanese competition in Southeast Asia. They informed the United States that the "Western powers should be resigned to the bad political influence which that trade would perforce have on Japan." Thus, on the eve of the Korean War, American policy was divided; political fears of Japanese-Chinese rapprochement contradicted the economic necessity of Chinese trade to ease the dollar gap. There was no clear solution to the problem.[46]

Neocolonial Alliances

Had the French allowed the development of Indochinese political nationalism while preserving Western commercial influence,

American policy in Southeast Asia might have been successful. French arrogance and racism, and their desire for a monopoly in Indochina, however, foiled American hopes for concessions to political nationalism. In March 1949, the Policy Planning staff completed its study of Southeast Asian policy, deciding that the United States could fully back neither colonialism nor nationalistic revolution. The answer was to pressure the Europeans to cooperate but, above all, to be discreet and let the Asians appear to lead the attack against Communism so as "to minimize suggestions of American imperialist intervention." It was important to downplay American sponsorship of Japanese economic expansion in Asia. In practice, however, Policy Planning recommended that the United States "seek vigorously to develop the economic interdependence between Southeast Asia, as a supplier of raw materials, and Japan, Western Europe and India, as suppliers of finished goods." Within the framework of prewar trade patterns the United States would also recognize "the legitimate aspirations of Southeast Asian countries for some diversification of their economies."[47]

The imperatives of multilateral goals and the dollar gap, reinforced by strategic concerns, ultimately drove the United States into an alliance with European powers to smother the nationalistic-Communist threat to their Southeast Asian interests. The United States, however, relied on diplomacy and discretion to avoid driving pro-Western Asian élites into an alliance with anticolonial militants. It may be recalled that in 1944 Bishop had warned that such an imperialist alliance would be doomed and would prejudice all Western economic goals in Southeast Asia. But when Asians discussed a regional political pact in 1949, Bishop, the assistant to Dean Rusk in the Far East division, warned that the United States had to intervene to counter Soviet influence. He said an exclusively Asiatic association would promote the idea of "Asia for the Asiatics," which would imperil Western influence. For example, the Pan American Union— the Latin American regional organization—he argued, would be worthless without U.S. participation.[48]

The British Commonwealth conference at Colombo in 1950 concluded that Indochina "[was] the key to holding the line versus Communism in Southeast Asia." The Commonwealth created the Colombo Plan to increase the region's economic development and to counter Communist economic appeals. Wary of American economic power, the British sought to limit American development aid while seeking military support. In 1949 and 1950 the two nations formed a natural military alliance with France to preserve the status quo in Southeast Asia. Acheson told the British ambassador in December 1949 that the United States would "be responsible for Japan and the Philippines, while Britain would secure Malaya and Burma, and to a lesser degree Thailand and Indochina." He urged military cooperation to protect the "Anglo-American arc of interest extending from Japan . . . to India," and pressed the British to take "greater initiative and responsibility for the mainland promontory of Southeast Asia." Both nations agreed that it was "essential [to] keep out of the limelight of Southeast Asian regional affairs but felt it absolutely essential to 'pull the strings' whenever necessary." The West, they concurred, would use ECAFE as a forum to teach Southeast Asian nations to "learn to help themselves" and not to expect significant American economic aid.[49]

Thus, the threat of militant Asian nationalism to American multilateral goals—like the impact of the European dollar gap crisis on the NSC 68 ideology—caused American policy to evolve from opposing formal colonialism in Asia to urging Britain and France to step up their military efforts. The State Department sought to ameliorate the contradiction between nationalism and neocolonialism by couching military intervention in anti-Communist rhetoric. Strategic fear of Communist gains thus neatly complemented the economic necessity of preserving Western economic influence. This again reflected the NSC 68 theme of Western "strength," which meant both economic prosperity for Europe and Japan and military power to crush revolutions.

For both Washington and the ESS in Tokyo, the often-dismissed domino theory symbolized a legitimate fear. The ESS staff reported that "the spread of communism throughout the Asian countries will have a significant and deleterious effect upon Japanese foreign trade. If communist governments take over, the stifling effect on trade will apply pressure on the economy which will have serious consequences. Japan may be cut off from supplies of food and critical raw materials which cannot be replaced except in dollar areas." Acheson's confidant, Joseph Alsop, wrote in January 1950 that Formosan trade was valuable to Japan: "By every possible test, however, whether economic, strategic, or political, Formosa is infinitely less valuable than the populous, incalculably wealthy Southeast Asian Peninsula." He urged the United States to stimulate trade between Southeast Asia, "with its great surplus of agricultural products," and "underfed, highly industrialized Japan."[50]

The domino theory was far more realistic in 1950 than it seemed to critics in succeeding decades after the United States built military and police networks to defend pro-American regimes in the area. Indochina was the strategic linchpin of Acheson's "Anglo-American arc of interest." It is possible that a French defeat in 1950, which would have been likely in the absence of American financial backing, might have sparked a revolution in Thailand and strengthened revolutionary movements in Malaya and the Philippines (Burma and Indonesia were both very nationalistic in the 1950s). The ultimate domino, of course, was Japan, and American military intervention in Indochina was of great psychological importance in assuring Japanese business that a future alliance with the West would not preclude trade with Asia.

Obstacles to Integration

The Dodge Plan for export recovery relied on the expansion of Asian sources of materials and markets to support Japanese production and on the initiation of domestic financial measures to suppress Japanese consumption. The Japan Management Association complained, however, about inadequate demand and Southeast Asian nations' lack of purchasing power. In January 1950 the Economic Stabilization Board completed its study on "Japan's Share in the Economic Development of Southeast Asia." "Japan will have no choice," it reported, but to rely on Southeast Asian trade in the future, but infrastructural development in the area, to increase raw materials exports and purchasing power, was a critical problem. The board thus renewed Ichimada's request for a Marshall Plan for Asia to stimulate trade and development, and sought help in promoting the expansion of Japanese business interests in Southeast Asia. If the United States could secure most-favored-nation status for Japan, it would "facilitate her central role in Asian development" and fulfill Hull's nine-year-old offer to Japan. Beginning in 1950, Japan imported more from Asia than from the United States, a milestone that marked only the beginning of a long transformation required to expand exports and balance dollar trade.[51]

Pessimism about prospects for expanding Southeast Asian trade marked official thinking in 1949 and early 1950. Army officials cautioned that as long as unrest in Asia prevented "normal intercourse with Japan, [there was] little, if any, assurance that the EROA Program [would] enable Japan to balance her foreign trade within the next few years." Bishop warned Butterworth that "backward nations are everywhere planning to increase their industry to reduce their dependence upon the vagaries of foreign trade, thereby rendering the life of the 'workshop' nation steadily more precarious." If the United States cut its aid, he added, it would force Japan to turn to China for survival; even at best, aid would be needed until 1954 or 1955. This problem, Bishop wrote, held the strategic key to Asia: "Faced with an overriding necessity to trade, Japan's international alignment must in the last analysis be determined by economic considerations where the facts are not in our favor." He warned that Southeast Asian nationalism and anticolonialism "lessen[ed] the ability of the Far East area in the coming decade to support a great industrial population such as is found in Japan." Prophetically, he suggested that Japan might have to exploit multilateral opportunities to expand into Latin America and Europe for its full recovery.[52]

Tracy Voorhees, the Republican lawyer from North Carolina, who in 1949 succeeded William Draper as under secretary of the Army, developed the most ambitious solutions to the problem. Overseer of the German and Japanese occupations, chief defender of the GARIOA and EROA programs before Congress, and after Draper's departure the strongest Washington advocate of Japanese recovery, Voorhees discovered the principle of "double dollar usage," or "coordinated aid," when the Army built military facilities in Okinawa. By employing Japanese instead of American construction firms, the Army boosted Japan's dollar earnings and reduced its need for GARIOA aid. Voorhees claimed that there would be steady progress toward ending the aid burden if Japan could earn dollars from other military and economic programs in Asia. One of the tasks of Admin-

Voorhees + the policy of recycling?

istration officials seeking Congressional appropriations was to convince Congress that the recipient nation was making progress toward a balanced dollar account and that aid could thus be decreased each year. To this end, Voorhees promoted the idea of Japan's gaining dollar-earning contracts for military and economic aid expenditures to narrow Japan's dollar gap.[53] The same results could be obtained by putting Occupation forces on a pay-as-you-go basis, which the Army had rejected in 1948. Voorhees's plans epitomized the pessimistic approach to Japanese recovery that called for coordinated regional aid programs to guarantee markets for Japan.

In January 1950, Voorhees presented to the National Security Council his case for a coordinated regional aid program, with "principal reliance upon the Japanese workshop." If the United States sent dollar aid to Southeast Asia that was tied to purchases in Japan, it would stimulate Japanese trade and cut GARIOA costs, thereby paying for itself. Without Chinese trade, he warned, "continuing, or even maintaining, Japan's economic recovery [would depend] upon keeping communism out of Southeast Asia, promoting economic recovery there and in further developing these countries . . . as the principal trading areas for Japan." He made assurances that Japanese–Southeast Asian integration would not prejudice European trade with the area; with increased primary production, Southeast Asia could indeed service both Japan and Europe. Lack of Southeast Asian purchasing power was the "chief handicap" to Japanese recovery. Japan "lack[ed] sufficient markets," he explained, and "major components" of her industry were producing at 50 percent of capacity. For "psychological" reasons, however, he suggested that the program be based in Manila rather than in Tokyo. He pleaded for a study of Asian economic aid that would be "linked with any military assistance programs in that area," and that would "employ the revived Japanese economy to the full." Coordinated aid was by 1950 a familiar topic in foreign economic policy circles, but Voorhees's link of military and economic aid was termed "novel" by one Treasury Department official.[54]

To support his claims, Voorhees sent his assistant, Robert West, and Agriculture Department expert Stanley Andrews on an eleven-nation, eight-week trip to Southeast Asia in January 1950. They sought "to normalize Japan's relations with Southeast Asia and cut GAR-

IOA expenditures." Earlier, the IBRD had also sent a mission to Southeast Asia, which explored the possibility of financing Thai purchases of agricultural equipment in Japan to increase Thai rice production. Voorhees assured MacArthur that the Andrews-West and IBRD missions had the potential "both of developing new Asiatic sources of food for Japan and of stimulating new markets for Japanese exports."[55]

Andrews and West claimed that in order to increase primary production, Southeast Asia had to gain political and military stability and infrastructural development. More specifically, they reported that the lack of credit facilities to finance the long lag time between ordering and delivering capital goods was the principal obstacle to expanded Japanese trade with the area. Japan lacked the foreign exchange reserves to offer credit terms, and thus lost the business to North Americans or Europeans. The mission suggested using yen credits, ECA or GARIOA funds, or a new aid program, which would cost nothing since it would allow GARIOA aid cuts. The situation demanded "a high degree of boldness and imagination in meeting a problem which [was] fundamental to any real stable trade development [in Asia]." The principle of coordinated aid was already being applied, they noted, since the level of ECA dollar aid to Indonesia used to purchase Japanese textiles determined the level of Japanese-Indonesian trade. Indeed, the Army had declared that ECA dollars were Japan's greatest dollar-earning sources in Asia. Without them Japan would have little dollar gains to show after two years of intensive recovery efforts. Andrews and West also noted European and American interests in the region. Indonesia, particularly, had "vast resources which the western world need[ed]."[56]

They attacked the "continuous and indefensible leakage of appropriated dollars in the Far East" caused by separate aid programs. Where separate aid programs led nations to hoard their dollars and stifle trade, coordinated aid would stimulate triangular trade and overcome the small imbalances that forced currency restrictions and import controls, and thus reduced trade. Their primary example of coordinated aid concerned a proposed $100 million Export-Import Bank credit to Indonesia. American law required that such credits be spent domestically, but Andrews and West said it was "appalling" not to tie the credits to capital goods purchased in Japan, which would reduce GARIOA requirements by $100 million and thus cost the United States nothing. They suggested the ECA, the Point IV Program, and the MDAP as other possible aid-dollar markets for Japan, and urged that the $189 million in non-arms MDAP aid to Asia be procured in Japan. The Bureau of the Budget already screened all procurement orders for Asian aid programs to determine whether the goods were available in Japan. They discussed another scheme whereby Japan would use her manufactured goods to pay for strategic materials, and then trade the materials to the United States for its stockpiling program in return for dollar imports.[57]

Andrews and West explained the theory of coordinated aid: "Japan would serve as the chief supplier of manufactures, other recipients the chief suppliers of foodstuffs and raw materials, and dollars would serve temporarily as the instrument to promote the production and exchange of goods among all participants." The Asian public, they were surprised to find, did not reject Japanese goods. "On the other hand, British and Dutch individuals, whether in government positions or otherwise, appear[ed] determined to oppose trade whenever possible." Europeans also publicized Japan's dishonest prewar trading practices in order to preserve European markets. But European sentiment notwithstanding, Andrews and West concluded on an "optimistic" note: because the prerequisites for industrialization were absent in Southeast Asia, "Japan can look forward to maintaining her position as the 'workshop of the East' for a long time to come."[58]

General Marquat, head of ESS, reacted somewhat bitterly to the Andrews-West report in March, since it implied that SCAP had overlooked such obvious and beneficial remedies for the Japanese trade dilemma. He said that in the postwar climate of intense Asian nationalism, the theme of the report would provoke anti-Japanese sentiments because it was "economically similar" to the former Japanese "Co-prosperity Sphere." On the other hand, he boasted that the ESS had so successfully promoted Japanese–Southeast Asian trade that it had aroused the "bitter reactions of the British." The logic of Asian economic integration based on Japanese industry was simple but compelling: American economic and strategic goals in Asia required a stable and prosperous Japan. William Draper, now a vice-president of the key New York investment house of Dillon Read, revealed the underlying workshop-integrationist strain of American policy when he told the National Foreign Trade Council in October 1950 that the "economic objectives" of the old co-prosperity sphere "were generally sound, and if peaceably and fairly pursued could have increased the per capita wealth and raised the standards of living throughout the area."[59]

In early 1950, Voorhees obtained commitments from ECA head Hoffman and Defense Secretary Johnson to procure supplies in Japan when practical. He pushed the logical link between military expenditures and dollar gap subsidies, advising MacArthur that "United States military forces themselves are potentially a much larger dollar market for Japanese products than they have been heretofore." American military purchases in Japan were "virtually mandatory in principle" in order to conserve dollars. Realizing that the military had close links with American arms makers, and no incentive to purchase in Japan because the GARIOA dollars saved did not come from military funds, he urged that it be forced to do so.[60]

He urged that SCAP and the Army Department in Washington "take the initiative in studying the market opportunities and affirmatively endeavoring to sell our products, treating the procurement section of G-4 as a customer whom we must sell rather than expecting the customer to take the initiative." Possible markets included Alaskan military construction for cement; military assistance programs to Southeast Asia; and, of course, the Occupation forces themselves, who would remain in Japan indefinitely and needed uniforms, vehicle repair, and food supplies. Voorhees argued that anything short of full coordination of all Asian funds would be a waste of tax dollars. He lobbied State, the National Security Council, Defense, and Gordon Gray, and told the Senate that his program was a "perfectly natural matching of Japan's industrial capacity and the raw materials of those areas." He left office, however, in April 1950, before concrete coordination plans were approved.[61]

Other Washington forces countered Voorhees's Japan-centric pleas. Congress vowed to prevent a flood of Japanese textiles from harming the powerful American textile industry. This limited a key dollar market for Japan. American glove and mitten manufacturers filed a complaint with the Tariff Commission against Japanese imports, and the Senate elicited an Administration pledge to continue the existing requirement that Export-Import Bank credits be spent domestically.

The bank, after all, was designed to promote American exports. Finally, although Voorhees attributed his difficulty in coordinating all Asian aid into a single program to State, Defense, and ECA reluctance to relinquish control of their funds,[62] the ECA had more concrete reasons to block the Andrews-West proposals.

Where American officials responsible for Japanese recovery viewed Southeast Asia as Japan's "backyard," the ECA viewed the area as Europe's "backyard." Europe's stake in Asian trade was still strong, as the ECA reported in 1950: "The trade of the Far Eastern countries continues to be concentrated to a remarkable degree along the lines of present or recent colonial interests." In a June 1950 critique of coordinated aid based on Japanese industry, the ECA charged that "many areas in the Far East had had much closer trading ties with Europe (and with the United States) than they have had with Japan. And some of the Far Eastern areas—far from operating through the Japanese monetary system—are integral parts of the European monetary systems." It urged the State Department to design programs to give full freedom of scope to the price mechanism to serve the "long range objective of efficiency through geographic specialization." While coordinating aid was acceptable in the sense of interagency cooperation to prevent dollar leakage, tying aid to purchases in Japan would discriminate against other industrial nations and contradicted multilateral principles.[63]

The ECA expressed sympathy for Japan's plight, but charged that Andrews, West, and Voorhees had ignored Europe's role in Far Eastern trade. If the United States granted yen credits, it would force dependent areas to rely on Japan and would hurt their terms of trade by preventing them from buying from the cheapest source. If Japan became the middleman for the stockpiling program, it would directly transfer Southeast Asia's dollars to Japan and prevent them from buying in America or Europe. The dollar gap was global, the ECA reminded officials: "Nearly all sources of strategic materials in the Pacific area are countries, or dependencies of countries, friendly to the United States and otherwise receiving United States assistance." The ECA recalled that prior to World War II Japan sought to dominate Asian trade, and if the United States promoted the revival of a new "Co-prosperity Sphere," it would alienate both Asia and Europe.[64]

The ECA took a global view because Europe had dollar-earning colonies and partners throughout the world. Global multilateralism would benefit the United States the most, because it would provide access to European colonial areas. Europe would lose exclusive privileges, but it would have an advantage because of its strong remaining ties to its former colonies. Japan would also benefit greatly, however, from its comparative advantage in Asian trade through geographic proximity, and also from its ultimate need to expand into Europe, South America, and Africa. As part of its attack on American economic nationalism, the ECA requested the NAC to revise the Export-Import Bank's tied-loan policy to increase dollar-earning possibilities for Europe.[65]

SCAP's Japan-centric plans, and the ECA's Eurocentric plans, illustrate the fascinating role of overwhelming American economic strength in formulating foreign policy. Because American interests required the revival of European and Japanese industrial allies, entire bureaucracies of American officials devoted their efforts to promoting Japanese and European trade expansion rather than to performing their traditional role of promoting American exports. American strength lay at the foundation of global economic disequilibrium, so the immediate task was to rebuild America's industrial competitors. SCAP officials became consumed by their task of securing dollar markets for Japan in the United States and promoting Japanese trade in Asia against European and American interests.[66] They and the Army devoted great energy to granting Japan full membership in the General Agreement on Trade and Tariffs (GATT) in order to secure most-favored-nation status for Japan. Sherwood Fine attended the 1950 GATT meeting on behalf of Japanese interests but, after Australia spoke out against admitting Japan, decided not to press the matter so as to avoid "arousing the smouldering passions" against Japan.[67]

The Tokyo Economic-Commercial Conference

By 1948 the difficulties of reintegrating Southeast Asia into Japan's expanded economy prompted Sebald, Marquat, Mac-Arthur, and Butterworth each to call for a Tokyo conference of United

States officials in Asia. The Chinese revolution prevented convening the conference in 1948, but Acheson instructed that it be held in April 1950, to formulate "concrete proposals for increasing intra-regional trade in the Far East with particular reference to increasing the mutually beneficial exchanges of goods between Japan and the countries of South and Southeast Asia."[68] The Department of State Tokyo Economic-Commercial Conference affords a fascinating and rare view into the perspectives of American officials in Asia in the critical spring of 1950. It vividly illustrates the Japan-centric views created by both the dollar gap and Asian nationalistic revolution.

SCAP officials welcomed the conferees by stating that a cure for Japan's dollar gap required the economic cooperation of Southeast Asian nations. Thomas Blaisdell, assistant secretary of commerce and a founder of the ERP, then presented an overview of foreign economic policy. He noted that Britain's dollar earnings derived principally from Southeast Asian trade. Historically, triangular trade enabled Britain to balance her dollar trade, and she would continue to rely on it in the future. The United States, he added, also desired recovery of production in Southeast Asia to help stabilize world finances and reduce the aid burden. He argued for American control of the world economy, and the responsibility of the officials present to promote American business: "[American business problems] are the tentacles of American life that reach out around the world in terms of our commercial needs. . . . Our problems here are the problems of American business. They are problems which, if we solve them adequately, will result in the benefit of American business. . . . Some people will tell you that is imperialism." He argued, however, that strong and productive business helps create strong and stable governments.[69]

Blaisdell warned that the United States had to "face its responsibility squarely. . . . We talk with great contempt about British imperialism, Dutch imperialism, somebody else's imperialism, which are nothing but the extension of commercial interests of one kind or another throughout the world. And yet, we find ourselves quite honestly and frankly faced with the building of a world trade system." Without American leadership, economic controls and restrictions would proliferate and American business would suffer. Currency inconvertibility was the principal obstacle to balancing Japan's dollar trade, because Japan could not convert sterling into dollars. Even though currency restrictions prevented national bankruptcies and their disastrous consequences for world trade, Blaisdell attacked them for stifling the profit motive. He said that the United States had to get tough, even if it meant taking over and administering the sterling bloc. Another official from Washington warned that "unless we get the economy of the world going as a whole, we shall suffer." The dollar gap would especially imperil American agricultural exports, but would also threaten all American exports and world economic prosperity. He expressed the essence of international multilateral Keynesianism: "The world economy is an expanding or contracting affair, and it is better to have a smaller slice of a much bigger pie."[70]

Blaisdell's blast at the British reflected the frustrations of the ambitious Treasury officials and New York bankers at being unable to assert their domination over the world economy in spite of American economic strength. In a study of post-ERP aid to Europe and aid to the Far East, the Treasury Department's C. J. Hynning attacked Britain's use of its far-flung sterling empire to restrict convertibility and discriminate against dollar exports. Hynning laid out the American opposition to colonialism: it was inefficient, restrictive, and, foremost in American minds, served to limit American business penetration of the colonial economies. He posed a fundamental question: Because the end of colonialism and the inevitable American takeover were imminent, should the United States hasten or retard the collapse? Continuing the traditional aggressiveness and conservative banking principles of the Treasury, as reflected in the Bretton Woods framework, Hynning said that all foreign aid should be canceled (except limited humanitarian aid based on food surpluses) until the British tore down their financial empire and welcomed American capital investment as the solution to the dollar gap. He charged that ECA aid made it too easy for Britain; she could reject the harsh terms of an IBRD loan and obtain ECA aid in its place. He also noted that since the excess profits tax had been repealed in 1945, American investors were strongly attracted to the domestic market, and that the necessity of increasing foreign investment had led to consideration of reimposing the tax.[71]

Reflecting the workshop strategy, the Tokyo conferees agreed that Southeast Asian industrialization was ill-advised. One complained that Southeast Asians shared a tendency to build steel mills through "artificial hot-house methods." It is thus ironic that Japan's own industrial development owed far more to "artificial hot-house methods" such as state subsidies for heavy industry than to foreign capital investment in Japan. He summarized the American position on industrialization:

> We don't take the position that a country has to industrialize. One of the points that the United States Government has been trying to put across in discussions on economic development in the UN is the point that you can have economic development along agricultural lines, along lines involving production of primary commodities. Of course the difficulty is that a lot of people conceive of economic development as involving industrialization, in many cases more than mere production of textiles or first stage processing of primary products.

The American challenge, he concluded, was to convince the Asians that their primary producing economies would not keep them in a "colonial status."[72]

A conference committee also decided that the United States had to persuade Asian nations that "expanding world trade [would] benefit them more in the final analysis than efforts to achieve a forced rate of industrialization by reliance on restrictive practices." Moreover, an official warned that granting aid not conditioned on acceptance of Western economic policies might do more harm than good; complementary rather than nationalistic development was necessary to match Japanese and European industry with Southeast Asian food and raw materials. The conferees discussed ways to increase American imports from Southeast Asia to expand Asian dollar reserves for Japanese exports, as well as ways to increase Japanese business presence in the area. The head of the ESS foreign trade and commerce division reminded them that, indeed, in the 1930s Japan had expanded into Asia to secure sources of raw materials, and reported that the technicians who had developed the mines were "willing and eager to go back" and would be "glad to give technical assistance."[73]

American officials had little respect for the new governments in Southeast Asia, emerging from decades of stifling colonial domination. One committee reported that, since good government was the key to development, the United States should condition aid on the acceptance of American advisors in all important government agencies, including those in British colonies. They proposed advisory boards, composed of Europeans and Americans—with "qualified Asians" permitted to participate—to oversee regional development. They believed that American expertise could overcome all development problems and counter Russian propaganda, and shared Acheson's deep frustration when anticolonial movements obstructed revival of the colonial trade that Europe and Japan so badly needed. Not surprisingly, they blamed anticolonialism on Russian propaganda, not on the oppressive colonial heritage of Asia. They projected their acquisitive approach to Asia onto Russian thinking: "An enemy method is to absorb surplus producing areas and leave to us the deficit regions." Russia "took" North Korea and Manchuria first, and now threatened Indochina. But, they hoped, "the enemy may have made a mistake in taking over the deficit region of China."[74]

The committee noted that whereas Malaya was successfully contributing to the global flow of raw materials under British rule, chaos reigned wherever the "natives" were in control. Their report concluded that it "would be best for the countries themselves if they were each to be placed under a United States or a UN mandate for the next fifty years." They believed that Southeast Asia would profit more from sound advice than from actual economic aid. In light of these attitudes, it is not surprising that a State Department official warned after a March 1950 trip to Southeast Asia that the "United States is feared throughout the whole area, [and] much of the fear is based upon the notion that our interests in the area originated in large part from conscious programs of economic imperialism." He noted that Asians no longer feared the declining Europeans. American policies, "however, [were] regarded with considerable apprehension," because Asians feared "our desire to replace European hegemony." Countering the thrust of the Tokyo conference, he cautioned: "We must be extremely careful not to overwhelm them with elaborate supervisory missions."[75]

Even at the conference, warnings were sounded against too much American manipulation. One official recalled a discussion with the chief Thai negotiator at a SCAP-Thai trade conference. The Thai had remarked that "apparently it is United States policy to secure through political pressure what the Japanese Army failed to secure in Asia." Another American official feared that Japan would quickly resume domination of Asia and remarked after listening to the plans to integrate Japan and smaller Asian states:

> It might be desirable that we should re-establish a Japanese empire which would be the equivalent of the Japanese empire which we had before. Perhaps that is in the world interest. Perhaps we should allow and encourage these forces to go on until Japan shall be the heart of a great empire which would include the agricultural resources in all of the surrounding countries. We here at this time are in a position to bend the twig that is going to be the tree of the future.

He charged, however, that the law of comparative advantage, the principle that underlay multilateral economic theory, contradicted the goal of Asian nations to create independent and viable economies. The new nations, he continued, could not be truly independent while being dominated economically by Japan; as Japan inevitably expanded, she would again view other Asians as inferiors. Sebald promptly blasted him for "meandering into speculation about a future co-prosperity sphere and whether that is good or bad." The POLAD explained that Japan's economic quandary required constructive solutions to "get trade off the dead end it is on today."[76]

The American tactic of using multilateral agencies, under Western, primarily American, control, to force undesirable policies on underdeveloped nations was commonly discussed at this time with respect to aid to Southeast Asia. One official at the conference said that one way to "avoid the charge of imperialism or economic domination of the countries" receiving aid was to channel it through the IBRD. This would shift the onus of domination to the international agency: "When the international bank requires certain actions by borrowing governments or requires certain conditions be met, it can do so far more easily than could the Export-Import Bank in terms of political reaction." In Washington, officials discussed opening a regional IBRD office in Southeast Asia, "which through its ability to offer unpalatable advice would be very useful in the area." The Treasury, too, was concerned that any unilateral American policy to end the Asian dollar gap would "meet with strong resistance." According to the Treasury, a nation could not have real "progress" without "controversy" (i.e., oppressive austerity policies).[77]

Coordinated Aid and Military Intervention

By the spring of 1950, the State Department had considered "many elaborate schemes to break up the log-jam" of Asian trade. Basically, it agreed with Andrews and West that the "lack of normal intermediate credit facilities for financing Japanese exports" blocked Asian economic integration. To solve this problem, and in response to Voorhees's pleas, John Allison, who was a 1947 advocate of coordinated aid, drew up a "Yen Fund proposal" in March 1950. After three months of departmental discussion, it was tentatively approved in June. The Philippines/Southeast Asia division said that the nations of the region would indeed accept credits or commodities from Japan, and that "even for the metropolitan powers which fear[ed] Japanese trade competition it would be extremely embarrassing to reject grants and only slightly less embarrassing to refuse to make use of presumably generous credit facilities." Within the Far East division, however, there were reservations, focusing on the drain on Japan's economy from shipping goods without repayments, the lack of an end date to the program, Southeast Asia's monumental economic and social problems, the fear that a White House foreign aid "Czar" (as proposed by Voorhees) would further bureaucratize and clog trade, and the great "ill will" which would be caused by American pressure to trade with Japan.[78] All these factors threatened the success of the proposal.

Under the scheme, Japan would pay in yen for its imports from the United States, and the United States would loan or grant the yen as aid to Southeast Asia. Since yen could be spent only on Japanese goods, the scheme would effectively tie American aid to Southeast Asian purchases in Japan. Even with such coordinated aid, the department's office of intelligence and research warned, "it will be at least five years before Japan achieves self-support and if the program is not carried out it is unlikely that Japan will be able to maintain politically tolerable living standards on a self-supporting basis at any time in the foreseeable future." In June the department presented SCAP and the Army with four alternate methods for coordinating aid. The United States could (1) aid Southeast Asia directly and either tie or not tie the aid to purchases in Japan, (2) send GARIOA dollars to Southeast Asia rather than to Japan, anticipating that Japan would earn the dollars through exports of manufactures, (3) grant yen credits to Southeast Asia, taken from Japanese counterpart funds, or (4) accept yen for aid goods sent to Japan and grant the yen to Southeast Asia. The Army's budget group, confused and skeptical about these "Rube Goldberg contraptions," vowed to reduce GARIOA aid only by the amount of Southeast Asian aid actually tied to purchases in Japan.[79]

The ESS staff recommended that credits be taken from counterpart funds in order best to "create an area economy" (integration), and to divert charges of U.S. imperialism, since the aid would appear to be from Japan. Kenneth Morrow, head of programs and statistics for ESS, said that since the first two alternatives focused much more on Southeast Asia than on Japan, using a yen fund (alternative 3) would be the preferable policy at least until the peace treaty.[80]

Allison's proposals, which took an aggressive and holistic approach to the Asian dollar gap, were opposed only by the cautious Treasury mentality. SCAP had largely been mesmerized by Dodge and by its own glowing public relations propaganda about Japan's "remarkable recovery." Its optimism was based on rising Japanese production, which would prove to be the least of Japan's structural problems. Chief of Staff General Almond told an April press conference that aid would assuredly end within two or three years. The ultraconservative and classically dogmatic Treasury Department, which had opposed all large-scale aid to Japan, claimed that Allison's schemes were based on invalid premises, were inadvisable, and were far too grandiose. Its skepticism about coordinated aid stemmed from the purely economic view that rock-bottom subsistence foreign living standards were the most desirable solution to the dollar gap. In November 1949, the Treasury had repeated its complaint about rising Japanese domestic consumption.[81] It blithely assumed that the Japanese would happily starve, be unemployed, and suffer a severe depression in order to do their part in creating international equilibrium. State and the Army, however, had to consider the possibility of social rebellion and, most crucially, the necessity of "positively" integrating Japan into the American-dominated world economy on terms that would satisfy Japan's highly insecure rulers.

The Treasury's Arthur Stuart, citing Almond's optimistic claim, advised his department on May 18 that using counterpart funds as coordinated aid was unnecessary. The funds would not necessarily stimulate the development of Asian raw materials to ease Japan's dollar gap, and would probably only make Japan more dependent on both American aid and subsidized, noncommercial trade with Asia. On May 22, Stuart recommended that, in lieu of Allison's plan, the department support Ikeda's recent proposal for an export finance corporation to finance Japanese trade with Southeast Asia. On May 20, Treasury attaché Dick Diehl, Dodge's greatest supporter in Tokyo, said Allison was simply being too pessimistic, since, he asserted, Japan had underlying economic strength.[82] No one doubted Japan's fundamental economic power—grounded in its extraordinary national cohesion, organization, skills, and energy—and Japan's subsequent recovery has verified the latent industrial capacity Japan possessed in 1950.

Diehl's critique, however, was flawed: Japan's productive capacity alone would not automatically ensure recovery and an end to the dollar gap. Indeed, it was Japan's unfavorable *external environment* that doomed quick trade recovery. Given outlets, financing, and sufficient demand over a period of time to allow industrial modernization, Japan would surely produce and compete. It was, on the contrary, the stifling of Japan's massive industrial capacity by the world dollar gap and the collapse of the Japanese empire that posed the greatest threat to the budding Pacific alliance. The Treasury saw the world as its banking customer, and sought solvency by pushing foreign consumption and living standards to the brink. Bankers primarily want customers that pay off their debts, but the strategic/economic crisis of 1950 demanded that the United States continue to subsidize Europe and Japan in order to maintain the industrial alliances.

Ultimately, the United States would use troop expenditures in Japan and military expansion in Asia to provide coordinated dollar markets for Japan. Voorhees suggested this in April, and, in Japan,

MacArthur and Yoshida made plans in early June to reactivate Japan's military plants to support American military intervention in Asia. Yoshida's anticipation of using Japan's idle military productive capacity to produce dollar-earning exports lends support to the theory that the Japanese, particularly Yoshida, subtly guided Americans toward recovery policies to launch Japan's postwar resurgence. MacArthur and Yoshida discouraged Dulles from pressuring Japan to rearm itself and proposed that the arms production from the idle arsenals be used instead as Japan's defense contribution in return for guaranteed dollar markets for the arms. Two interdepartmental offspring of the MDAP and ECA (the Foreign Military Assistance Coordinating Committee and the Southeast Asian Aid Policy Committee), each established prior to the Korean outbreak, held promise of increased, coordinated military and economic aid to Asia to provide markets for Japan. Dodge advised MacArthur in May that plans to integrate foreign military aid with economic aid were growing in Washington and "[would] directly affect the dollar gap." Military and economic aid "seem[ed] on the move toward much larger totals," he reported, since the "good sense" of coordinating aid to save dollars seemed "to be gaining friends in official circles."[83] After three years of discussion, the coordinated aid proposals were finally implemented with the Korean War.

American officials viewed Southeast Asian "stability" as the vital element in the recovery of Japan. Moreover, they undeniably gave priority to cementing the alliance with Japan over any other aspect of Asian policy. Since the success of the alliance depended on Japan's prosperity and satisfaction with its situation as a member of the capitalist bloc, the United States was forced to guarantee a non-Communist Southeast Asia to Japan. The actual decision to intervene was made in February 1950, when a State Department working group agreed that, because the Soviets had recognized Ho's government, the United States either had to back Bao Dai or had to accept the loss of Southeast Asia. In April 1950 the Joint Chiefs of Staff pleaded for immediate aid to Indochina and "long-term measures to provide for Japan and the other offshore islands a secure source of food and other strategic materials from the non-communist areas held in the Far East."[84]

The State Department–sponsored Griffin mission to Southeast Asia in March 1950, led by the ECA's R. Allen Griffin, studied uses for the aid funds appropriated for the "general area of China." The mission focused primarily on the threat of Communism, but also recognized that, owing to the world dollar gap, "the United States had an important financial interest, as well as a commodity interest in the economic recovery and progress of Southeast Asia and in open access thereto by the non-communist nations of the world." The mission met with Voorhees and discussed the Yen Fund proposal. Under SCAP prodding the mission urged Southeast Asians to employ Japanese technicians, but received "negative" results; in Indochina, the mere suggestion was considered an "affront." They advised SCAP that "political and trade relations might be unfavorably affected if we press the matter at too early a time," but promised that channeling orders for Southeast Asian military and economic aid programs would lead to a "considerable amount of business for Japan."[85]

Russell Fifield, in a study sponsored by the Council on Foreign Relations, has, more accurately than others, captured the essence of American policy in Southeast Asia. Concurring with the insightful analysis of the Elliott Committee in 1955, he concludes that American postwar policy in the Third World was primarily shaped by "indirect interests"—the economic needs of its industrial allies—rather than by fear of Communism: "The importance of Southeast Asia to the United States clearly had acquired broad dimensions. Direct and indirect values were significant since the United States had to bear in mind the effect of Southeast Asia on American friends with deep interest in the area." Indochina was the Greece of Asia, the strategic flank of the southern mainland which guarded all communication routes between the Pacific and Indian oceans. Its strategic value thus loomed large in American eyes because of Southeast Asia's economic potential and immediate importance to the industrial nations: "The economic value of Southeast Asia was greater for some of the allies of the United States, like Japan in Asia and certain others in Western Europe, than for itself. Traditional patterns of investment banking and trade once involving colonial areas and metropolitan countries had not disappeared."[86] Only within the context of the global ERP-NSC 68 policy of economic revival and within the Asian context of Japanese recovery and dependence on Asian markets and materials does the inescapable logic of intervention become clear. From 1950 to 1954, as U.S. involvement grew in Southeast Asia, the problems of economic recovery in Japan also increased, and the two became even more closely entwined.

4. The United States–Japan Economic Cooperation Program

> *The Japanese must be assured of a satisfactory livelihood, and yet from the American point of view it is essential that this be achieved without placing Japan in a position of dependence upon the communist-dominated mainland of Asia.*
>
> —*Council on Foreign Relations Study Group,*
> *October 23, 1950*

> *Mr. Dulles stated his view that the two major problems facing the United States in foreign relations were Japan and Germany, of which the former was far the more difficult. The problem of weaving Germany into the economy, industry and security fabric of Western civilization was infinitely easier than that of first bringing Japan into that fabric and keeping her there against the promise of contiguous Asia.*
>
> —*Dulles, Ridgway, and Sebald meeting,*
> *April 22, 1951*

"Sent from Heaven": The Korean Boom

The Korean War was the decisive event in postwar international relations. The war spurred military spending to a new level and enabled the Truman Administration to launch an aggressive military policy in Asia. The North Korean attack thus fulfilled Acheson's strategy to escalate the cold war, as planned in NSC 68; no longer would Congress impose major restraints on military budgets and foreign aid programs with military overtones. Acheson advised the embassy in Moscow that in the Korean hostilities "an excellent opportunity is here offered to disrupt the Soviet peace offensive, which, as the Embassy is aware, is assuming serious proportions and having a certain effect on public opinion." Acheson had counted on a conflict he could blame on the Soviet Union. NSC 68 brilliantly laid the groundwork for bureaucratic acceptance of aggressive foreign policies, and the Korean War furnished the opportunity to implement them. The 1947 Truman Doctrine reaffirmed traditional American anti-Communism and began the practice of intervention in support of weak, reactionary regimes; NATO and MDAP had introduced rearmament and alliances in 1949, but NSC 68 and the Korean War were responsible for the massive arms race and the global tensions associated with the cold war since 1950.[1]

The war also heartened John Allison and other Far Eastern planners. Allison wrote that the war "served to hasten the day when the true nature of the Communist threat will be recognized by those Asiatic nations now unable to believe the truth." Dulles expressed the hope that the war would frighten the Japanese into rearming themselves, and other American officials cited the necessity of polarizing cold war attitudes in Japan and of weakening Japanese neutrality as motives for American intervention in Korea. The war had the intended effect, as the conservative Japanese press began to label the Chinese army as "bandits" and "puppets" and as pressure for trade with China eased temporarily. Dulles encouraged Acheson to launch an anti-Communist offensive in Asia to fully exploit the great opportunities afforded by the conflict within Korea.[2]

The Korean War profoundly affected world recovery and American foreign economic policy in the 1950s, but its greatest impact was on Japanese recovery. The war enabled MacArthur and Yoshida to implement their plan to activate idle Japanese arsenals in support of American military activities in Asia. SCAP and the State Department exploited two loopholes in the FEC's 1947 "Prohibition of Military Activity in Japan," especially that which permitted Japanese military production to supply the needs of the Occupation at the discretion of the supreme commander. MacArthur cited the Korean

War as a threat to the Occupation and invoked his authority to commence "emergency" procurement of military services and supplies for South Korea.[3] Japan was the most logical source of supply for Korea for three reasons: because of its geographical proximity, because American industry was strained by rearmament orders, and, most critically for Japan, because it could furnish dollar-earning markets for Japanese industry.

By the end of 1950, the global economic stimulus and the military procurement orders caused by the war dramatically improved Japan's structural trade position. Initially, Japanese business reacted with caution to orders for weapons, jeeps, trucks, clothing, tents, ammunition, and so on. Many believed they would be temporary; either the war would end quickly, or the United States would procure only at home, or the U.S. Congress would limit arms funding. Others, however, argued that the war would drag on and that Japan would continue to be a logical supply source. By September, the orders, which reached $149 million by year's end, had reduced the inventories which tied up capital and "weighed heavily" on business.[4] Procurement orders constituted a dollar export market, which directly reduced Japan's dollar shortage. Just as important, however, was the shift in the United States and Europe from the production of export goods to the production of arms and the rapid growth of world trade caused by panic buying. Thus, the world buyer's market became a seller's market, world prices rose, and Japan competed successfully for the first time since 1945. Furthermore, Southeast Asia earned its first significant postwar dollar reserves through its increased sales of strategic raw materials to the United States, enabling Japan to earn many of these dollars through increased exports to the region. Thus, at a stroke, the Korean War improved Japan's competitive position from a marginal, overpriced supplier in highly competitive world markets to a prime producer with competitive prices in rapidly expanding world markets. Japanese manufacturing and export indices shattered postwar records each month in late 1950, as commercial exports rose 50 percent.[5]

Observers have overwhelmingly proclaimed the Korean War as the decisive factor in Japan's postwar industrial recovery. *U.S. News and World Report* reported that "military orders and other business stemming from the war [had] lifted the country out of a depression that six months ago [had become] critical."[6] Chalmers Johnson later agreed:

> The Korean War was in many ways the equivalent for Japan of the Marshall Plan. Between June 1950 and 1954 the United States spent close to $3 billion in Japan for war and war related supplies. The Tokuju Keiki, or Tokuju Boom (from the name of the procurement orders, called special needs or Tokubetsu Juyo) overcame the depression caused by economic stabilization and started the economy on its upward course. The Tokuju boom saved the regime of Prime Minister Yoshida from almost certain discredit as a Japanese Hoover Administration and saved the United States occupation from possible charges of monumental bungling.[7]

The Pacific Rivals, by the staff of the *Asahi Shimbun,* recalled the dramatic psychological effect of the war orders on Japanese economic fortunes:

> Just in the nick of time, a new windfall blew Japan's way in the form of procurement orders to supply the United States forces fighting in the Korean War. Japanese business picked up at once, but even today Japanese businessmen shudder at the thought of what might have happened if there had been no war in Korea at that time. . . . There can be no question that the procurement orders of the Korean War were exactly what the Japanese economy needed to tide it over depression and direct its course away from the "stability panic" that was expected. The procurement orders led to the biggest economic boom in the nation's history and paved the way for the late high economic growth rates. "Divine aid" was what Naoto (sic) Ichimada, Governor of the Bank of Japan, called the procurement orders.[8]

Heavy industry was especially blessed. For instance, the Toyota Corporation had been on the verge of folding: "from April 1949 on automobile makers in Japan came to find it impossible to maintain production." War orders revived the industry. The president of Toyota, which received a large share of vehicle orders and boosted production 40 percent, recalled that "these orders were Toyota's salvation. I felt a mingling of joy for my company and a sense of guilt that I was rejoicing over another country's war."[9]

The entire Japanese business community may have shared his feelings, as the war revived the entire economy. Japan historically had been dependent on exogenous stimulation for economic growth—especially the Sino-Japanese and Russo-Japanese wars, World War I, the imperialist expansion of the 1930s, and World War II. In the summer of 1950, the Keynesian domestic multiplier effect rippled through the economy, as falling inventories stimulated production and employment, prompting the *Oriental Economist* to report that procurement and export orders created "benefits to Japan's economy far beyond their actual face values."[10] Most critically, the boom advanced Japanese industrial modernization, the key to subsequent export recovery. Under the Dodge Plan, industrial rationalization meant slashing wages and cutting back on employees; during the Korean War, with sound conditions for investment, the *Nippon Times* reported that industrial rationalization could mean modern equipment instead of layoffs.[11]

The startling turnaround in Japan's fortunes led some American officials to false optimism about Japanese recovery, since Japan's treasury was "bulging with dollars" in comparison with early 1950. A July State Department study concluded that the war would have "heavy net favorable effects" in Japan, despite causing raw materials inflation. It predicted a drop in Japan's commercial dollar gap (from $270 million to $165 million), which, the report said, would enable Japan to stockpile dollar-area supplies.[12] The most optimistic, and least realistic, appraisal was the Gray report to Truman on the dollar gap, which finally appeared in November after the global war boom greatly eased the immediacy of the dollar gap crisis. Gray declared that Japanese recovery reduced her need for dollar aid, and the Bureau of the Budget and the Senate Appropriations Committee also called for aid cuts. Others were not deceived by the dramatic recovery triggered by the war boom, especially the Army and the Japanese themselves. The Army complained to the White House that the unwarranted optimism should be deleted from the Gray report and termed aid cuts the "antithesis of economy," since they would hinder long-term Japanese solvency and thus necessitate larger dollar grants later.[13]

To ensure continued dollar gap financing, Truman and MacArthur agreed on Wake Island in December 1950 to initiate a pay-as-you-go system of financing Occupation costs with dollars, to begin in July 1951. It may be recalled that this form of coordinated aid had been suggested by the State Department but rejected by the Army in 1948. Acheson advised Defense Secretary Marshall to use the pay-as-you-go system to bolster Japan's foreign exchange position and complement the "substantial orders for military equipment" that the United States would place in Japan. American dollar expenditures in Japan for Occupation expenses would be calculated to cover the commercial dollar gap. Dodge wrote that pay-as-you-go could also be used as a dollar gap payment beyond the Occupation to finance American military installations in Japan.[14] The United States used expenditures by American military personnel and bases in Japan (as in Europe) as the third method, alongside military procurement and economic aid, to fill the commercial dollar gap, with military expenditures replacing economic aid to a large degree after 1950.

The artificial stimulus of war orders kept the economy afloat and financed modernization, but, as Dodge warned in Tokyo in October 1950, it did not constitute commercial trade recovery: "Japan has not yet answered its need and proved its ability to earn its own living with normal exports in increasingly competitive world markets." He urged investing profits generated by procurements and increased exports in modernization and increasing financial incentives for exporters. Dodge's actions on this trip reflected the necessity of exploiting the boom to strengthen basic industries. He approved the release of 82 billion yen in counterpart funds to the telecommunications, railroad, electric power, and shipping industries, and designated 7.6 billion yen of counterpart funds to finance the Equipment Import Trust Account. The account would finance long-term credit offerings by commercial banks to enable export industries to purchase modern equipment abroad. He also helped establish the Japanese Export Finance Bank to cover the time lag on capital goods export deliveries, thus providing the long-sought intermediate credit facility for Japanese exports. The bank, restructured as the Japan Export-Import Bank in 1952, opened in February 1951 and was also partly financed with counterpart funds.[15]

The fundamental weakness of the Japanese economy and its position in world trade were best evidenced in late 1950, when, despite the most fortuitous possible circumstances and a complete reversal of trends since the Dodge Plan, Japan still found itself in a precarious situation. The Japanese well recognized this structural yoke and knew that their political independence rested on freeing themselves from American aid. Having secured beneficial economic terms from the United States, the goal of the conservative Japanese government after 1950 was to secure some degree of autonomy within the American sphere.

By late 1950, the boom had essentially reversed Japan's recovery problems. Instead of inadequate foreign demand, what now presented serious problems were import shortages, raw materials inflation, and production bottlenecks. In late 1950 and early 1951, the Economic Stabilization Board developed two self-support studies emphasizing a gradual reduction of the dollar gap through 1954. The reports assumed that subsidies from procurements and economic aid would continue through 1954. Even so, they warned, balanced Japanese trade required global currency convertibility, imported capital to finance modernization, and more plentiful and inexpensive raw materials imports and electric power supplies. If heavy manufacturing demand slackened (dependent as it was upon American orders), the board warned that the critical mining and manufacturing sectors would suffer from low production, poor economies of scale, and retarded modernization. The only ways to cut import costs were to increase domestic food production and to keep living standards at suppressed levels, both of which were long-standing self-support concepts with limited promise, since Japan could not hope to feed itself and since living standards were already at politically dangerous levels.[16] By 1951, however, such self-support ideas, which had constituted economic policy since 1947, were no longer in American plans.

The Concept of Economic Cooperation

Spearheaded by peace treaty architect Dulles, American planning shifted in 1951 from the theme of "self-support" to that of "economic cooperation." Economic cooperation meant offering Japan economic incentives and dollar gap subsidies in the form of war orders and American sponsorship in Southeast Asia, in return for Japanese adherence to American policies in Asia, especially the non-recognition of China. His world view shaped by the Versailles treaty and its aftermath, Dulles cleverly catered to Japanese economic interests to cement the alliance on a long-term basis, as required by American global strategy. A top Yoshida aide, Jirō Shirasu, had suggested that the United States "utilize Japanese industrial capacity to the full. . . . There can be no more effective way of firmly binding Japan to the free world."[17] Though American documents suggest that the United States took the initiative, the Yoshida government certainly encouraged and fostered the shift from economic aid to heavy industrial orders placed by the American government. Thus, there was a reciprocal relationship between Dulles's strategy to placate Japanese business and Yoshida's strategy to turn military defeat into economic victory by exploiting the cold war and the global dollar gap, exploiting Japan's very weakness to the hilt.

The equation of cooperation was simple. Japan had four possible trade outlets: trade with China for primary products (which was severely limited by American strategic policy); trade with Southeast Asia for primary products (which was supported by American policy and Japanese business, but was only a long-term solution [see Chapter 6]); greatly increased Japanese sales to the dollar area (which was considered an impossibility in 1951, since Japan's meager success in exporting textiles and tuna to the United States was met with congressional calls for protection); and, finally, military markets to earn dollars (which was the best interim solution and the basis of economic cooperation). In addition to providing immediate benefits with war orders, the United States sought a longer-term cure by accelerating its efforts to achieve Japanese economic integration with Southeast Asia. Sebald echoed Dulles's thoughts and the essence of American Asian strategy when he wrote: "The action of the Japanese government will presumably be motivated by what it considers its own best interest. The chief instrument of economic cooperation will doubtless become those specific economic opportunities which the United States will be able to offer in procurement and trade."[18]

The most active proponent of economic cooperation with Japan was Kenneth Morrow, head of the programs and statistics division of ESS. Morrow lobbied incessantly for Japanese economic interests, especially procurement orders and aid to Southeast Asia that would be tied to purchases in Japan. He advised Marquat on February 6, 1951, that in Washington "SCAP/ESS should be represented by a vigorous group of persons who will concern themselves with active promotion of Japan's overall economic welfare before all agencies and groups." Noting that the Mutual Defense Assistance Program (MDAP) agencies had $4 billion to spend after a flood of congressional arms legislation (funds, moreover, not subject to Buy American Act restrictions on government purchases abroad), Morrow wrote: "These agencies should be worked with continuously to develop the MDAP program in the Far East, primarily on the foundation of Japan's industrial potential." He suggested that American military research-and-development personnel develop "specialized war materials for the Far East which would utilize the Japanese industrial potential." Morrow recognized that despite both the economic logic of purchasing in Japan and the support of Dulles, Dodge, and SCAP, "an adequate program for Japan [would] not just grow," but had to be actively pursued.[19] For the next year Morrow represented Japanese business interests in an effort to cement the Pacific alliance through the economic cooperation program and to pave the way for the final phase of Occupation policy—post-treaty economic cooperation planning.

Morrow, Marquat, Dulles, Dodge, the Army, and the State Department all viewed procurement as a way to continue to subsidize Japan's economy without economic aid. Until Southeast Asia developed sufficient raw materials supplies and until world currency convertibility was restored, dollar subsidies for Japan were necessary to preserve American markets and ensure that the strong forces in Japan which supported extensive trade with China did not prevail. Economic aid was both unpopular in Congress and demeaning to the Japanese. Economic "cooperation," however, removed the stigma of aid without removing the subsidy. The cooperation program culminated the efforts of Voorhees, Draper, and SCAP to stimulate Japanese industry on a long-term basis. Joseph Dodge wrote in 1951 that Japan's role in economic cooperation was to restrict its living standard until exports recovered, and "to promote that pattern of foreign trade calculated to support the objectives of the free world" (i.e., not to trade with China). For its part, Dodge continued, the United States would "recognize Japan's need for access to food, essential materials and strategic raw materials and continue to support Japan's production for the UN effort in Korea and participation in Southeast Asian rehabilitation and economic aid procurement. The further development by Japan of markets within its normal economic orbit will be recognized and assisted."[20]

The most revealing American thinking about the interrelationship between the Asian dollar gap and the cold war was developed in the programs and statistics division in 1951 and 1952. Under Morrow, the division produced a five-part series of top secret reports entitled "Japan's Industrial Potential" (JIP). MacArthur and the Munitions Board in Washington each had ordered studies of Japan's idle industrial capacity in early 1951 to evaluate the feasibility of military procurement in Japan. JIP I, issued on February 21, 1951, took as its premise Japan's willing and skilled labor force. Idle plants meant unemployment, which threatened conservative electoral supremacy; rearmament orders and raw materials imports, however, would revive the economy and raise living standards. Reminiscent of Administration arguments on behalf of the ERP bill in 1948, JIP I warned that failing to subsidize Japan in 1951 would increase American military burdens in the future: unless Japan was

> provided with markets and sources of materials to continue satisfactory industrial and commercial progress both military and economic aid would be a necessity. The obvious solution [lay] in having Japan contribute to the international military effort by utilizing the surplus economic potential to the fullest extent possible, thereby providing for its continued economic sufficiency.[21]

War orders would keep Japan "psychologically adjusted to anticommunist doctrines," the report continued. Conversely, if Japan's capacity lay idle, "it may be made a means of ingress of subversive influences [if] Japan [were] faced with economic deterioration following attainment of independent national existence."[22] This was the basic, if publicly unarticulated, theme of postwar American foreign policy: the inability of Japan and Europe to prosper in their postwar circumstances. The most immediate threat to American interests in Japan, as well as in Europe, was not a Russian invasion, but economic collapse and the social radicalism that would prevail with a prolonged depression.

The report was essentially a lobbying effort directed at Washington officials who controlled the purse strings of foreign aid and procurement. Perhaps the key argument was that the procurement program had to include military supplies for Southeast Asia—in addition to Korea—so that a Korean truce would not threaten the capital invested by Japanese financiers in arms plants. The report stated frankly that the United States should view procurement primarily as a policy of economic stimulation and dollar-gap subsidies rather than as "defense of the occupation": "It is the opinion accepted here that a more adequate initial basis for engaging in production of military items by Japan is that of insuring economic survival as described heretofore. The production of military equipment as a marketable export commodity . . . would permit continuity of contractual obligations into the peace treaty period."[23]

Contrary to official claims that war damage caused Japan's economic downfall and impeded recovery, the report showed that Japan suffered remarkably little loss of its wartime industrial capacity. One-half of Japan's machinery and metal capacity and 86 percent of railroad stock capacity lay idle. The report claimed that Japan could produce explosives, ammunition, "and virtually any type of material required in chemical warfare." Moreover, it said that Japanese business had a right to share in the war profits enjoyed by American and European manufacturers. Realizing that the Japanese placed economic opportunity ahead of other considerations, the report warned: "Exclusion from the program . . . could be construed as discriminatory and unjustifiable. It could result in serious disruption of international good will. . . . With sizeable idle industrial capacity, unemployed by reason of exclusion from available military exports markets, the probability of attractive offers by the Communists is not entirely remote. Under the capitalistic system the profit motive is difficult to control."[24] This fear reinforced American determination to cater to Japanese business interests as the only certain way to ensure the continuation of the alliance.

The Marquat Mission to Washington

The success of the cooperation program depended on the ability of SCAP and its Washington allies to alert the Administration and Congress to Japan's vulnerability and desperate economic situation. Armed with JIP I, Marquat led a mission to Washington in April 1951, to lobby for expanded procurement orders geared to the needs of Japanese industry and coordinated aid to Southeast Asia. Prior to his departure, Morrow advised Marquat that if procurement orders were programmed in advance to allow Japanese business to plan ahead, they "could contribute in a major degree to sustaining Japanese economic stability by providing a sizeable increment of the foreign exchange earnings needed to achieve a balance of international payments." With this goal, the mission met with the mushrooming cold war bureaucracy—the Munitions Board, the departments of State, Treasury, and Defense, the Army, the Joint Chiefs of Staff, the Office of Emergency Procurement Services, the Committee on Supplies and Requirements, the Office of Defense Management, the Federal Reserve Board, the ECA, and the Export-Import Bank—and with Dulles, Dodge, and Harriman.[25]

On May 16, Marquat announced the results to an anxious Japan. He expressed Washington's deep concern that Japan be given world markets, sources of materials, and ongoing procurement orders. Washington officials, however, had rejected orders programmed in advance to ease planning problems for Japanese business, insisting that the global rearmament program was too vast to program, and that each order had to be bid upon separately. Japan's prices would thus dictate the extent of its orders, but Marquat warned that Japan had already lost 40 percent of her possible procurement opportunities because revised procedures, established on December 24, 1950, required that the services procure domestically unless foreign prices were within 10 percent of American prices (still a very generous provision, which would subsidize foreign producers by 10 percent). He promised Japan American assistance in securing raw materials and IMF and GATT membership and noted that American business had "indicated hearty approval" for sales of their technology to Japan, through either patent sales or equity ownership. He advised Japan to seize Southeast Asian markets quickly while American and European producers had their production for export diverted to arms markets. Finally, he heralded an American commitment to aid Japan after a peace treaty, but warned that this did not include bailing out Japan if inflation got out of hand.[26] While his announcement was vague, the Marquat mission proved to be successful, as procurement rose from $141 million in the first half of 1951 to $241 million in the second half despite peace talks in Korea.

Washington responded quickly to Japan's obvious plight and the U.S. need to exploit military tensions to put aid on a permanent basis. The day following Marquat's announcement in Japan, May 17, the National Security Council drafted NSC 48/5 on Asian policy, which pledged the United States to "assist Japan in the production of low-cost military material in volume for use in Japan and in other non-communist countries of Asia." The paper also called for "appropriate psychological programs designed to further orient the Japanese toward the free world and away from communism."[27] The essence of cooperative planning, as Marquat wrote in early 1951, was that Japan's losses from the end of the Korean War and the end of the Occupation in 1952 would be offset: "The United States–Japan Economic Cooperation Program, the United States MDAP operation in Asia and the United States–Japan industrial mobilization planning will all be in a state of rapid acceleration."[28]

Post-Treaty Cooperation Planning

Despite such support from Washington, Morrow pressed his campaign through 1951 to ensure post-treaty cooperation policies. Writing to a responsive Averell Harriman, then representative to NATO, he warned that a Korean cease-fire would cut procurement orders for Japan by 75 to 85 percent of the $1 million-per-day 1951 figures. Morrow felt that procurement could "make or break" Japan as an economic entity: "If a coherent plan is followed, the United States can have greatly increased procurement and at the same time raise the Japanese standard of living," as well as finance Japanese trade with Southeast Asia. In Washington, before the Interdepartmental Committee for Far East Mobilization, he charged that "there is no evidence to date that Defense now has a long-range purchasing program for end-products in Japan." End-product orders referred to offshore procurement, the program which replaced ERP economic aid to Europe.[29]

In July 1951, the interdepartmental committee drafted a letter for Office of Defense Management head Charles Wilson to send to Defense Secretary Lovett asking how defense planned to "develop procurement in volume" for post-treaty Japan. Dodge and SCAP had also urged Wilson to ask the Washington agencies to consider Japan's economic needs. Wilson explained to State, Defense, and the ECA that Japan's idle factories, comprising one-third to one-half of Japan's capacity, should be put to work in the cold war effort.[30] Dulles also lobbied for the cooperation plan, advising the Senate Foreign Relations Committee, in executive session, that procurement would be necessary after the Korean War to support Japan's balance of payments: "MacArthur has made out a long schedule of things which he thinks Japan can do to our advantage much more cheaply than can be done anywhere else." By November 1951, MacArthur's successor, Matthew Ridgway, came to an agreement with Wilson, Lovett, and William Foster (the acting secretary of defense) that an integrated procurement program would have to be continued after the Occupation. SCAP, moreover, kept pressuring the Army Department to continue procurement for both economic and military strength in Japan, and warned that because Japan had more idle plant capacity than Europe, Japan was the most likely ally to seek East-West trade and weaken the alliance.[31]

Morrow recommended that a small ESS staff remain in Japan after the Occupation, to oversee the industrial mobilization program. Only the ESS, not the military services, he explained, understood the vital role of procurement in Japanese recovery. Procurement by the services was "fraught with real dangers," he warned; they treated Japan like a department store and regularly purchased 15 to 20 percent of Japanese production without considering the needs of the economy. Dodge concurred with Morrow that "if the orientation of Japan toward the United States [were] to be maintained," the "special relationship" had to be continued by providing Japan with a sympathetic American presence to which it could turn to express Japan's economic needs.[32]

POLAD William Sebald, however, was skeptical about the post-treaty cooperation scheme. He warned the State Department that Morrow planned to maintain a full-scale ESS contingent in Japan, prompting Morrow to assure Washington that only a small staff would be necessary. Sebald, playing the devil's advocate, complained that "Japan's role as a sub-contractual agent of the United States, unless developed in light of Japan's long-term trade requirements, will prove merely a temporary expedient. The Japanese will be the first to recognize that such an economic arrangement subjects Japan to the political inconsistencies of Congressional appropriations and the economic cycles of American business." Sebald was of course correct that the cooperation scheme—like the ERP and the entire American foreign economic policy—rested on undependable congressional funding, a long-standing problem largely overcome by military aid programs. Sebald admitted that continued Japanese dependence on American aid would "to a large extent automatically assure her alignment with the free world." Sebald also complained that the Japanese left would profit from continued procurement, since their strategy was to portray military orders as American exploitation of Japanese labor for imperialistic ends and to charge that orders would lower standards of living by fueling inflation.[33]

Sherwood Fine, responding to Sebald's critique of the cooperation scheme for ESS, easily dismissed this latter fear. Without trade with China, he said, and with the existence of the world dollar gap, procurement would mean higher living standards, employment, and profits for Japan. The orders "obviously" solved Japan's "urgent requirement" for dollars and "constituted perhaps the most profitable trade Japan [had] enjoyed in the postwar period."[34] Sebald probably objected not so much to the cooperation scheme as to the large role of the military bureaucracy (ESS) in planning future relations between Japan and the United States. A Defense Department consultant, Ernest Tupper, was also surprised by the blatantly "opportunistic" campaign by Morrow and ESS to use the cold war to stimulate and subsidize the Japanese economy. Tupper informed Washington that ESS saw procurement strictly as a way to raise Japanese profits, employment, and living standards, which, he admitted, it did quite effectively.[35]

The Truman Administration wholeheartedly supported the Dulles-ESS strategy of economic cooperation with Japan in early 1952, as the United States prepared to end the Occupation. NSC 125, drafted by the National Security Council in February, stated that the American-Japanese alliance would succeed "only if Japan, in its own self-interest, fully recognize[d] its stake in the free world," and developed "close political, military and economic cooperation with the United States and other free nations, particularly in Asia." The council further recognized that Japan's dollar gap "require[d] that every effort be made to expand Japan's earnings from normal commerce and from programs of United States military and economic assistance to other countries, with a view to avoiding if possible any requirement for direct economic assistance." It pledged that the United States, however, would constantly monitor Japan's trade balance and would grant "direct economic assistance when and if necessary." The primary obstacle to expanding the combined military-economic offensive in Asia using Japanese factories was the lack of authorization of military sales to Southeast Asia. The United States did include a provision to procure MDAP supplies for Southeast Asia in Japan in the administrative agreement with Japan signed in February 1952.[36]

Post-treaty cooperation planning was institutionalized by the establishment of a "Joint United States–Japan Committee," formed under the administrative agreement in February to oversee the military presence of the United States. In addition, a joint economic council, composed of American embassy officials, other American personnel, and Japanese representatives, directed industrial mobilization and economic cooperation schemes. A "Procurement Coordination Sub-Committee" of the joint committee included officials of the procurement and development branch of the economics division of the American embassy. The staff of eleven was financed by MSA funds. Morrow and several former programs and statistics division colleagues remained on to implement post-treaty cooperation plans. They used American influence to assist Japan in negotiations with Third World countries, and used American labor relations expertise to help foil a Japanese coal miners' strike. The staff also compiled volumes IV and V of "JIP" on pre- and post-World War II Japanese trading patterns. When Joseph Dodge was appointed consultant to Secretary of State Acheson, it assured that the Japanese view would be well heeded in both Washington and the Tokyo embassy.[37]

Japan Affirms the Alliance (1951–1952)

Japan faced a critical choice in 1951 and 1952 as it emerged from the Occupation and total American control: whether to cast its lot with the American bloc by exploiting aid and procurement opportunities or to embrace a neutralist-independent course and open relations with China and the Soviet Union. Without the presence of American troops, the economic and technological opportunities afforded by aid, the American military umbrella in Southeast Asia, and an Occupation-developed subservience to American diplomacy, which all stifled Japanese nationalism, Japan would likely have emulated India as a fiercely independent Asian power.

Indeed, there were compelling economic and strategic reasons for the conservative Japanese élite to shirk the American partnership. Cooperation with the United States afforded great technological advantages for manufacturing, but large-scale Chinese trade offered inexpensive raw materials and large markets. The American strategic offensive in Asia offered a conducive environment (enhanced by U.S. military markets) for Japanese corporations to penetrate Southeast Asia; yet, neutrality would allow Japan to trade with all of Asia and would alleviate the risk that an American military collapse in the region would leave Japan isolated from a socialist mainland. The depth and complexity of the development of post-treaty Japanese diplomacy are far beyond the scope of this work; suffice it to say that American policy to reverse Occupation reforms and soothe conservative rulers with war orders and military moves in Asia proved to be a complete success.

To greatly oversimplify, Japan opted to cooperate with the United States because the large monopolies/corporations which emerged from the aborted deconcentration program were best served by the rapid technological modernization offered by the United States. They easily overruled the longings of Osaka textile merchants for vast Chinese markets for textiles and other low-technology items and resisted the public resentment at the continued presence of American troops and fealty to American policy. Nonetheless, although Japan remained committed to American cold war strategy, even the conservatives strained at their leash to open nonstrategic trade with China and to minimize the Japanese military buildup, which drained capital and offended the pacifistic electorate.[38] These issues created constant tension within the Pacific alliance and shaped Japanese-American relations in the post-Occupation period.

Two other forces significantly shaped the Japanese policy of co-operation with the United States: Japan's continued economic fragility and great dollar dependence; and the long-standing Yoshida strategy to convert defeat into victory by exploiting Japan's poverty to gain American subsidies. Many Japanese and others gave Yoshida credit for the long-term success of his strategy of economic recovery—to subtly guide the Americans into aiding Japan by pleading Japan's utter economic deprivation.[39] In this view, it was more a matter of the Americans' taking the bait than Japan's accepting its subordinate role in the alliance. Japan, after all, had profited from its junior role in the 1902 partnership with the world leader, Great Britain. Yet, the weakness of the economy and the reemergence of the monopolies created the conditions for Japan's pro-American policy.

It was commonplace to refer to Japan's economy in the early 1950s as a "shallow economy." This referred to the dramatic impact on Japan of slight price fluctuations abroad, either of competitors' goods or of raw materials. Such changes could drastically affect Japanese production costs and would price Japanese goods out of world markets. Japan was extraordinarily dependent on world market conditions; thus, when the world boom generated by the Korean War gave way to depressed markets in mid-1952, Japanese business again became uneasy about its prospects. In a buyer's panic during the Korean boom, Japanese importers had stocked up on high-priced raw materials, only to see their prices plunge in 1951. This left Japanese manufacturers with overpriced raw materials and crippled Japan's export competitiveness: Japan was more vulnerable than any other nation to raw materials inflation. Moreover, Japan was vitally dependent on the dollar area for grains, minerals, sugar, oil, and cotton. Thus, it was not surprising that manufacturers welcomed the American war orders to sustain the economy after the boom. While Marquat negotiated on behalf of Japan in Washington in April, the "Dulles Line [economic cooperation] was keenly discussed" by Japanese businessmen. Marquat's timely May announcement ensured that "new special procurement orders" (as they were called by Japanese businessmen) stemming from the post-treaty cooperation program were on the way.[40]

The challenge facing American cooperation planners was to soothe the fragile psyche of the Japanese investment community. JIP III, issued in February 1952, stated that the Japanese would cooperate with the United States only if "they [could] be supplied with an adequate incentive by means of United States end-product orders so that the Japanese [could] see the opportunity to realize on their investments." The capital outlays necessary to rebuild and modernize heavy industry would not be forthcoming unless the investors felt that American military orders would continue for the foreseeable future; otherwise, the investments would be unsound financial risks. The uneasiness of investors about the permanence of military markets was explained in the *Oriental Economist:*

> The Japanese Government before the outbreak of the Korean War had no policy whereby to keep the depression from going from bad to worse. The Japanese economy was saved by the special procurement orders born of the Korean conflict and the speculative demands from abroad. The subsequent remarkable progress in production and the rapid increase in profits in industry—these were the products of chance.[41]

Japan, of course, had profited greatly from foreign wars in the past and chose to do so again. Yet the underlying fear of peace, which was best displayed when the Japanese stock market plunged at the hint of progress in Korean peace talks, placed great pressure on the United States to assure Japan that the orders would continue indefinitely. As the Treasury representative in the embassy informed his superiors in June 1952, Japan's reliance on procurement orders was so great that the "psychological repercussions" of a cut would outweigh the actual economic effect.[42]

The Yoshida government responded quickly to the American shift from self-support to cooperation. Two weeks after the government had rejected the final self-support plan, on February 5, 1951, the Economic Stabilization Board issued its first economic cooperation program. The board planned to keep Japan's economy flexible enough to adapt to changing procurement orders. It requested American capital and credits, along with technological assistance (especially thermal electric power equipment), and also shifted their goal from food self-sufficiency to reliance on American agricultural imports to maintain food consumption. They further requested that Japan be included in American and British plans to develop Southeast Asia—another bonus of cooperation. Their expressed strategy was to expand Japanese shipping and business abroad and, as befitting a "workshop," to export "those commodities which require[d] a high degree of fabrication."[43]

In February 1952, the Economic Stabilization Board called for emphasis on "increasing the volume, extending the scope, and prolonging the duration of off-shore procurement." The Japanese feared that an end to the Korean War would prejudice $700 million in annual dollar earnings, and that expected Korean rehabilitation orders would not be sufficient compensation. In June 1952, the board said that "long-ranged and big-sized procurements" were necessary "to make the modernization of domestic plants attainable."[44]

Japanese strategy since early in the Occupation had been to obtain American capital and technology to catch up to Western industry. Such requests poured forth in the early years of the cooperation program, especially for electric power equipment—the key industrial bottleneck. Indeed, the political parties had long campaigned on the pledge that they would obtain more American investment and assistance than their opponents. The military production program greatly facilitated such linkages; by the end of 1952, 211 technical assistance contracts had been signed in the areas of communications, electronics, optical goods, and fuel tanks. Yoshida, moreover, was anxious to secure a symbolic loan to display the success of his "economic diplomacy."[45]

Yoshida's loan request was considered by Dodge on a return trip to Japan in late 1951. Dodge no longer held control of Japan's domestic economic policy, but he remained outspoken on the necessity of government economic controls to channel all capital into basic industrial development. Japanese business was opting for quick profits with luxury hotel and restaurant investments, which squandered vital capital funds. Dodge and Marquat agreed that the government sacrificed sound credit policies because of political pressure by business for easy loan terms. Dodge also advised the government to allocate all raw materials imports to export production and not allow them to be used for domestic construction or consumption. This is one of Dodge's enduring legacies in Japan; for the sake of economic growth, conservative Japanese governments deemphasized social infrastructural development—roads, sewers, parks, hospitals, and other public services. Even SCAP's tax experts complained that the "severe tax burden" imposed on the workers to subsidize capital accumulation was unfair. Japan's corporate tax rate, at 35 percent and with accelerated depreciation allowances, was one of the lowest in the world, another policy encouraged by Dodge.[46]

Despite his disappointment with Japanese liberal economic policies, on his 1951 trip Dodge was careful to temper his criticism of the Yoshida cabinet, in the fear of strengthening the hand of the opposition conservatives, the "pro-inflationists" Ichirō Hatoyama and Ishibashi. Yet Dodge did not agree with Morrow that the United States should develop its policies strictly in accordance with Japan's needs. Morrow echoed the repeated Japanese pleas to coordinate procurement orders so that they matched Japan's capacity, but Dodge insisted that Japan would have to adapt its economy to match the needs of the United States. He summed up the American position on cooperation when he assured the Japanese government that there was no contradiction between political independence and economic dependence on the United States. Finally, Dodge disputed Japan's economic necessity for a loan (dollar reserves from procurements were adequate), but agreed that it would be beneficial symbolically to cement the alliance.[47] Washington directed Japan to the IBRD, and Japan became the bank's best customer and thus ultimately found the capital infusion sought by political leaders from an international source.

By 1952, the slump in the wake of the Korean boom had wiped out many of the gains against the dollar gap made in 1950 and 1951, both in Japan and worldwide. Shigeo Horie, executive director of the Bank of Tokyo, noted the pervading fear of depression in business circles in early 1952, "comparable" to that which existed on the eve of the Korean War. As in the autumn of 1950, the corporate community was divided into pessimists and optimists: the pessimists feared an American recession and a reduction in defense spending; the optimists believed that cold war tensions would maintain Keynesian stimuli. Both, however, feared the plague of overproduction and unemployment. The slump also reversed the progress of the sterling area, and led a British economist to lament that the dollar gap was worse than in 1947 and that the American policy of using foreign aid to finance "expanding equilibrium" and prevent contracting disequilibrium was in jeopardy. Global multilateralism, a key to Japanese export success, was impossible until the sterling area approached a dollar balance.[48]

By the spring of 1952, poor economic conditions led Japan's basic industries—steel, shipbuilding, machinery, and textiles—to cooperate openly in order to regulate markets and prices and to share the burdens of overproduction. The Ministry of International Trade and Industry (MITI) initiated and institutionalized the collusion among producers, and approved the use of prewar Zaibatsu trademarks. Against the wishes of small- and medium-size businesses, the Diet revised the antimonopoly law on August 6, 1952. Ridgway sealed the doom of the reform programs and assured the triumph of the reverse course when he encouraged the Japanese to review all Occupation reforms for revision. Even before the Occupation ended, Mitsui and Mitsubishi had reconsolidated their vast corporate dominions.[49]

In mid-1952, the powerful Federation of Economic Organizations purged small and medium businesses and looked to American military orders to revive industry. Removal of the Japanese Chamber of Commerce and Industry enabled the federation to represent only the large industrial combines. The federation, giving "the highest priority to defense production," eagerly lobbied for procurement orders, suggesting to the United States the many items that Japan could produce. The cycle of war production/defeat/war production became complete when the Occupation was terminated in April 1952. SCAP returned to the Japanese government the weapons plants that had survived the aborted reparations program. Then, under federation pressure, Yoshida returned 859 arms plants to their wartime corporate owners. The cooperation program was institutionalized on the Japanese side by the creation of the federation's Economic Cooperation Council and the government's Supreme Economic Cooperation Conference. By August the federation's Defense Production Committee, chaired by Kiyoshi Gōko, head of Mitsubishi Heavy Industries, became the most influential force in Japanese business. Finally, in September, the government designated the weapons industry as a major "national policy industry," and gave MITI the task of stimulating and protecting it through subsidies, tax breaks, and procurement.[50] The American embassy staff worked closely with the federation's Economic Cooperation Council, and reported to the State Department in September: "Private Japanese business circles are keenly aware of the desirability of adequate organizational arrangements to promote maximum utilization of Japan's industrial potential in connection with the defense production efforts of the free world."[51]

Despite the strong support of American policies by the giant corporations, many Japanese were uneasy about Japan's prolonged dependence on and subservience to the United States. Shigeto Tsuru, a Harvard-trained former head of the Economic Stabilization Board under the Social-Democratic Katayama cabinet, expressed the fears of opponents of Yoshida's solution to Japan's "chronic" dollar gap: "So long as Japan has to depend upon America, for filling her dollar gap in the balance of payments, she is likely to be all the more politically dependent on America, which in turn will make it more and more difficult to open free economic intercourse with the continent of Asia." He also feared that the economic benefits of the Korean War were "exactly that kind of stimulus which is likely to resuscitate those motive forces which led Japan into the road of militarism in the past."[52] His first fear was confirmed, as Japan failed to benefit greatly from Chinese trade for two decades; his second fear, however, misread the total dedication to economic growth and eventual economic dominance which has characterized Japanese policy and stifled state militarism now for at least three decades.

5. The Workshop Realized: The MSA and Japan

The history of the 1930's should be a warning to the West, and especially to the United States, that failure to make sufficient economic opportunity for the expansion of Japan's exports and for Japanese economic growth can be disastrous for the security of the West and the peace of the world. The logical way to open this opportunity would be to make possible greater Japanese participation in the development of Southern Asia.

—*Elliott Committee, 1955*

Southeast Asia is one of the markets that Japan must have. But until Southeast Asian markets can be opened up, as an interim measure we must permit Japan to enter into the open world competitive market with us, the British and Germany. The question of Japanese trade is one of great difficulty. I would like to remind you of one of the last things Stalin wrote before he died. He said the free world would find itself in the position where it could not absorb the industrial capacities of Japan and Germany; that the free world would try to set up trade barriers between Germany and Japan and would fall apart eventually on this question, and all the Reds would have to do then would be to pick up the pieces.

—*Dulles to the Cabinet, August 6, 1954*

The crux of Japan's economic problem, now as in the interwar years, is that its energetic, self-confident and ambitious business class lacks sufficient outlets for its talent and energies at home. . . . In the interwar period, the Japanese industrialists threw in their lot with

166

*the militarists in an effort to solve this problem through
imperialism. Today the same problem faces them again
in much aggravated form.*

—*Elliott Committee, 1955*

Cementing the Alliance: Post-Treaty Economic Cooperation (1952–1955)

After the April 1952 enactment of the peace treaty with
Japan, U.S. policy sought to strengthen the bonds of economic cooperation that tied Japan to American cold war policies. In order to
protect the Pacific alliance against the divisive forces of pressures
for Chinese trade and Japanese resistance to American rearmament
pleas, the United States had to continue to subsidize Japan's huge
dollar gap and seek more permanent solutions. From 1952 to 1954
Japan's economy staggered and the dollar gap mushroomed, while
Europe's dollar gap shrank. By 1954, therefore, Japan had emerged
as the most critical foreign economic policy problem for the Eisenhower Administration. Southeast Asian penetration, greater American imports from Japan, and freer multilateral trade were all solutions sought in this period.

A third phase in the attack on the dollar gap began in 1953. Coined
by the British chancellor of the exchequer as a critique of American
trade surpluses, the phrase "Trade not Aid" characterized the new
phase. From 1947 to 1950, economic aid subsidized the dollar gap,
and from 1950 to 1953 the explosion of overseas military expenditures replaced economic aid. After 1953 the Eisenhower Administration sought to increase American imports to cure the global dollar
gap while continuing to rely on military expenditures to ease payments crises, especially in Japan. Offshore procurement of military
supplies continued as one form of the "Trade not Aid" approach.
The more direct form was the Japanese effort to tap the huge American market to resolve its seemingly perpetual dependence on American imports. The final phase of the economic cooperation program
was marked by the incorporation of Japan into the lucrative Mutual
Security System. The Mutual Security Program had already replaced
the ERP in Europe, and also used offshore procurement of military

material to finance the dollar gap. A series of mutual security arrangements with Japan in 1954 consolidated the Pacific alliance. Japan thus became formally locked into the American cold war bloc, in return for military protection, continued procurement subsidies, and an American military protectorate in Southeast Asia.

Japan's Economy Falters (1952–1953)

Despite a staggering $800 million in dollar earnings from American military procurement, Japan's economic position failed to improve in 1952. The special income equaled 64 percent of normal exports and 37 percent of all foreign exchange receipts. Yet Japan continued to be hurt by the post-Korean business lull. Exports, which held firm in the first half of the year, fell by $80 million in the second half, causing observers to fear a sharp increase in the payments deficit. In 1953 the worst fears were realized when exports rose a paltry $3 million, while imports increased to $2.4 billion. The trade deficit grew from $150 million in 1950 to $600 million in 1951, $750 million in 1952, and a staggering $1.1 billion in 1953. For the second straight year, procurement orders reached $800 million—38 percent of foreign exchange receipts and 70 percent of commercial exports.[1] Procurement orders allowed Japan the luxury of increased consumption, industrial production, and machinery manufacture, and of maintaining a huge commercial trade deficit.

Japan's structural economic problems did not improve by 1953, even though the vast American military spending program helped refurbish industry, which later reaped great dividends for Japan. Japan had achieved only 40 percent of its prewar trade level; Europe had reached 150 percent. Japanese business feared the possibility of global overproduction, with the newly elected Republican Administration threatening to trim military spending. The Japanese business press noted that "to worsen this gloomy situation, the Soviet peace 'offensive' ha[d] been stepped up at a time when most forecasts predict[ed] high probability of a recession in the United States." Finally, the greatest fear—a conclusion to the Korean War—haunted Japan through 1953. The *Oriental Economist* warned: "Should there be a tapering off of U.S. spending in Japan as a result of the truce in

Korea, untold suffering may be caused." Indeed, "near panic" set in as stock prices plunged 37 percent during the last stage of peace talks. The Japanese government and American observers agreed that the "artificial prosperity of the Korean War" was pushing the economy to disaster.[2] James Reston charged that the Japanese had done nothing to prepare for a cut in the $2 million-per-day subsidy; he said that neither the American nor the Japanese government had yet faced the problem. Both were living in a "fool's paradise," reported the *New York Times,* which added that a Japanese collapse would be the equivalent of a major military defeat for the United States.[3]

Concern about Japan and the cooperation program increased among American officials and observers through 1953. Dodge blamed Japan's export problems on her inability to procure inexpensive coking coal and iron ore and warned that an end to the Korean War, the projected American defense phaseout, and Buy American policies in the United States all boded ill for Japan. Jerome Cohen wrote:

Obviously a cessation of UN procurement in Japan without a corresponding increase in dollar area purchases of Japanese goods would wreck Japan's trade and her economy. Since such a step would be unthinkable, a gradual tapering off of special procurements would have to be followed by either (a) large substitute expenditures in Japan for Korean Rehabilitation, or (b) a book of orders for military end-products placed over a period of, say, five years, falling off as commercial trade with other areas expanded.

Cohen placed his faith in a trading boom with the Third World, aided by expanding American foreign aid programs, which would, he hoped, allow Japanese expansion without crippling British trade. To move in the opposite direction (to cut aid, increase trade barriers, restrict international loans, inhibit foreign investment, and retain inconvertibility) would lend credence to Stalin's prediction that the Western trading bloc would be unable to "absorb the export capacities of Japan and West Germany."[4]

The State Department feared more than ever that any failure of the cooperation program would drive Japan into the hands of China. In December 1952, Merrill Gay of the Far Eastern division prepared a comprehensive summary of the bleak prospects for Japanese prosperity. He said that the plight of Japan was so grave that it was "unique," and warranted intense American aid considerations. Noting that Japanese industry suffered from a demand insufficient to maintain efficient, high-volume production, Gay said that "under present circumstances off-shore procurement of both military and non-military items offers an effective means for stimulating and directing the use and expansion of Japanese productive resources." He also stressed the omnipresent concern that the pivotal American market would cease to grow through military-related production, thereby causing a greater dollar gap: "A doubling of Japan's trade with Southeast Asia might hardly touch in magnitude the impact on Japan of a serious United States depression." Agreeing with many knowledgeable observers that Southeast Asian trade would not provide a near-term solution for Japan, Gay stated that Japanese sales to America held the solution to the dollar gap. Thus, he found it especially disconcerting when Japanese sales to America drew more protest from American manufacturers than those from any other nation.[5]

American nationalism, a key obstacle to solving the global dollar gap, imperiled the cooperation program. Large American corporations viewed Japan as a trading partner and backed cooperation and increased American imports. Weak American manufacturing interests directly threatened by Japanese sales, however, joined with their British counterparts to resist even small-scale Japanese exports. American producers of tuna, gloves, mittens, toys, and other goods filed complaints against Japanese exports. The Japanese faith in American goodwill was shaken when their products were attacked, despite Japan's enormous purchases in the United States. The Japanese complained that the *Saturday Evening Post* and *Collier's* had editorialized against imports from Japan under pressure from their advertisers. Moreover, American shipping interests fought for policies that would limit Japanese shipping.[6]

The most serious dispute arose when the United States doubled its tariff on tuna—after Japan had doubled its tuna exports to the United States. American fleet owners complained to Congress that they had to pay their workers $1.75 per hour, while the Japanese earned only $8 per month. Ridgway protested that the tariff hike would cost Japan $11 million in dollar sales, and that the psychological impact would be even greater. Tuna was Japan's first successful postwar export to the United States, and the tariff issue "represented in the spiritual field to the Japanese people what the Asiatic Exclusion Act did years ago," Ridgway warned. He said that American protectionism would drive Japan into an "isolationist mentality": "If the United States [is] now undermining Japan[ese] efforts to earn their own way, what nation in [the] free world would permit Japan to do so?"[7]

Indeed, this was the great fear of the Eisenhower Administration. If Japan could not gain access to markets in the United States, how could America force other nations to open their markets to Japan? American tariffs averaged 12 percent, but tariffs on Japanese goods averaged 26 percent. In 1953 the Administration, recognizing that Japan was the weak link in the American industrial alliance system, lobbied business and the public to accept Japanese goods. Harold Linder, of the State Department, told the House Foreign Economic Policy Subcommittee that the Administration had to counter the great pressure put on the Japanese government to implement trade with China; Western markets had to be opened to replace procurement orders, or the cooperation scheme would fail. Dulles also warned Congress of the necessity of Western markets for Japan: "With the end of active hostilities in Korea, Japan foresees serious difficulties in being able to obtain the dollars it needs to feed and clothe its population at minimum levels of subsistence." Clarence Randall's Commission on Foreign Economic Policy, the spearhead of the campaign to increase imports, also concluded in October 1953 that the success of the cooperation program rested with increased Japanese exports to the West. The United States had to set the example for other nations, but the commission feared that the tuna industry and makers of china, silk, textiles, footware, toys, novelties, and optical goods would obstruct that strategy.[8]

The United States moved in April 1953 to respond to conservative fears precipitated by socialist electoral gains in Japan. On April 2, the United States granted most-favored-nation status to Japan in a commercial treaty, and on April 15 the State Department authorized the embassy to assure Japan that procurement would continue at a "relatively high level" through 1955. Still, the socialists gained ground.[9]

In the summer of 1953, as Korean peace talks neared their conclusion, Japanese business once again faced a critical decision. Shipping, textile, and fishing interests called for an independent foreign policy (i.e., trade with China). Heavy and chemical industries and the financial and trading sectors continued to back cooperation with the United States. The latter "were counting on close American-Japanese cooperation to develop full-scale defense production activities as a means of weathering the economic crisis." [10]

The Japanese Federation of Economic Organizations was anxious that Japan be incorporated into the lucrative mutual security nexus, both to share in Europe's good fortune and to receive long-term American aid. In July, the federation, representing Japan's largest corporations, issued its "General Recommendations Regarding Reception of MSA Benefits": "It is undeniable that with properly planned procurements in Japan as the basis of MSA aid, the foundations can be laid for an industrial structure which, in the future, would contribute in no little way to augumentation of Japan's competitive capacity in international markets." The federation expressed "great expectations" for transfers of high technology, and requested economic aid in addition to military orders. Admiral Takuo Godō, a private confidant of Yoshida, urged the United States to grant all foreign military procurement orders to Japan to advance technological modernization, saying that an MSA agreement would "have great significance for the reconstruction of Japan's industrial economy." Finally, the director of the federation, Tokuju Uchiyama, expressed the corporations' desire for orders: "It is extremely doubtful whether there is any way for Japan to recover economic independence without accepting the call for defense production. The shortest and quickest way to economic self-support lies in the acceptance of the new procurements to replace the Emergency Korean War Orders." [11]

Thus, when Dulles announced to the Senate Foreign Relations Committee that the Administration planned to include Japan in future MSA aid programs, the effect in Japan was similar to that of Marquat's announcement in May 1951. The *Oriental Economist* reported a flurry of enthusiasm among business circles, and that "the defense industry showed tremendous activity." The final obstacle to MSA talks was removed when the United States assured Japan that Japanese troops would not be required to fight American wars in Southeast Asia. Such an arrangement had been mentioned in Congress but was unacceptable to Japan. Negotiations on the future shape of the alliance commenced in Tokyo on July 15, 1953.[12]

The Ikeda-Robertson Talks

Perhaps the most critical negotiations between the United States and Japan took place in Washington, when Yoshida sent his chief aide, Ikeda, to discuss Japan's role in the mutual security aid system with Far East division head Walter Robertson. The talks took place against a backdrop of Japanese business pressure for offshore procurement orders similar to those granted to Europe, insufficient trade with Southeast Asia, and an imminent end to the extremely lucrative Korean War. Thus, the United States had to offer incentives to Japan to prolong the cooperation scheme, as a Treasury Department official reported: "There may be great pressure to plan something favorable for Mr. Ikeda to take home which no one has yet come up with."[13]

American officials had already made general assurances that a Korean peace settlement would not drastically decrease war orders, fulfilling the American side of long-term economic cooperation. Korean rehabilitation orders, however, long expected by Japan to substitute for war orders, were not forthcoming. The orders never materialized because Syngman Rhee refused to abandon his lifelong antipathy toward Japan—the former colonizer of Korea. When a dispute flared up in November over fishing rights and the Japanese treatment of Korean nationals, trade talks broke off between Japan and South Korea and did not resume until 1960. This situation placed even greater pressure on the United States to develop alternate markets for Japanese goods.[14]

The Japanese had a clear conception of how to overcome the loss of markets in Korea. Ikeda first presented the standard portrayal of Japan's economic plight: a vicious cycle of insufficient capital, retarded modernization, inflation, and slumping exports. Japan then requested maximum military procurement orders for American forces in Asia, help in easing sterling trade restrictions and reparations snags, and relaxed limits on trade with China. Ikeda reported that the economic crisis had led to a "strong nationwide desire" to lift Chinese trade restrictions: "As export competition becomes severe Japanese traders are inclined to look for trade with Red China." The Diet had unanimously approved a bill that called for stepped-up trade with China, and the conservatives feared that the socialists would make further gains if the United States failed to consider Japan's needs. Finally, Ikeda called for MSA "defense support" economic aid similar to that received by Europe (he also termed it "non-direct military aid") and expressed Japan's "great concern about the future of procurement."[15]

The American delegation to the talks responded that procurement was actually more beneficial economically than direct aid grants: "Off-shore procurement in fact stimulates the rebuilding and modernization of industry and is preferred by most countries to aid of other kinds." Moreover, Japan's large procurement earnings precluded economic aid. Robertson expressed American disappointment with Japan's high inflation and domestic consumption and her half-hearted effort to rearm. Congress would not look kindly on Japanese requests, he insisted, until Japan enforced rigid austerity measures and allocated a minimum percentage of gross national product to the national defense budget. Europe also had to meet these terms in order to receive MSA aid, he explained. Like the Europeans, however, the Japanese gave definite priority to economic recovery over rearmament. Ikeda warned that the Japanese public had stubbornly adopted the pacifism imposed by the Occupation in Article IX of the Japanese constitution, which forbade Japan from establishing standing armed forces. The United States delegation said the public had to be reeducated to support rearmament, and pressed Japan to doubled the two percent of gross national product allocated to defense.[16]

The strains latent in the cooperation scheme emerged vividly when the Ikeda mission resisted the American call for rearmament and domestic austerity. The Japanese well knew the value of their China trump card, which precluded the withholding of American aid. Rigid American punishment of Japan would plunge the economy into chaos, cripple American exports to Japan, strengthen opposition parties, and possibly instigate a Japanese-Chinese alliance that would greatly diminish American influence in Asia. As John Allison, ambassador to Japan during this critical period, recalled, the Japanese government "seemed confident the United States would bail it out of any economic trouble."[17]

Nor did Japan seek rapidly to rearm. Pacific Commander Mark Clark confided to the Joint Chiefs that the "Japanese may be aware that Communist land forces pose relatively little threat to her security." The Japanese delegation would not budge above a figure of 180,000 troops, while the United States insisted on 300,000. Ikeda also resisted Joseph Dodge's stern advice to slash manufacturing costs and apply strict credit and consumption controls to boost export competitiveness. When Dodge suggested that declining procurement orders might force Japanese business to rationalize its production (and thus cure the economy), Ikeda replied: "Patient will die instead of 'cure.'"[18] Yet, the Yoshida government eventually did take deflationary actions at the end of 1953.

The conflicts over austerity and troop strength continued into 1954. The American strategy was to reencourage Japanese military sentiment. In Japan, Vice-President Richard Nixon bluntly defied the Japanese government's policies, as expressed in the MSA talks, by suggesting that the Japanese change their constitution to allow for war. The American embassy, however, replacing SCAP as lobbyist for Japanese interests, convinced Washington that it would be counterproductive to humiliate the conservatives in the Japanese public eye by forcing rearmament on Japan. When the Mutual Defense Assistance Agreement was finally signed on March 8, 1954, it set no target figure for Japanese troop strength and committed Japan to rearm only when her economic strength allowed. The embassy also attempted to halt growing Washington criticism of Japan's "profligate" living standards. Conservative Washington financiers such as Dodge, who complained that the world was sacrificing solvency for "political considerations" (i.e., jobs and wages), self-righteously lectured the Japanese to tighten their belts. The embassy suggested that actually withholding some procurement orders to force austerity would be less dangerous to the alliance than Washington's public attacks on Japan, which fanned Japanese anti-Americanism.[19]

As part of the mutual defense agreement, signed in March 1954, the United States pledged "substantially larger" offshore procurement orders for Japan. Congress, however, had made the aid less appealing. In 1953, reacting to the renewal of the historical glut of

American farm products caused by the recovery of European agriculture and the end of ERP aid tied to purchases of American agricultural surpluses, Congress wrote Section 550 into the Mutual Security Act of 1951. All postwar aid programs had featured the dumping of agricultural products, and Section 550 required that MSA aid recipients take part of their aid in surplus agricultural goods. The products would be sold locally for counterpart funds, which would be spent in the manufacture of arms. This policy continued to stimulate arms and other heavy industries, but reduced direct dollar earnings used to balance international payments.[20]

The mutual defense agreement was another triumph of Yoshida's economic diplomacy. Japan succeeded in downplaying rearmament and obtained $50 million in Section 550 aid. It was too late, however, to obtain MSA aid for fiscal year 1955, because the agreement was not formally ratified until May. Yet the agreement did grant Japan equality with Europe in the MSA system of defense and industrial subsidies. The agreement was rather more symbolic than directly lucrative. It paved the way for long-term American interest in financing Japan's arms industry. The *New York Times* reported that the Federation of Economic Organizations' Defense Production Committee planned in 1954 to emphasize the key economic role of arms production: "Japanese industrialists have developed long-range plans to restore this nation to its position as the arsenal of Asia."[21] The agreement was a final step in cementing the Pacific alliance, yet the strains within the cooperation rubric persisted.

The 1954 Dollar Gap Crisis

In late 1953 the Yoshida government imposed a strict austerity program. The Bank of Japan cut loans and raised interest rates. The results were as expected. On the one hand, imports and production costs dropped, as depressed wages had "remarkable" benefits for business. On the other hand, however, the program sparked a wave of bankruptcies: "By 1954 the deflationary policy brought the Japanese economy to a virtual standstill. Thousands of enterprises in consumer goods and service lines, which had sprung up in the era of the 'divine wind' [the Korean War boom], were forced to close." Again, the Japanese feared that a world depression would wipe out the gains made since the outbreak of the Korean War.[22] And, again, the Eisenhower Administration feared for the stability of the alliance, as Japan ran a $1 billion deficit in 1953.

On May 20, 1954, the embassy in Tokyo alarmed Eisenhower about Japan's desperate situation. On June 21, he told the cabinet that Japan was the "key" to Asia and her payments problem had to be solved, but "of course we do not want to ruin our own industries to keep Japan on our side." Further consideration was given to the theory that carefully planned trade with China would save Japan and would also help lure China from the Soviet orbit. Eisenhower also reiterated what had been true since the founding of the ERP in 1948— that congressional obstruction was the heart of the problem. On June 21, 1954, he described four sets of congressional groups, whose principles were, respectively, no trade with China, no intervention in Southeast Asia, no liberalization of trade, and limited trade with Japan. He said, "If we didn't do a little of some of these, we would lose Japan." He declared publicly the next day that "even our current concern with Southeast Asia . . . was largely motivated by Japan's need to trade with the area if it was to 'make a living' and be prevented from going to the Communists." Further, several governors sent to study Korea concluded that the one "simple and inescapable" fact about the Far East was that "Japan must be kept out of the Communist camp" and that steps had to be taken to bolster her economy. On Capitol Hill, Mike Mansfield glumly predicted that Japan would need American aid forever unless adequate trade outlets were found.[23]

Administration studies outlined the bleak structural outlook for Japanese trade in mid-1954. The austerity program had to be continued "if it [could] be done without bringing about either political chaos or depression," advised the Commerce Department. It added that the only solution was for the Japanese to "submit to a cut in their real standard of living." Yoshida, however, could not be pushed too hard, the department recognized, because American pressure would endanger his rule, already under seige for implementing austerity measures and showing submissiveness to the United States. If he responded to American pressure he might be ousted, and the United States would have to deal with an unfamiliar and less responsive government. It warned that the West failed to recognize that Japan had to export or, by "sheer desperation, be compelled to regard Communist offers and eventual Communist domination as more attractive than economic collapse."[24]

The Japanese expressed their concern with their role in the American system, complaining that procurement receipts were falling at a critical time. The government presented a paper to the embassy in July, entitled "United States Procurement in Japan: Recent Trends and Requested Countermeasures." They feared that troop expenditures would drop by $40 million compared with 1953, since fewer American troops remained in Korea to take leaves in Japan. Moreover, the master labor contract for procurement by the United States Forces, Japan (the American military stationed in Japan), had been changed to provide yen instead of dollar payment to Japanese labor, which would cost Japan another $60 million: "In view of the recent and rapid downward trend in special procurement receipts as set forth above and the importance of this income to the Japanese economy, it is imperative that positive measures be adopted to prevent further decline, and if possible assure some increase." The government sought guarantees that, as American troops withdrew, offshore procurement and Foreign Operations Administration (FOA—the 1954 successor to MSA) orders for Southeast Asia would increase. The Commerce Department shared Japanese fears, advising President Eisenhower that procurements would likely drop to $200 million per year and remove the "most important prop to the postwar Japanese economy."[25]

The fears and strains in the Pacific alliance reached their peak in an August 6, 1954, cabinet meeting. Secretary Dulles gave a vivid portrayal of the American predicament in Japan. He first reminded the cabinet that Japan expanded militarily in the 1930s "to get control of their own markets and their own materials." If the United States allowed tariff concessions, he continued, it could "keep Japan on our side"; without new markets, "Japan could very soon go bankrupt." He cited Britain's obstruction of Japanese revival: "They wanted to keep Japan alive through what would amount to doles so that Japan would have no chance to compete with British goods in the world markets." He then explained that the American market also offered no solution: "In the United States there is no enthusiasm for

Japanese goods. We don't need or want many of their items since they are really cheap imitations of our own goods, so in the long run the future of Japan must be found in markets in the underdeveloped areas of the world. In return Japan can get the raw materials she so desperately needs." He insisted that every agency support tariff concessions to Japan.[26]

Eisenhower agreed, adding that East-West trade would also help Japan: "I have always believed that this kind of trade should not only be allowed but encouraged, particularly as far as Japan is concerned with the neighboring Red areas in Asia." He suggested that the Chinese might come to depend on cheap Japanese consumer items, weakening the Moscow-Peking axis, and that Japan could acquire its most essential iron ore and coking coal imports much more cheaply. When Assistant Secretary of Commerce Anderson said that the answer was to return Japan to its mid-1930s standard of living, Eisenhower agreed that wages had to go even lower, but warned: "We can't force them back beyond the point of no return. If we do, they will say 'To Hell with you' we'll go Communist. That's what this is all about. We must hold Japan for the free world or we must go to war to keep it in the free world. This is a world problem. We have got to work on a broad front. We have got to do a considerable job of education."[27]

Americans and Europeans had to be educated to the fact that the immediate sacrifice of accepting Japanese goods paled before the long-term threat of a Communist Japan. American business interests were represented in the cabinet meeting by Secretary of Commerce Weeks and Treasury Secretary Humphrey of Ohio's massive Hanna Mining empire. Eisenhower termed the 1955 tariff negotiations with Japan "critical" and said that "to bar all competitive products would result, in the long run, in the disaster of war." Secretary Weeks replied that he understood, but noted the drastic difference in wage scales between Japan and the United States. He insisted that the United States reserve the right to use peril point tariffs and escape clauses to protect beleaguered companies. He also "preferred an examination of alternative methods such as military aid, quotas, etc." Humphrey warned that the United States could not alone bear the burden of Japanese imports; electrical goods makers already suffered from Japanese imports, and the American workers could not compete against the delicate hand labor of the Japanese. Eisenhower acknowledged the problem of American unemployment, but concluded: "Don't let us let Japan reach a point where they want to invite the Kremlin into their country. Everything else fades into insignificance in the light of such a threat."[28]

In addition to "a maximum amount of economic and military aid," the Administration's prime goal was to obtain GATT membership for Japan. Such membership would automatically confer most-favored-nation status for Japanese goods. Germany had recovered through strict stabilization policies and quick acceptance into Western trade through GATT. Japan had to repeat this formula. The United States could either win GATT approval for Japan or grant unilateral most-favored-nation status. The former approach would have to overcome the opposition of Britain, Burma, France, Italy, and South Africa to multilateral tariff negotiations with Japan. Unilateral negotiations with Japan, however, would place great pressure on America's own industry, and the Administration expected "unusually severe" opposition from the American business sector. Also among the potential solutions for Japan were economic aid and Keynesian stimulation of the American economy to increase imports. A study entitled "Importance of Successful Trade Agreement Negotiations with Japan" ruled out long-term economic aid on the grounds that it would be too demeaning for the Japanese; economic aid was "not a satisfactory way of building partners."[29] The Republican Administration also adopted a policy of sustained military spending as part of a concerted effort both to avoid being tagged as another Hoover Administration and to sustain imports.

Crisis in the Cooperation Program:
The Yoshida Visit of 1954

The United States and Japan held consultation meetings in August and September 1954 to rectify the sharp drop in procurement orders which followed the Korean peace. The Japanese cited the Ikeda-Robertson talks, Harold Stassen's January 1954 statement in Japan, and an American embassy letter of March 8, each of which had promised $100 million in offshore procurement in fiscal year 1954. They complained that only $64 million in orders had been placed. The Americans answered that they had allotted $40 million in counterpart funds from surplus agricultural sales for offshore procurement. The Japanese, however, refused to use the counterpart funds for offshore procurement because the $100 million commitment had been breached. The Americans blamed the shortfall in orders on Rhee's persistent refusal, despite great American pressure, to lift the ban on United Nations Korean Rehabilitation Agency orders for Japan, as well as on Japan's inferior production quality and inflation. Inflation alone prevented $30 million in orders. Because Congress was unreliable, the Americans warned that Japan could not depend on offshore procurement orders. They also argued that the change in the master labor contract had freed dollars for the procurement of goods and services. But the Japanese countered by saying that labor procurement constituted Japan's most stable and lucrative dollar earnings, since no imports were required (unlike arms production) and since Japan did not have to outbid other nations on labor procurement. The "Consultation Report" issued in September "clearly indicated that any further heavy decline in special procurement would deal a crippling blow to Japan's economy," and might require "drastic measures."[30]

Seeking to bolster his sagging political fortunes, Yoshida traveled to Washington in November to enlist "American help in speeding up Japan's economy recovery." The Yoshida mission said that Japan's arms industry could not grow without a "steady supply of orders," and suggested using Japan's arms industry to supply Southeast Asian military efforts. Yoshida continued the "economic diplomacy" that marked postwar Japanese policy. The Treasury Department reported that the major objective of the mission was "to obtain assurance from the United States that if the economic position of Japan deteriorates to a dangerous level the United States will take whatever action is required to stabilize and strengthen Japan. . . . There is still a deep and basic Japanese point of view that the United States interest in Japan may be exploited on the basis of 'you provide and we receive for that is your basic self-interest.'" The Japanese, like the Europeans, knew the United States had to fund their deficits for both economic and strategic reasons. The Japanese lacked confidence in continuing high levels of American military expenditures, and requested coordinated aid, aid to establish a productivity center, and trade with Communist China for "purely economic" reasons. They warned that bankruptcies and serious social problems caused by the austerity measures had increased the public clamor for Chinese trade, as confirmed by a U.S. Information Agency poll of Japanese.[31]

In late 1954 the Japanese made the American market their primary export target. The Yoshida mission proclaimed, "What Japan desires most is that the United States market be stabilized for Japan's export goods so that her export industries can depend on it over the long-term." Yoshida told the Japanese Chamber of Commerce in New York that Japan's large dollar gap necessitated reducing American tariff barriers, especially on tuna, cotton goods, lace, glass, furs, linenware, leather goods, and raw silk. American officials argued that despite Japanese complaints about American protectionism, there had been only five successful pleas for escape clause protection under the Reciprocal Trade Agreements Act. Moreover, they assured the Japanese that efforts were under way to liberalize the Buy American Act, and that a special GATT session had been set for February 21, 1955, to consider Japanese membership. They suggested that Japan adopt strict curbs on unfair trade practices to defuse American and European protectionism. Finally, they approved the use of yen counterpart funds for Southeast Asian integration and development projects, and rejected $29 million in "defense support" economic aid, because of Japan's continued dollar holdings.[32]

Agricultural Surplus Disposal: PL 480 and Japan

From the American point of view, economic cooperation increasingly came to mean that Japan would absorb large quantities of American surplus agricultural products. On July 10, the powerful farm lobby, led by Walter Judd and Hubert Humphrey (both representing Minnesota wheat interests), pushed through PL 480, the Agricultural Trade and Development Act of 1954. PL 480 ultimately proved to be a main feature of cold war economic policy. Senator Fulbright had noted that American policy depended on supplying Europe and Japan with the agricultural goods they formerly obtained in Eastern Europe and China. This disposed of the American farm glut and locked industrial competitors into the American economic orbit PL 480, in an ingenious application of coordinated aid (virtually identical to Section 550 of the 1951 Mutual Security Act), stipulated that 95 percent of local currency counterpart funds from agricultural sales finance offshore procurement orders for rearmament. The other 5 percent would be spent to promote the sale of American agricultural products to establish permanent market penetration. At a stroke the United States thus dumped its costly and burdensome agricultural stocks and financed the creation of a global military network to prop up Western and Third World capitalist governments. Even so, the powerful American Farm Bureau Federation complained that the PL 480 budget ($400 million for fiscal year 1955, with $100 million for Japan) fell short of their $1 billion target (at a minimum, $2 billion over three years). They demanded a bill to link more aid to dollar sales of agricultural goods, to use export credits more extensively to boost foreign purchasing power, and to use more than 5 percent of the counterpart funds to create permanent foreign markets for agriculture.[33]

As part of the mutual defense aid package signed on March 8, Japan and the United States made agreements on "Economic Arrangements" and "Purchase of Agricultural Commodities," in which the Japanese agreed to absorb the agricultural surplus goods in return for offshore procurement orders. The new Intradepartmental Committee on Agricultural Surplus Disposal, established by the Administration to study the immense problems of agriculture, viewed Japan as its primary target. The State Department strongly resisted the Agriculture Department's desire to dump rice in Japan, because this would cut Japan's rice purchases in Southeast Asia. Since Japan needed to cut dollar imports and increase its trade with Southeast Asia by increasing the area's purchasing power, rice dumping in Japan would directly hurt Japanese interests.[34]

In November the Japanese termed the PL 480 proposals "most disappointing." The proposals served American interests, but did little for Japan, which had always viewed agricultural aid as a way to generate yen counterpart funds for economic development. Japanese critics charged that if the Americans proposed genuine "aid," the Japanese should control all yen counterpart funds to be used in domestic investment or to stimulate Southeast Asian trade. MITI Minister Kiichi Aichi presented a plan for $130 million in PL 480 aid to be controlled by Japan, saying that if offshore procurement paid in PL 480 counterpart funds replaced offshore procurement paid in cash dollars, then Japan would lose the dollar earnings from procurement—which was the only reason for accepting the orders. He insisted that if PL 480 counterpart funds were not "invested entirely" in economic and trade expansion, they should be cut to a bare minimum. The Japanese also complained that the United States forced them to take the surplus agricultural stocks in addition to "normal exports" from the United States. They correctly noted that in the chaotic postwar years there could be no level of "normal exports." The Americans, of course, desperate for agricultural outlets, were trying to freeze Japanese commercial purchases at the artificially high postwar level. The Japanese said that this would deprive Japan's other trade partners of markets in Japan and thus reduce Japanese exports and nondollar trade.[35]

The Japanese rejected one triangular coordinated aid scheme concocted to dump American agricultural goods. The United States proposed sending surplus agricultural products to Japan; Japan would then send cement to the Philippines; and the Philippines would in turn send chromite to the United States. The Americans would obtain chromite for nothing (since the agricultural surplus was a liability, not an asset), but Japan would receive no foreign exchange for her cement exports. Nor would her dollar gap be reduced. Although Japan provided the greatest market for American agriculture (the very largest for rice, wheat, cotton, and soybeans, purchases that helped sustain America's very prosperity), the Japanese voluntarily had to restrict their exports to the United States. The conferees finally agreed on $85 million in grants for counterpart funds, 30 percent of which was to be controlled by the United States for housing in Japan, agricultural market development, and third-country procurement in Japan, and the remaining 70 percent to be loans to Japanese industry. An additional $15 million was granted without stipulations. In 1956, 75 percent of the counterpart funds went to Japanese industry.[36]

The global PL 480 program is a fascinating example of coordinated aid. It had a devastating impact on Indian agricultural development, when the billions of dollars of grains dumped on the Indian market made it impossible for Indian farmers to receive reasonable prices for their products. By far its greatest success in long-term agricultural market development was in Japan. Counterpart funds paid for cooking shows to demonstrate to Japanese women the art of using wheat flour instead of rice flour to bake bread and make do-nuts. Because Japan absorbed much of the American agricultural surplus after 1954, critical American and European battles over ag-ricultural protection were less bitter than they would have been oth-erwise, thus sustaining the overall alliance system. In 1956 the United States and Japan signed another PL 480 agreement for $66 million. Even after American agriculture lost the price advantages it held in the postwar decade over Australian and Canadian grain producers, the United States used export subsidies (universally considered an "unfair" trading practice) to preserve its huge Japanese market. When Japan sought to switch to Australian grains in 1957, the United States granted revolving credits and Export-Import Bank loans to maintain its grip on Japan's market. An ironic result of these subsidies was that Japanese textile manufacturers paid less than American textile makers for American cotton. Moreover, taxes paid by the American textile industry helped finance this subsidy.[37]

The joint communiqué concluding the Yoshida mission reaffirmed American policy to help Japan in Southeast Asia and backed limited trade with China, which would be "resolutely barred to Communist ideological influence." The *Oriental Economist* reported that Yo-shida brought back a "present" for Japan: "Whether this gesture will serve to help the tottering Yoshida Government in the way that the promise of continued off-shore procurement for at least two years, made just prior to the general election of 1953, aided the Liberal Party to remain in power remains an open question." The matter was quickly resolved when Yoshida resigned in December 1954 and Ha-toyama became prime minister, with Mamoru Shigemitsu as deputy prime minister.[38]

Japanese exports and economic activity began to recover in mid-1954, but Administration concern continued. Clarence Randall's fi-nal report to the president on foreign economic policy cited Japan as the major foreign economic problem—the weakest link in the indus-trial bloc: "The economic plight of Japan is desperate; unless she can find a way to live, she may be driven into the camp of the enemy." The United States had to ensure multilateral acceptance of Japanese goods.[39]

Long-Term Cooperation (1955–1959)

The year 1955 was one of transition, from four years of economic cooperation to sustain Japanese modernization (1951–54) to four years of continuing cooperation and genuine export recovery (1955–59). Familiar American concerns about Japan's trade deficit, sustaining procurement subsidies, and Southeast Asian integration combined with the new policy of opening world (and to a limited extent American) markets to Japan. As exports improved and special procurements continued, Japan ran a balance-of-payments surplus from 1955 to 1960 (except for 1957, when the international recession cut sales). The surplus, of course, did not signal the end of the commercial dollar gap, since procurement earnings still subsidized Japan's payments balance. Indeed, in 1955 Japan entered the phase that Europe had entered in 1952, in which commercial recovery and military expenditures allowed an accumulation of gold and dollar reserves. Such accumulation over a period of years was the prerequisite to genuine multilateral economic relations—the long-term goal of American foreign economic policy.

In 1955 Japan still warranted great concern in Washington. Harold Stassen and Raymond Moyer, director and Far East program director, respectively, of the FOA, explained Japan's continuing weakness to Congress. Moyer advised that "Japan has a very serious and fundamental economic problem. . . . When the payments we are making as a result of the military spending there cease, they will be in real trouble." Senator Mansfield asked: "If the Japanese do not find markets and if we do not continue to subsidize them enough, how long do you think it is going to be before they will go Communist?" Moyer replied: "I think unrest would develop very soon if that situation should come about. It has not come about yet economically because of our spending." He assured Congress that the small FOA mission established in 1954 was "following the situation quite closely to be sure steps are taken in time to prevent that." Charged with finding a "fundamental" solution in Japan, the mission helped establish a productivity center and signed a technical cooperation agreement in 1955.[40]

American efforts finally paid off when Japan became a full member of GATT in September 1955. Eleven nations, however, led by Great Britain, invoked Article 35 of the GATT accords—the "escape clause"—to avoid granting most-favored-nation status to Japan. The United States also signed a bilateral trade agreement with Japan in September. Even though accepting Japanese goods was viewed as a "distasteful" choice, the Americans did realize that importing from Japan was inevitable given the huge Japanese purchases in the United States. In order to "share the burden" of Japanese exports, the United States signed fourteen trilateral agreements with Asian and European nations, in which the United States granted tariff concessions to the third party in return for that nation's granting concessions to Japan. The United States thus begrudgingly granted Japan more favorable trade rights after years of huge surpluses in trade with Japan. Stassen, however, told the nationalistic Congress not to fear—the United States would not absorb all of Japan's increased exports, and the rest of the world would have to do its part.[41]

Perhaps the most fascinating aspect of long-term economic cooperation was the continued subsidization of Japan's arms industries. In 1955, Japan complained that American procurement cuts threatened the foundation of its "defense industry." The United States replied that the purpose of offshore procurement was merely to "prime the pump," and that it was Japan's responsibility to furnish arms orders to the companies to sustain production. After announcing in March that Defense Department arms and ammunition procurement orders in Japan would plunge to $10 million in fiscal year 1956, American officials (including Irving Ross of the Defense Department and the embassy staff) met with the Japanese to discuss the future of defense orders. The Americans advised Japan to show interest in the industry to impress Washington and justify further subsidies. The Japanese responded with a request for stopgap aid and a pledge to finance microwave communications systems and "defense" roads, both of which would augment Japan's economic strength. The Japanese claimed that 126 corporations and 75 contractors depended on arms orders, which "played a very valuable role in accelerating the recovery of Japan's machinery industry suffering from the pressures of mammoth idle facilities." Forcing the plants to close would have a general depressing effect on economic production, so they requested contracts to supply forces in Southeast Asia to keep the plants operating. Nothing, however, came of the 1955 talks.[42]

Japanese industry turned to its financial connections on Wall Street to help stop the decline in arms production subsidies. In June 1950, Tetsuji Atarashiya, president of Japan Steel, wrote to Wall Street consultant Frederich P. Rich about the "serious impact" on the steel industry and economic recovery. He said there was no civilian market to take up the slack, that procurement orders provided the "slim margin" between solvency and bankruptcy. Rich assured him that Washington understood Japan's difficulties, but that the increase in atomic weapons capacity diminished Japan's role in American eyes as the fortress of Asia. Washington intended to reduce troop levels and cut procurement, he advised, because the United States could not continue to be the "Atlas" of the world indefinitely by propping up other economies. He pledged that Washington would contribute to keep the arms industry functioning if Japan increased its military spending.[43]

The United States was especially interested in the Tokyo Akanabe Works owned by Japan Steel, the principal American repair facility in Asia. The facility was a major strategic factor in Asia, and Rich suggested that Japan and the United States cooperate to keep it active in support of Southeast Asian military efforts. Another friend of Japanese arms makers, H. Frazier Kammeyer, of Wall Street's O. G. Innis Corporation, lobbied before Dodge and Defense Secretary Wilson in support of the arms production program in Japan. He advised Gengo Suzuki of the Japanese Ministry of Finance that Washington wanted to use Japanese ammunition and weapons in Southeast Asia, and that by importing scrap iron to boost production Japan could compete with Germany for forthcoming American war orders. The Japanese economy never completely adjusted to a peacetime economy, and the American military expansion into Asia proved to be a substantial boost to Japanese industrial modernization and recovery.[44]

The international trade boom which began in mid-1955 lifted Japan's economy out of the postwar structural trap of insufficient international demand. Exports increased by $400 million in 1955. Procurements, however, dipped only $26 million (to $570 million) and held firm at $596 million in 1956 and $524 million in 1957. Japan's export boom was led by textiles, iron and steel, invisible earnings, and, especially, the highly successful shipbuilding industry. Japan now ranked second in the world in shipbuilding, and her second largest export market became the favorite flag of shipowners, Liberia. Exports were also favored by inflation in Europe and by MITI's drive to form export cartels and authorize dumping practices. The ultimate solution for Japan was rapid multilateral trade expansion. As during the Korean boom, Japan and Germany far outstripped world export growth, and Britain again bore the brunt of the competition.[45]

Despite the many plans that were never fully implemented, and the many fits and starts, the recovery concepts that had been discussed since 1947 were largely realized in the late 1950s. Japan was truly a "workshop nation," which imported 70 percent of its primary goods and exported 90 percent of its manufactured goods. Moreover, coordinated aid, in the original sense of financing Southeast Asian purchases in Japan, assumed a greater role in American procurement. As expenditures by American troops diminished from $307 million in 1954 to $280 million in 1956, and official United States Forces, Japan, purchases fell from $236 million to $173 million, FOA procurement for Southeast Asia in Japan increased from $37 million to $126 million. (In 1956 the FOA was transferred to the State Department and was renamed the International Cooperation Agency, ICA.)[46]

In the late 1950s American nationalism remained a problem for American-Japanese relations and became the last remaining obstacle to a final solution to the Japanese dollar gap. On April 21, 1956, in off-the-cuff remarks to American editors, Eisenhower said that each week he received complaints from business about Japanese sales to the United States. Noting that Southeast Asia was too poor to support Japan, he asked: "Where are we chasing Japan? . . . Unless something is done, Japan has to, now, begin to look rather longingly to China."

The Japanese had cause to be pessimistic about penetrating American markets. In 1956 the Japanese Chamber of Commerce in New

York and the Cotton Textile Association of Osaka established the Council for Improved United States–Japanese Trade. The council's director, Nelson Stitt, testified before the House of Representatives against pending legislation to restrict Japanese textile imports. He noted that Japan was the largest buyer of American agricultural products, and that barring Japanese goods would eventually hurt American farmers. Also in 1956 Japan lodged a formal protest against a South Carolina law which required stores carrying Japanese textiles to display the fact openly on the front of the store. This blatant commercial discrimination violated the "Treaty of Friendship, Commerce and Navigation" between the two nations.[47] Yet, despite its continuing large commercial trade deficit with the United States, Japan bowed to American nationalism and voluntarily restricted textile sales in 1956 (although this had a crippling effect on many small and medium businesses).[48] The restriction set a precedent for later Japanese voluntary export restrictions to appease American protectionism.

The year 1960 marked the end of the fifteen-year struggle to overcome Japan's dollar gap. For the first time since the war Japan began to liberalize its own import controls, no longer able to claim exemption from GATT provisions as a deficit nation. Procurement still continued at the $500 million level in 1960, enabling Japan to add to her exchange reserves. In aggregate, the United States spent $5.6 billion in military orders in Japan in the 1950s. Japan's dollar exports increased from $300 million in 1950 to $1.4 billion in 1958, thus approaching a new equilibrium after thirteen years of aid and "economic cooperation." The case of Japan vividly illustrates the structural disequilibrium facing American foreign economic policy after World War II and the decisive and monumental role of military expenditures in overcoming the failure of economic aid to revive the world economy.

6. Cooperation in Southeast Asia, 1950–1954

*The fall of Southeast Asia would underline the apparent
economic advantages to Japan of association with the
communist-dominated sphere. Exclusion of Japan from
trade with Southeast Asia would seriously affect the
Japanese economy, and increase Japan's dependence on
United States aid. In the long run the loss of Southeast
Asia, especially Malaya and Indonesia could result in
such economic and political pressures in Japan as to
make it extremely difficult to prevent Japan's eventual
accommodation to the soviet bloc.*

> —Annex to NSC 124, February 13, 1952

*There could hardly exist a multilateral world economy
without Southeast Asia.*

> —R. Allen Griffin, ECA, 1951

*We view the situation in Southeast Asia with great con-
cern and feel a strong need for an intensified common
effort to prevent the communist danger, not only because the spread of communism threatens the independence and welfare of the free peoples of this region, but
also because the future development of our economy is
dependent to a large extent upon the development of
trade with that area.*

> —Japanese government position paper, 1954

Japanese economic integration with Southeast Asia remained central to American policy in Japan after June 1950. Kenneth Morrow told the ESS and MITI staffs that Japan's exports had
doubled and that production had increased 50 percent as a result of

191

the Korean War boom: "If we want to go beyond that point it is necessary to seek out new sources of raw materials. That is why we have to turn to Southeast Asia and the Southeast Asian development problem." The Americans had to convince Japanese leaders that, with development, Southeast Asia could outproduce China. Morrow said the ESS would seek capital in Southeast Asia, Japan, and the United States as well as from the Colombo Plan, the British Colonial Development Corporation, and the IBRD. He went on to describe the essentially primary processing industries the United States envisioned for Southeast Asia: gunny-bag factories, textile plants, sugar mills, pulp mills, iron foundries, and transportation facilities to move the goods to waiting ships. He predicted that Japan would gain "vast new markets" through an integrated, regional economy: "We expect that Japan will make long-term contracts with potential sources of supply in Southeast Asia. What we are trying to do is to tie together existing facilities in Japan with sources of supply in Southeast Asia."[1]

Southeast Asian integration and military procurements each formed half of the economic cooperation program. With Chinese trade barred by the Korean War and Battle Act restrictions imposed by Congress, the United States was forced to promote Southeast Asian trade aggressively to keep Japan wedded to the alliance. Congressional cold war fervor again limited the administration's flexibility in solving the dollar gap. As with procurements, Morrow spearheaded the campaign to gain Washington support for coordinated aid to Southeast Asia and for diplomatic efforts to break down Southeast Asian hostility toward Japan. The corollary to promoting economic integration, of course, was military intervention in Southeast Asia to preserve the region for Western and especially Japanese strategic and business interests. Ultimately, military intervention mushroomed, while economic integration faltered somewhat in the 1950s. In the long term, however, the alliance rested on Japan's willingness both to forsake extensive trade with China and to rely on the American military protectorate in Southeast Asia to preserve a favorable business climate for Japan. The riches of Indonesia and Malaya and the potential markets of that populous area were a powerful lure for Japan, which, of course, had expanded to the south in 1941.

The grand design for Asia, which reflected Japan's central economic role, was developed largely by John Foster Dulles, whom

Acheson assigned to make peace with Japan in 1950. Dulles warned Congress in 1951 that the future of Japan was precarious without trade with China and with the threat of Communism spreading throughout Southeast Asia; compounding Japan's weakness were the large freight charges incurred by the shipping of heavy raw materials from the distant United States (the United States subsidized the higher cost of its exports through its aid and procurements, but Japan needed inexpensive industrial raw materials to compete in world export markets). Dulles advised that only Southeast Asian stability and raw materials development could solve this problem. He called it the greatest challenge the United States faced in Asia. He also advised the head of the Office of Defense Management, Charles Wilson, that the United States "would have to make certain military and economic commitments to the Japanese of a general nature"; the United States had to share iron ore and coking coal supplies with Japan and had to "reactivate" the Philippines and Southeast Asia as supply sources.[2]

By 1951, after lobbying by Morrow and Marquat, Washington officials well recognized Japan's need for access to Southeast Asia. JIP III summarized ESS thinking:

> Japan must have markets to replace those lost to communist aggression. Temporarily, a partial substitute had been found in the emergency procurement for the UN forces. . . . Two things are now needed: The placement of a long-range book of orders which will permit the Japanese to schedule production and realize a reasonable value-added-by-manufacture, and an acceleration of the United States programs in Southeast Asia.[3]

In Washington, Morrow warned that local Southeast Asian capital was fleeing the region because of the revolutionary wave. Without capital, raw materials development was impeded, which further aggravated the instability. The situation was analogous to that of Europe in 1948, a situation which had partially influenced the formation of NATO and the MDAP. He suggested that each Asian ECA mission "have attached to it one person of good quality who can be assigned to the Japanese program in that particular country." In November 1950, ECA Far East head R. Allen Griffin assured Marquat that the ECA had begun to finance a "considerable amount of trade for Japan." He shared SCAP's views: "It is our common interest that ECA do the maximum amount of business possible with Japan . . . and to reinstate within the limits politically advisable in Southeast Asia the trade that Japanese industry formerly had in that region." In July 1951, the ECA announced a plan for the "fullest utilization" of Japanese industry for its Southeast Asian aid programs and set up a field office in Tokyo to coordinate the effort.[4]

Acheson also responded to Morrow's pleas. In December 1951 he sent a message to American officials in Southeast Asia, entitled "Relationship with Japan and Production of Essential Materials," citing Japan's need for materials to prevent dependence on China. He also reflected State Department recognition that tact was required to avoid inflaming anti-Japanese sentiment; this recalled the 1947 dispute between State and the Army over the bluntness of reverse-course pronouncements. He advised the missions to laud the mutual benefits of trade and to assure Southeast Asians that Japan was trustworthy enough to "overcome [their] continued suspicion of Japan [and] ill will generated by [the] war and non-settlement of reparations claims." He further stipulated that all cooperation plans be approved by the diplomatic mission in each country, "in view of the political sensitivity surrounding the entire concept of the Japanese position in Far Eastern affairs."[5]

If there was any dissent during the height of cold war thinking in Washington in 1951, it came from Southeast Asian experts aware of the potency of Southeast Asian nationalism. The *New York Times* reported on Wilson's plan to put Japanese industry "to work on the materials of Asia": "Those interested in restoring the economic health of Japan, for example, were more favorable to the proposal than those working directly with or having a more intimate knowledge of those Southeast Asian countries regarded as sources of raw materials." Although the latter warned that Southeast Asians would be reluctant to join a new co-prosperity sphere in their drive to industrialize, the "predominant view" was that the United States should channel raw materials to Japan and procure 95 percent of Southeast Asian aid goods there.[6]

The Interdepartmental Committee on Far East Mobilization represented Washington's effort to obtain raw materials for Japan, primarily from Southeast Asia. It considered over a hundred iron ore properties in the region, assigned ECA and Technical Cooperation Administration personnel to advise on mineral deposits, and sought financing from various American and international sources. The welter of planning produced few concrete results in the early 1950s. In October 1951, the Economic Stabilization Board, ESS, and the Far East mobilization committee put together a deal to develop iron ore in Goa. The Japanese Export Bank loaned $1.6 million to Japanese companies to develop the mine, and the United States helped finance the construction of shipping piers. The Economic Stabilization Board, in its February 1952 three-year plan to develop Southeast Asian resources, looked primarily to mines developed by Japan during World War II. The Japanese government committed $91 million to such investments. When it sent a mission to Southeast Asia in 1951 to study development projects, the ESS consulted Japanese engineers who had worked the mines.[7] Finally, by 1955, nine major raw material development contracts had been signed with Thailand, India, Pakistan, Goa, and the Philippines.

Administration spokesmen argued the strategic case for intervention in Southeast Asia before Congress in 1951. Dean Rusk, head of the Far Eastern affairs office, placed the Administration's anti-Communism into perspective: "Even without a communist threat . . . it seems to us that we should have to be deeply interested in the strength and stability of these nations and we would want to bind them to us in ties of friendship in whatever ways we could, and in a more practical sense to serve our mutual advantage by developing a lively exchange of goods and services with them." He warned that the "loss" of Southeast Asia would embolden the Communists and sap Western raw materials resources: "The absorption of additional countries in Asia would bring about a severe dislocation of the economic patterns which are of the greatest importance to the strength and well-being of Western Europe and the United States and particularly of course to countries like Japan." R. Allen Griffin added that rearmament required ever-increasing quantities of raw materials, and that "Southeast Asia [was] one of the greatest producing areas in the whole world." Dulles later placed into perspective the significance of Indochina, terming it "of no great importance" except as a "staging area" for Indonesia, "which is very rich in natural resources."[8]

In 1951, Truman, the Joint Chiefs, and the National Security Council approved the policies that underlay American intervention in Southeast Asia based on Japanese needs. NSC 125, signed by Truman on July 27, explained the strategic domino theory:

Japan's basic national objectives will be to rebuild its national strength and to enhance its position in the Far East. . . . The continuance of Japan's alignment with the United States will depend in large degree upon maintenance by the United States of a strong military posture in the Pacific and the pursuance of policies by the United States and other free nations which encourage the growth in Japan of basic economic strength. . . . In the long run, Japan's access to raw materials and markets for her exports will significantly affect Japan's basic operation.[9]

On July 28, the Joint Chiefs of Staff agreed on military action in Southeast Asia. They advised the secretary of defense that Japan's prosperity would dictate the extent of her cooperation with the United States:

This in turn will be significantly affected by Japan's ability to retain access to her historic markets and the sources of food and raw materials in Southeast Asia. Viewed in this context, United States objectives with respect to Southeast Asia and United States objectives with respect to Japan would appear to be inseparably related. Moreover, the Joint Chiefs of Staff are of the opinion that Japan's security and Western orientation are of such importance to the United States position in the Pacific area that . . . (1) the United States must take into full account Japan's dependence upon Southeast Asia for her economic well-being; and (2) the loss of Southeast Asia to the Western World would almost inevitably force Japan into an eventual accommodation with the Communist-controlled areas in Asia.[10]

Among the highest circles in Washington, the explicit rationale for military intervention was thus the overriding importance of the alliance with Japan. Strategic planners could not segment areas of the world and form disparate policies. Foremost when developing any aspect of Asian policy, they had to consider Japan's strategic significance as the economic workshop of Asia, and the overwhelmingly economic nature of Japanese insecurity about the Pacific alliance.

Development and Underdevelopment in Southeast Asia

Colonialism left an indelible mark on the economy of Southeast Asia, which ultimately frustrated Japanese and American attempts to foster Asian trade. Japanese imports from and exports to the region were indicative of Southeast Asia's extreme economic backwardness and dependence. Japan exported textile machinery and parts, pottery, porcelainware, metal and metal products, chemicals, drugs, paper, steel, locomotives, electrical equipment, and some consumer goods in return for wool, cotton, wheat, jute, salt, hides, cereals, fruits, rice, copra, oils, iron ore, manganese, chrome, logs, and rattan.[11]

Naturally, the neocolonial trade pattern and the generous peace treaty with Japan angered Southeast Asian nationalists. Carlos Romulo, representing the Philippines at the peace conference, delivered a scathing attack on the lavish American efforts to rebuild Japan as the dominant economy of Asia. Ambassador to the Philippines Myron Cowen explained the problem to Acheson in August 1951: "To Philippinos, as to other Asians, [the] status of raw materials suppliers connotes colonial subservience. Any Western tendency to discourage indigenous industrial development therefore is automatically suspect as [a] ruse to retain dominance economically despite [the] relinquishment of political control." He warned that Southeast Asians preferred local industrialization over dependence on Japan. Even State Department officials recognized that primary goods producers faced a vicious spiral of dependence and underdevelopment, although this understanding was never reflected in policy since it contradicted the goal of a multilateral world economy based on workshops trading with primary producers and the short-term interests of the industrial nations. A departmental study concluded in 1955: "Under the system of exchanging raw materials for processed goods and manufactured products, Southeast Asia remained industrially backward and undeveloped." The report explained that Southeast Asians were dependent upon the West for the prices set on their raw materials, and that "the rise or fall of a few cents in the prices of these raw materials makes a difference of millions of dollars in the producing countries."[12]

Yet Western and Japanese voracity for industrial materials dictated opposing Third World economic nationalism. One official, testifying before the House of Representatives in 1953, said:

> One of the principal concerns in those areas is the rise of nationalism which translated economically means a desire for rapid and sometimes uneconomic industrialization and development. By that I mean there is a strong tendency to build a steel mill when the best interest of the particular country would be served by growing a little more food, whether it be rice, or coffee or whatever it might be.[13]

Undoubtedly, many development projects were "uneconomic," yet uncolonized Japan had used massive government subsidies to foster Japanese heavy industrial development since the Meiji period with spectacular results. Growing "a little more food," while desirable, would not constitute sound, integrated national economic development.

Since 1945, there had been two American responses to Southeast Asian economic nationalism: economic aid and diplomatic "tact." Significant economic aid programs had continually been rejected. Thus, diplomatic tact (i.e., talking Southeast Asia out of nationalistic policies) characterized American "development" policy. American policy sought to divert Southeast Asian nationalists from their fundamental struggle against colonialism and economic dependence toward anti-Communism, a clever but impossible goal. Dulles wrote to Acheson in August 1950 suggesting that the United States should simply ignore economic dependence, as, of course, it had: "It seems to me that we may not get much sympathy in the UN with our Asiatic policy unless we emphasize that the colonial struggle for independence has now been won." He said that Southeast Asians lacked capitalistic values and had no fear of Communism. Thus, the United States should instead play up the fear of Russian intervention and influence. An Institute for Pacific Relations conference in October 1950 indicated the differing concerns of Southeast Asians and Americans: the *New York Times* reported that where Westerners were obsessed with the threat of Communism, Asians attacked the evils of colonialism.[14]

George Kennan's approach diametrically opposed that of Dulles. Kennan suggested that the United States tell Southeast Asians that it could do without their resources—which would force the region inevitably to resist Communism on their own. Kennan also believed that a Communist Southeast Asia would still be a good trading partner for Japan, and thus the strategic loss of Southeast Asia would not be as severe as the Administration claimed. American policy toward Japanese trade with China in the 1950s, however, rejected extensive trade with Communists because of the American fear that Japan would be ideologically corrupted by depending on Communist materials.[15]

[handwritten margin note: No BRUSH FIRE,]

Kennan's argument recalled the concern of Southeast Asian desk officers in the 1940s that the United States was prostituting itself in Southeast Asia by being so quick to support pro-American forces. In 1951, Charlton Ogburn wrote that American policy "seems to produce the opposite results from what we intend." Indeed, Ogburn's complaint goes far to explode the cold war myths of direct and aggressive Soviet military expansionism:

> Ho Chi-Minh's "Democratic Republic of Vietnam" declared its independence in August 1945. Yet it was not until early 1950 that the Soviet Union even recognized it. By contrast, it will be remembered that we recognized Bao Dai's Government the moment the French gave the all-clear. Soviet official stand-offishness with respect to the Chinese Communists was a conspicuous feature of their relationship until the autumn of 1949. The scale of assistance with which the Soviet Union has provided the Peiping regime after recognizing it has been minor by our standards of foreign aid. Indeed, for some time it appeared that the Soviet Union was taking more than it was giving. This, indeed, seems to be a common feature of Soviet relations with non-Russian communist bodies. To a degree that must be really astonishing to us, who conceive of support of non-Communist elements in

terms of prodigious outlays by the United States, the Asian Communists have been left to fend for themselves materially. With its very large production of gold and with what must be its huge quantities of weapons, it would seem that the Soviet Union could do far more than it has done for the Communists in Indochina, Burma, Malaya, the Philippines, etc.[16]

By withholding aid, he continued, the Russians avoided the possibility of "backing a losing horse." The United States, however, leaped to support pathetic leaders: "If Bao Dai is as deficient in the qualities of leadership and determination as we are told, one would imagine that what he needs is incentive—such as the winning of American recognition—and not the satiation of his desires, including those he has presumably not even expressed." Ogburn went on to explain the vibrancy of Communism in the region:

The practice of the Russians in giving guidance, instructions, and orders to Communist elements in other countries but withholding large-scale material assistance tends to bring out real leaders among these elements and to develop among them the qualities of determination, resourcefulness, and fortitude. It gives them the incentive of advancing a cause in which they believe. They have the position of contributors, not beneficiaries. They are supporting the Communist cause, not being supported by it. The effect on them, if one may judge, is exhilarating.[17]

By contrast, American officials felt intense frustration, Ogburn continued: "We are continually hurt and bewildered because the more independent minded Asians refuse to recognize their Communist fellows as puppets of Moscow but persist in regarding other Asians whom we are supporting as puppets of the United States." He concluded in anger: "Darn it, they are the ones who are threatened with a fate worse than death—not we."[18]

Southeast Asian skepticism about American policy stemmed from the colonial past. Moreover, the decline of political colonialism had not altered economic relations. The ECA reported in 1950 that Far East trade continued to be concentrated heavily along the lines of present or recent colonial interests. Southeast Asians were locked into the colonial economic nexus, and this confinement limited their economic options. Indeed, despite their fear of Japan, they were forced to turn to Japanese trade to solve their dollar gap and supply problems in 1950. SCAP was delighted when ECAFE's Secretary General Lokanathan came to suggest the use of counterpart funds as coordinated aid. ECAFE studies, however, revealed a familiar problem: Japan could easily produce capital goods but Southeast Asia was too underdeveloped to absorb them.[19]

While officials like Ogburn could discern the frustrations of American policy, only cold economic and strategic realities were important at the National Security Council level. NSC 141 in 1952 represented the global perspective that shaped American policy, a perspective based exclusively on the economic needs of the industrial capitalist bloc. It called for "additional economic programs for the underdeveloped countries to stimulate the production of raw materials and foodstuffs and thereby benefit the Western European countries and Japan and strengthen the economic base of the whole free world." From the National Security Council view, the problem was not economic backwardness but "the prevailing prejudice against colonialism and western 'interference' and the insensitivity to the danger of communist imperialism."[20] One is forced to conclude that the U.S. government failed to recognize the development aspirations of Southeast Asians and insisted on imposing American values through military means.

The vicious cycle of primary production and underdevelopment ultimately crippled integration plans. Leon Hollerman, a one-time SCAP trade official, concluded that falling raw materials prices in the 1950s (which of course greatly enriched and fueled the growth of the industrial nations) were the root of Japan's inability to boost exports to Asia: "The corresponding adverse terms of trade sustained by primary producers in Asia resulted in a shrinkage in their income and thus in the demand for Japanese goods."[21] There was no escaping the curse of underdevelopment.

Underdevelopment also crippled American economic aid schemes. In November 1951, the previously rejected concept of a "Marshall Plan for Asia" reemerged when ECA Far East director Harlan Cleveland proposed an "Action Program for Asia." John Allison, who had long proposed Asian aid tied to Japan, charged that Cleveland's plan was too ambitious in committing the United States to raising Asian living standards. ECA head Richard Bissell had recently described Asian poverty as too massive a problem for a frontal attack. Moreover, Allison warned that Southeast Asian nationalism would prevent American control of domestic finances in the region; he advised that Indonesia was already sensitive about the number of American advisors there. Because Congress would not appropriate the funds and the plan would inevitably fail, he continued, the only result would be a lessening of American prestige in Asia. Reaching the heart of the American predicament in relations with underdeveloped areas, he said that the United States had to develop a strong bargaining position to force Asians to adopt Western policies without an aid commitment.[22] As the IMF expanded its role in the 1950s and 1960s, the West did develop such power. IMF loans to Asia came due in the 1960s, and needed repayment extensions depended on whether Asian countries adopted currency devaluation, austerity measures, and favorable terms for foreign investors.

The issue of coordinated economic aid to Asia arose again in 1955. FOA director Stassen, reflecting the Eisenhower Administration's concerns about Asia on the heels of direct intervention in Vietnam, proposed a $200 million "President's Asian Fund." The fund would attract European and local capital to thwart Communism and "enlist the industrial production capacity of Japan with the raw material markets of the vast area." The aid would be tied specifically to Japanese needs, "particularly in ways that will help them get into the Southeast Asian market." Japan was already receiving $15 to $25 million per year in ECA (later MSA and, by 1954, FOA) aid. Later, under the International Cooperation Agency and Agency for International Development, Japan received even larger orders for coordinated aid to Southeast Asia. Through 1960, approximately 10 percent of Japan's exports to the region were financed by American aid; the highest figure was $147 million in 1960. Japanese integration with Southeast Asia was also promoted by technical ties financed by the International Cooperation Agency. In 1956 the Technical Assistance Program paid for 199 Southeast Asians to receive technical training in Japan.[23] Coordinated aid thus played a relatively minor yet still significant role in Japanese recovery. When we consider the grandiose planning since 1947, however, the results were mixed at best. The underdevelopment of the region, limiting its ability to absorb capital imports, was partially to blame, along with limits on aid funds, nonsettlement of reparations claims, and Western competition with Japan in the region.

Reparations and Integration

Dulles and the State Department cleverly exploited Japan's obligation to pay war reparations in order to facilitate integration with Southeast Asia. Dulles said it was "doubtful whether these channels could be satisfactorily reopened unless the trade was on a basis sufficiently advantageous to these countries to appear in the guise of reparations." He noted that cheap Japanese manufactured goods sent as reparations would stifle industrialization in the area, but said that it would be good business for Japan. The reparations formula in the peace treaty was simple: Southeast Asia would provide raw materials, to which Japan would add labor and return the finished goods. Acheson assured Yoshida that the reparations formula would "in fact be of benefit to the Japanese economy in that it would enable Japan to employ its excess industrial capacity, give employment to the people and reestablish trade channels."[24]

Nonsettlement of reparations claims led to Japanese disappointment in trade with the region. Neither the Philippines nor Indonesia had ratified the peace treaty, pending settlement of their reparations claims. In December 1951 an Indonesian delegation in Tokyo proposed an $18 billion settlement, and a month later a Philippine delegation proposed $8 billion. While these claims reflected Japan's destruction of life and property, the figures were unrealistic in light of Japan's poverty. The Japanese viewed reparations as a way to promote economic integration, as the Americans had intended at the San Francisco conference. Some Japanese economists, however, "expressed concern over the long-range effect of reparations payments on their country's normal exports, fearing that large shipments of textile plants and other industrial machinery would create competition for Japan's own industries." Textiles did constitute 40 percent of Japanese exports, but heavy industrialists disagreed and "were concerned that reparations must open the door to rich raw materials and new markets for equipment, spare parts, and after-services." In 1953, Japan agreed to salvage ships in the Philippines to acquire scrap iron, and in 1954 the two nations tentatively agreed to the Ono-Garcia reparations plan for Japan to invest $400 million in Philippine resource development. The agreement failed, however, to pass the nationalistic Philippine congress.[25]

Americans urged Japan to settle the reparations negotiations quickly in order to improve relations with Southeast Asia. When Senator Mansfield asked whether reparations would facilitate Japanese "penetration" of Southeast Asia's markets, Raymond Moyer of the FOA said that they "will immediately get the Japanese into business, as it were, in some of these countries to a great extent, and trade will follow." On May 9, 1956, Japan agreed on $800 million for the Philippines, with $550 million in goods and services over twenty years and $250 million in private loans. Business expectations that reparations were "seeds from which a great harvest [could] be expected" were realized. During the first five years of the agreement, trade increased fivefold. In 1954 Japan concluded an agreement with Burma for $200 million in goods and services over ten years. And, on November 27, 1957, Japan signed an agreement with Indonesia for $400 million in loans, cancellation of Indonesia's $170 million debt to Japan, and $223 million in reparations. In the short run the deals were mutually beneficial because Southeast Asians received valuable machinery, "in the long run it consolidated Japan's role as a supplier of replacement parts, new equipment, and technical advice."[26]

Japan and the British Empire

The American "capitalist bloc" economic strategy of isolating Germany and Japan from their trading areas in Communist hands had profound effects on Britain and the world economy. Asian development was stunted when American policy kept the tremendous complementary resources of China and Japan artificially separated. Indeed, Japan had to turn to distant world markets for export success, causing the recent phenomenon of Japanese global domination of many segments of international trade. Congressional anti-Communism in the 1950s thus contributed significantly to the Japanese domination of some American markets that so antagonized Congress in succeeding decades. Moreover, Britain could not survive the competition of German and Japanese industry in the far-flung sterling area after the two industrial powers were forced out of their traditional trading patterns. Britain resisted the American global strategy, especially the anti-Chinese peace treaty with Japan and the American attempt to integrate Japan with Southeast Asia.

Dulles and Allison labored from May 1950 to September 1951 on a treaty that would both prevent Japanese-Chinese reconciliation and place no limits on Japanese industry and trade. The British, feeling with some justification that their national livelihood was at stake, opposed both objectives. After long negotiations in 1951, they agreed to the treaty terms only after Dulles stipulated that Japan would be free to recognize either Peking or Taipei. The American Congress, however, demanded assurance that Japan would recognize only Taiwan, which prompted Dulles to write a letter proclaiming such a policy for Yoshida's signature. The "Yoshida letter" understandably infuriated the British, who expressed "shock" over Dulles's duplicity. British interests greatly feared that if Japan were deprived of trade with China, it would expand into sterling markets. Acheson and Dulles, however, knew that the treaty had to please only one party, and that, ironically, was Japan, not the Allies.[27]

Many members of Parliament and other British observers reacted strongly to the capitulation of the British government after the American arm twisting on the peace treaty terms. One lord charged that the United States had insulted the British public when an American official read the treaty terms over British radio even before the government could publicly announce its retreat. He charged that the United States would never have submitted to such treatment, and that, had the treaty been submitted for approval, Parliament would have altered it "drastically in many ways."[28]

The *New Statesman and Nation* denounced the United States for forging a cold war treaty opposed by the Asian neutrals—Burma, Indonesia, and India. The *Times* described Dulles's series of bilateral deals to obtain prior approval for the unpopular treaty as humiliating to Asians: "If this is not a 'Whiteman's Treaty', it may mean at least the virtual demolition of the British-built bridge between the non-communist countries of Asia and the West."[29]

Opposition to American strategy stemmed from the fear on the part of British pottery and textile interests that the "reverse course" against Japanese labor doomed their hope for strong unions and progressive wages in Japan. They logically feared that the Dodge Plan to make Japan ultracompetitive would ensure future Japanese economic aggression, that is, illegal dumping policies. Lancashire vividly recalled Japan's notorious prewar economic policies and opposed multilateralism as a threat to Britain's right of economic self-defense.[30]

Members of Parliament twisted the American moral justification for multilateralism to attack American strategy. Whereas the State Department preached the moral virtue of complete freedom for business to operate across national borders, the British charged that GATT denied Britain the freedom to protect her own population from economic ruin. MPs urged the government to "take steps to restore our commercial freedom and safe-guard our interests." One lord, however, viewed Japan's unsavory trade practices (stealing designs and copying British goods) as the least of Britain's worries: "We do not want protection against Japan's unfair trade practices; we want protection against her fair trade practices. . . . [We must] encourage them to concentrate on those particular forms of their activity that do the least harm to everyone else's industries." His ideal Japan would produce silk, toys, and sandals. He argued that only absolute quotas on Japanese goods would suffice, that tariffs alone would be ineffective. Japanese expansion threatened to transfer Japan's dollar gap to Britain, weaken the pound, and gradually impoverish the British Isles. The lord said that the only answer to this "most urgent problem facing Britain" was to gain a bargaining position over Japan through the peace treaty and exploit it to survive: "It is essential that we should have somewhere the power of total exclusion of Japanese goods from the British Commonwealth."[31]

Americans countered with the rhetoric of multilateralism and the international theory of comparative economic advantage. Dulles pontificated that the British were merely protecting their own inefficiency: "Nations have no right to legislate against a neighbor's industriousness."[32] Had the roles been reversed, however, it is likely that the United States would have generated an equally virtuous argument for saving its jobs and preserving its social stability.

Dulles warned Congress of British resistance to tying Southeast Asian aid to purchases in Japan and manipulating the sterling bloc to keep Japan out. Whitehall had advised Dulles that "provisions should be included in the Treaty which would reduce Japan's impact on the commercial relations existing in the Far East." Eugene Dooman, reflecting the lessons of Versailles that Dulles held so dear, expressed the American view that such restrictions would stifle Japanese initiative, antagonize Japan, and drive Japan to Communism.[33]

The British still retained some commercial privileges to thwart Japan. Marquat had to advise the Japanese that the United States could not sign a bilateral trade agreement with Japan in 1951 for fear of antagonizing Britain. Admission to GATT, he assured Japan, would automatically confer most-favored-nation status on Japan by all members. In a 1951 aide-mémoire to the State Department, the British opposed GATT membership for Japan and her expansion into Southeast Asia, citing the need to protect British interests and the antagonism of Southeast Asians toward Japan. The British also argued that since it was the United States that prohibited Japanese trade with China, the United States should compensate by accepting Japanese products instead of forcing them onto the sterling area. Even staunchly pro-American British leaders insisted that Japan's shipping capacity was bloated and should be reduced and permanently restricted.[34] United States multilateral policy dictated, however, that world economic development follow the "natural course of events," which, in this instance, clearly worked against Britain.

In the spring and summer of 1951 Japan and Britain negotiated their first postwar trade agreement. SCAP had negotiated the 1948 Overall Payments Agreement between Japan and the sterling area, and had insisted on the right of the Occupation to convert sterling into dollars if Japan's holdings rose above 17 million pounds. This clause was never invoked, but the fear that it would be used helped to limit sterling-area purchases in Japan. At the 1951 payments conference, SCAP's presence as an observer considerably bolstered Japan's bargaining position. Japan had three choices: she could join the dollar bloc, the sterling bloc, or the transferable account area. As a dollar or hard-currency nation, Japan would trade on an unrestricted multilateral basis, with settlement of imbalances made in gold or dollars. This, however, would enlarge the dollar gap, because sterling nations would have to limit their trade with Japan in order to avoid losing dollars, making Japan more dependent on dollar raw materials. The advantages to the United States of enlarging the hard-currency area and preserving markets in Japan would not outweigh the large amount of aid required to subsidize Japan's hard-currency status. As a bilateral account nation, on the other hand, Japan could greatly increase her exports to such sterling nations as South Africa, Pakistan, Ceylon, and India. If Japan could not procure an offsetting amount of primary materials from the sterling area, however, she would merely accumulate sterling balances that she could not spend. Both the Japanese and the Americans feared such a result if Japan agreed to abandon the dollar conversion clause.[35]

The talks dragged on through the summer, with the British refusing to agree to a dollar conversion clause. Reminding Japan of her dollar gap and need to expand nondollar trade, they said that by dropping the dollar clause Japan would gain access to the "vast territories contained in the sterling area." They argued that the dollar clause restricted exports to the many sterling nations which were anxious to buy in Japan for reasons of lower prices and shipping charges. The Japanese finally relented on August 31 under pressure from a business community which was anxious to boost sales. Japan chose to join the transferable account countries, which allowed her to settle nonsterling imbalances through the British treasury. Japanese fears were realized in 1952 when sterling primary goods were either unavailable or overpriced relative to dollar goods; Japan's sterling reserves mounted, and the Japanese government began to limit sales to the sterling area over the objection of business interests. Sterling representatives admitted that their primary products could not compete with American prices. Britain, too, they argued, would prefer to buy cheaper goods in the dollar area, but could not because she lacked dollars. They told the Japanese that they were fortunate to have the special procurement dollar income that enabled them to afford the luxury of purchasing in the dollar area. Britain, of course, received its own defense support aid, which, however, was not as lucrative as Japan's.[36]

Some Americans feared that the Colombo Plan was designed to consolidate Southeast Asian economic integration with Britain at the expense of Japan. Americans also viewed the attitudes of British officials in Southeast Asia as a great impediment to Japanese expansion in the area. SCAP charged that Malaysian officials had agreed to admit Japanese to work their former mines, but that British colonial officials had rejected all visa applications submitted by Japanese since the San Francisco Conference. The British mine owners, of course, feared competition from the Japanese mines. It was characteristic of Occupation politics that, to gain Japanese admission to Malaya, SCAP urged the Army to prod State to pressure the British.[37]

In late 1951 the Japanese formally asked the United States to secure Japanese admission to the Colombo Plan, as long as the British were not to use Japanese affiliation to their advantage in payments negotiations, and as long as Japanese participation were to be limited to "fields which will benefit Japan." Morrow and his aides agreed that Colombo membership would help Japan put a "foot in the door" of Southeast Asian markets. Japan could provide technical aid and capital goods to create export markets, and membership would help break down barriers to Japanese market penetration: "If you get them in the Colombo the others will fall in line." In London, in December 1951, Morrow queried the British about Japanese membership. The Foreign Office responded, diplomatically, that it would be "splendid," although premature. Officials in the Colonial Office, however, less graciously revealed that they were being compelled to "go along" with an American plan for Japanese "domination of Southeast Asia." British hesitation was well founded: previously, Southeast Asian dollar earnings went into the central sterling pool, but Southeast Asians were now seeking their own pool, independent of London, and petitioned for permission to spend their dollars on Japanese manufactures. This trend led one Indian observer to warn that "the present structure of the sterling area might be completely undermined."[38]

Such fears compounded Britain's desire to open trade between China and Japan. The American strategy of subsidizing Germany and Japan in order to direct their trade away from Eastern Europe and China meant integrating them into the "free world economy" (i.e., the sterling area, Latin America, and the nonsterling areas of Asia and Africa). Since these new sources would extend German and Japanese supply lines, both Germany and Japan would have to cover the higher costs with increased exports. German and Japanese revival came entirely at the expense of British and American exports, something the United States, but not Britain, could afford.

Sino-Japanese Trade

Japanese leaders received conflicting advice from British and American diplomats on the economic necessity and value of trade with China. On the one hand, Americans sought to counter Japanese business pressure for ties with China, which would weaken the Pacific alliance. On the other hand, the British feared that the Japanese export surplus would be dumped into both Southeast Asia and other sterling areas if Japan could not trade with China. The British advised Japan that its hope for recovery through Southeast Asian trade was "wishful thinking," because of the region's underdevelopment and its nationalistic thinking. They said that Japan's only alternative to Chinese trade was long-term dependence on American subsidies.[39]

American officials did their best to convince Japanese leaders that Chinese trade would be insignificant because of China's new revolutionary government. The greatest American fear, of course, was that trade would indeed become significant and that China would use its leverage to withhold raw materials to blackmail Japan into political accommodation with the Soviet bloc. Among themselves, Americans remained skeptical about Southeast Asian trade, but only ambivalent about Sino-Japanese trade. At a Council on Foreign Relations meeting, Eugene Dooman said that Southeast Asia would be unable to absorb 35 percent of Japan's exports, as had China. Dulles, however, answered that he was confident that Southeast Asia could do so if it were provided with development assistance. William Sebald later raised the Chinese blackmail issue as part of his critique of the ESS post-treaty economic cooperation scheme. Sebald said that British and Japanese opposition to Dulles's polarization of Asia would inevitably lead to Chinese trade. Sherwood Fine countered that the "more enlightened" Japanese opposed an alliance with China, and that Japan would suffer economically if it broke relations with the United States. A Japanese move toward China, he said, would blackmail the United States, and, in that instance, the United States would be forced to call Japan's bluff to protect its international prestige.[40]

Walter Robertson explained to the Commission on Foreign Economic Policy in November 1953 that the United States resisted East-West trade "to the greatest possible extent," in hopes that China would collapse from famine as a result of the embargo. Clarence Randall, however, noted that Sino-Japanese trade would protect the markets of American textile producers from a flood of Japanese textiles to the United States. Robertson agreed, but cautioned that it would be impossible to limit trade with China once it gathered momentum. He warned that it was "greatly against our interest" to allow Japanese economic dependence on China; it was safer to accept Japanese goods into the American market.[41] Given the alternate export markets for Japan (i.e., China, the United States, or Southeast Asia), it was logical for the United States to force Japan to trade with Southeast Asia, where American sales would be least affected and the "free world" economic bloc best preserved.

American policy was contradictory. If, as it maintained, Chinese trade would be insignificant because Japan would not enjoy the profitable concessions it had enjoyed in the 1930s, how could a dangerous dependence be created? Faced with great Japanese business pressure in 1953, the American ambassador to Japan, Robert Murphy, warned business not to become excited about Chinese trade, because it would indeed be insignificant. Yet, paradoxically, he also warned that with Chinese trade Japan could possibly create a dangerous dependence on Chinese sources. To ameliorate the opposition of Japanese business to American policy, he was forced to promise that procurement of $400 to $500 million per year would continue "for some time."[42] Marquat informed Ridgway that although the United States could not tell the Japanese for fear of arousing business protest, "it is considered [that] the United States position in the Pacific can best be served by reducing the economic contact between Japan and Red China to the greatest possible degree."[43] Recognition of and trade with Communists were counter to Acheson's psychological cold war strategy of moral supremacy, which Dulles carried on to heighten global polarization and weaken neutralism. Even if the Administration had sought such trade, it would have had to overcome stiff congressional opposition.

Yet the Japanese had to realize a vital truth in the American argument. Revolutionary China would use far more of its own raw materials in its quest for industrialization than it had prior to World War II, and would never grant colonial concessions to Japan, like the lucrative Kwantung leasehold. On the other hand, the two governments could have planned large and mutually profitable trade, which would have reduced Japan's raw material costs and hastened China's modernization. The Japanese felt that Chinese trade was vital and blamed Japan's economic problems on the United States and its tendency to use trade as a political weapon. Governor Hisato Ichimada of the Bank of Japan told Dodge that, for example, the United States should directly subsidize the higher freight charges Japan incurred by importing from North America rather than from China.[44] The United States did, of course, indirectly subsidize Japan's imports through procurements and military expenditures.

Indeed, the entire American strategy of replacing Chinese with Southeast Asian trade conflicted with Japan's economic needs. A 1954 foreign office study by Takeshi Yamazaki termed Southeast Asian trade and development a failure; the region had insufficient purchasing power, and Japan could not successfully compete with American and European exporters. He blamed the high Japanese steel production costs on Japan's forced alienation from China, and the consequent unnecessarily high shipping charges incurred through iron ore and coking coal imports from North America. The Japanese steel industry had been "developed on the premise that raw materials would be available from nearby countries." Half of Japan's iron ore came from the dollar area, and, although Southeast Asia could fill Japan's iron ore needs (with "development"), only China could provide cheap coking coal. Yamazaki charged that the result of American policy was to cripple Japan's exports and subsidize American companies. The U.S. embargo on China subsidized American manufacturing corporations because it kept competing Japanese manufacturers' costs artificially high. Moreover, Japan's great dependence on American primary products helped subsidize the American oil, coal, mining, and agricultural industries.[45] For Japan to divert its imports from the dollar area because of its inability to pay would have severely hurt key American producers, especially in agriculture.

Acceptance of the cooperation program did not necessarily mean that Japan would not attempt to resist the American embargo on trade with China. SCAP began screening all export applications to China on January 1, 1951, to fulfill Battle Act requirements. On February 4, 1952, SCAP stopped monitoring each application and began issuing export licenses to shippers. But even after Japan received its sovereignty on April 28, 1952, MITI still had to issue the licenses. The Japanese government came under great pressure from small- and medium-size companies, especially Osaka textile interests, to defy the United States. The Japanese argued that nonstrategic trade would not hurt American interests, and that it was wrong to hinder trade over political differences. Yoshida also tried to convince Dulles that Japan could wean China from the Soviet Union with trade offers. Dulles informed him that it was American policy to starve China until she submitted to Western terms, and that trade would only make it more tolerable for China to exist under Russian control.[46]

Despite American sentiment the Japanese government allowed three Japanese trade groups to sign an informal trade pact on June 1, 1952, with the China Committee for the Promotion of International Trade. From 1952 to 1954 only five Japanese missions visited China; in 1955, however, nine trade missions went, with one signing a new barter agreement. Americans were concerned. *Fortune* reported that Ambassador Allison's "basic diplomatic task was to deter the drift of the Japanese Government toward some degree of political and economic accommodation with the Soviet Union and Communist China." The Japanese were naturally sensitive about having their policies dictated by the United States. When the United States issued a warning about Chinese trade in March 1955, it "shocked" the Japanese business community. The foreign office said that the loss of Chinese trade was "great," but estimated that it would grow only from a paltry 1.5 percent of Japanese trade to a significant, not decisive, 10 percent even if decontrolled. Fearing Japan's continued dependence on procurements, the government decided to relax controls on Chinese trade on July 16, 1957, to help replace American orders. Nevertheless, Prime Minister Nobusuke Kishi's firm loyalty to American policy in Asia subsequently alienated the Chinese; when, in 1960, Kishi refused to display the Chinese flag in Japan, China cut trade with Japan.[47] When after two decades of limiting Japanese diplomatic sovereignty, the United States recognized China in 1971 without first consulting the Japanese, it severely angered Japan and strained the alliance.

Mixed Results in Southeast Asia

Southeast Asia became an important trading partner for Japan in the 1950s, but the trade never quite fulfilled expectations. Jerome Cohen observed in 1957 that "the frequently voiced hope that this area would prove the main factor in improving Japan's trade position has hardly been realized." Southeast Asia's failure to develop balanced, integrated economies and its continued reliance on primary production for export income limited its ability to absorb manufactured goods. Moreover, Japan was undersold in the capital goods market by Germany, in fertilizer by Italy, in textiles by India; it faced British obstruction and competition, reparations snags, trade and exchange controls, quotas, currency inconvertibility, and infant industry tariffs. Japan remained the lone industrial nation without a currency bloc to afford the advantages of multilateral trade.[48] Yoshida returned from a trip to Southeast Asia in 1954, and after noting the area's lack of purchasing power and its many requests for aid from Japan, said that Japan should trade with "rich men, not beggars." His remark vividly illustrates Japan's reasons for switching its primary emphasis to the American market in 1954. The rich American market had staggering purchasing power, especially in contrast to the sharply limited buying capacity of Southeast Asia. The American policy in Asia to perpetuate colonial trade patterns helped doom Southeast Asians to poverty in the 1950s. Rubber prices dropped from 88 cents per pound to 20 cents from 1951 to 1954, and tin dropped from $1.81 to 84 cents. These stark shifts help explain the lack of Southeast Asian purchasing power.[49]

Although Southeast Asian trade disappointed recovery planners in Japan and Washington, their interest remained great. In 1954 they continued their plans to help Japan in Southeast Asia and their military efforts to secure the area. Everett Drumwright of the Far East division told the House that Southeast Asian trade would go "far to compensate for Japan's lost markets in China." In July the Tokyo embassy "urged integrating Japan and Southeast Asia both politically and economically and pointed out that in the long run, and short of war, the greatest source of weakness in Japan was the fear that it would not be included in the future of the Far East." In 1955, Dulles told the Senate Foreign Relations Committee that the area had "fabulous potential wealth" in raw materials: "We feel Japan has a very important economic problem and one that can be best solved by their relations with other Asian countries rather than by a situation where the United States has to take vast quantities of Japanese goods that we may not want." He advised that Southeast Asia was too backward to absorb much economic aid; what the area needed was greater raw materials production and trade with Japan, not nationalistic policies.[50]

Prior to 1952 the United States seemed to be taking the initiative in planning aid to promote integration with Southeast Asia. As evidenced by the important Ikeda-Robertson talks in Washington in 1953 and the 1954 Yoshida trip to the United States, however, the Japanese increasingly came to voice their mounting frustration with Southeast Asian trade, interim solutions to the dollar gap (especially their great dependence on special procurement orders), and the failure of the United States to provide a massive Asian aid program to promote integration. Some elements of the Japanese élite, including Yamazaki, suggested rejecting American military cooperation in Southeast Asia, since Asians would not appreciate Japan's profiting from their internal conflicts, and since such cooperation would preclude Japan from creating an independent policy of peaceful relations with Asia.[51]

Generally, however, Japan backed American military intervention. Yoshida told the National Press Club that Japan "[could not] survive unless the free nations of the Asian community also survive[d], and unless there [were] free trade and friendly cooperation among us." The 1954 Yoshida mission warned the United States that the domino theory was indeed relevant: "From a political point of view, if a greater part of Southeast Asia should be put under Communist sphere of influence, Japan will find it impossible to stand alone"; stability and development in Southeast Asia were "very important" factors in "strengthening Japan politically and economically."[52]

Disappointment with Southeast Asian trade, and resentment at American sanctions on Chinese trade, only heightened Japan's desire for bold trade and development programs in Southeast Asia. "Backed up if not inspired by the Zaikai" (the Japanese corporate élite), the Yoshida mission requested a "Marshall Plan for Asia" to realize Japan's "high hopes" for Southeast Asian trade. Yoshida also approached the British high commissioner for Southeast Asia, Malcolm MacDonald, about Anglo-Japanese cooperation in the region in 1954.[53] The Japanese warned that China would invest in a massive development effort and capture Southeast Asia through sheer economic power. Japan thus pressed for a $4 billion annual aid program (ten times greater than the combined 1954 contributions of the Colombo Plan, the IBRD, and the FOA) to match Chinese investment. They labeled the American policy of relying on local capital to develop Asia as "negative" and ineffective, and cited the integrated and coordinated aid success of the ERP, comparing Japan's plight to that of Europe in 1947. They also renewed their request for an Asiatic payments union. Japan had no multilateral clearing arrangements with Southeast Asia, and such an institution would thus be the most effective way of integrating Japan and the region financially. The Southeast Asian sterling countries, having use of London's clearing arrangements, opposed an Asiatic payments union.[54] In Washington in August 1955, Prime Minister Shigemitsu again proposed a payments union and establishment of a training center for Southeast Asian officials in Japan to orient them toward Japanese technology and business. The United States, however, said that multilateral clearing arrangements were neither necessary nor desirable. When India convened a conference at Simla in 1955 to discuss Stassen's Asian aid proposal, the Japanese boldly proposed using the funds to promote regional integration that would be based on Japanese industry; the pleas, however, largely "fell on deaf ears." American officials assured Japan that they were "acutely aware of the importance of economic development in South and Southeast Asia to Japan," and said that Japan could make suggestions on how to use the aid fund and could bid on contracts. The United States, finally, never seriously considered a large Asian Marshall Plan, but did intensify its military and development programs in Southeast Asia to reassure Japan.[55]

The Japanese still prized Southeast Asia because of its economic potential and because it was a local source of materials. Prime Minister Kishi launched a new integration campaign in 1957, reflecting Japan's ever more aggressive international stance and the popular cry for "vigorous prosecution of economic diplomacy." His proposal for a Southeast Asian development fund was rejected by the Southeast Asians, Europeans, and Americans. He still requested massive American coordinated aid to Asia to subsidize Japan's exports, and visited the United States to request this aid, "particularly through tie ups with Japanese industrial techniques."[56]

In the late 1950s, Japanese plans turned from seeking direct American aid to seeking American support for an Asian development bank. Although Japanese prime ministers strongly promoted the idea, it was premature because Southeast Asia was not eager for Japanese leadership, and the United States had definitely cooled on the idea, preferring the use of IBRD and local funds. In 1959 the United States described as "a bad idea" a proposal for a large American grant to the Japanese Export-Import Bank to finance trade with Southeast Asia and Latin America because Japan was no longer considered a weak nation.[57] The idea that the United States would be directly subsidizing foreign companies in competition with American firms now had become a real consideration, since the dollar gap had finally been conquered.

Even though they kept suggesting them, the Japanese were losing hope in the long-debated, large-scale coordinated aid plans. The *Mainichi* reported in 1957 that Japan was cynical about coordinated aid plans because of the "long history of past failures" of the Yoshida and Hatoyama cabinets to evoke American interest in coordinating U.S. aid funds with Japanese reparations and technical assistance.[58] The idea of a Marshall Plan for Asia never reached the level envisioned in the plans. If there was a Marshall Plan, it was, as Chalmers Johnson has remarked, the Korean War and subsequent procurement programs, which far outweighed coordinated aid to Southeast Asia and led to the industrial resurgence of Japan. In light of the many "coordinated aid" suggestions made since 1947, it is ironic that Walter Robertson told the Cleveland Council of World Affairs in 1954 that Japan's exports to Southeast Asia could be "increased by devices to tie Southeast Asia's economy to Japan. But these are out of the question." He thus reflected State's sensitivity to charges that America was sponsoring Japanese imperialistic domination of Asia.[59] The United States, of course, consistently considered such devices, though it never implemented them on a scale sufficient to satisfy Japan.

The ultimate judgments on the coordinated aid attempts to reintegrate Japan and Southeast Asia must be mixed, in almost every sense. Disappointment mounted after 1952, especially on the Japanese side. The United States had never been able to commit large sums for nonmilitary aid to Asia, although Japan-centric and Southeast Asia-centric officials naturally concocted such schemes periodically for circulation, and diplomats trumpeted them in order to assuage the Japanese business community. Indeed, schemes of this type were under varying degrees of serious discussion from 1947 to 1960, and drew the attention of powerful forces in the Truman and Eisenhower administrations. Ultimately, American policy evolved toward military solutions. The Japanese wanted to attack Asian poverty, strictly for their own economic interests and the stability of the region, but American cold warriors, astride their military machine, and a Congress and public weary of foreign economic aid but supportive of military adventures wanted to attack Asian revolutionaries. Moreover, with large funds diverted to the military, there was no surplus remaining for Asian economic aid. In addition to its military approach, the United States also recognized the short-term futility of economic aid to underdeveloped Southeast Asia and well understood that pouring large sums of development aid into the region was a slow-yielding investment.

The increasing American military intervention in Asia paid off in handsome profits for Japan in the 1960s, when $2.6 billion in war supplies were procured in Japan between 1964 and 1969 alone. Ironically, though these coordinated aid orders effected profits for the Japanese industrial sector, they also enabled the United States to pursue its military intervention with printing press dollars used to pay foreign contractors. The dollar outflow became so great that massive inflation and the sharp drop in the value of the dollar became inevitable. In 1963, Russell Fifield wrote that Japan and the United States had similar objectives in Southeast Asia: "Japan wants the region to have a much more important place in its economic future, believing that relations on a mutually profitable basis can be strengthened, and it realizes that maintaining the independence of the states in the area free from communist domination is an essential prerequisite."[60] The policy of multilateralism—economic freedom for Western and Japanese business—dictated that the United States and, to a lesser extent, the British form a military protectorate in Southeast Asia.

By the 1970s Japanese expansion into Southeast Asia had reached the saturation point. Through the Tokyo-based Asian Development Bank (1966), and Japanese yen aid to South and Southeast Asia, Japan had become the dominant power in the region. She had granted over $400 million to Korea, the Philippines, Indonesia, and India, and over $150 million to Taiwan, Burma, Thailand, and Pakistan. She had placed 32 percent of her foreign investment in the area, including $810 million in resource-rich Indonesia. Southeast Asians, however, began to fear that Japan's dependence on Asian materials was "irreversible," and that if the Asians tried to resist Japanese control and assert nationalistic goals, Japan's growing military might be called upon. The aggressive and dominating character of Japanese corporate practices in the area, moreover, alienated the Southeast Asians. Prime Minister Tanaka's tour in 1975, which attracted massive protests, symbolized the resentment toward Japanese economic domination.[61] Japan's absolute superiority led to massive trade surpluses with the area, creating a yen gap similar to the dollar gap of the postwar decade. Southeast Asia remained underdeveloped, but, by the 1970s, the promise of its vast mineral wealth was being fully exploited by Japanese and Western consortiums. Thus the long-range strategic and economic plans of 1947 to 1955 served to fulfill Japan's economic needs of the 1960s and 1970s.

Conclusion

In the words of Sherwood Fine, Japan faced an "unprecedented array of harrowing economic problems" after World War II. The aggregate aid and dollar gap figures illustrate the dimensions of the obstacles confronting Japanese revival. Through 1955 the cumulative dollar gap stood at $6.2 billion, balanced by $2 billion in economic aid and $4 billion in military expenditures. By 1964, military procurement alone reached $7.2 billion. Government transfers of dollars to Japan thus averaged $500 million per year for twenty years. By 1970 the Vietnam War and continued military expenditures in Japan pushed the military total near $10 billion.

Military demand played a significant role in Japanese recovery. Shigeto Tsuru, in a 1953 lecture, suggested that the American "reverse course" dictated that Japan recover "in the manner consistent with American capitalism," which would negate the possibility of the socioeconomic transformation necessary to expand the Japanese domestic market. He said that the Japanese economy "prospers in the circumstances of war or war-like situation. That is to say its mechanism of prosperity and growth is still geared to circumstances which favor the production of commodities useful for the prosecution of war."[1] This conclusion is ironic in light of the often-repeated statement that Japan's postwar development proves that industrial capitalist economies do not require military demand to sustain production.

Other observers have also pointed to the conclusion that the procurement orders served a unique need in Japan's troubled economy. Jerome Cohen explained that there was a "circular inter-relationship" in the Japanese economy between external stimulation (exports or war orders) and industrial growth. According to Leon Hollerman, procurements were the equivalent of "high-powered" exports, because they yielded foreign exchange receipts both for goods not normally exported and for labor, which had no import component foreign exchange cost. Dodge understood that Japanese domestic expansion automatically raised imports and increased the dollar gap. Limited domestic raw materials resources meant that each increment in consumption required an increase in imports. Without sustained export demand, only procurements could provide the industrial stimulation required by Japan to sustain rapid industrial growth from 1950 to 1955, when exports finally recovered.[2]

Had not Japan enjoyed the massive stimulation of procurements that enabled her to finance industrial modernization in the early 1950s, it is possible that her later commercial export success would have been far less spectacular. Japan had no "normal" peacetime markets for heavy industrial goods in the postwar decade. Japan's export competitiveness depended on increased economies of scale and massive capital investment, which required great industrial demand. Moreover, as previously noted, this demand had to come from external sources to pay for imported food and raw materials. The leap in production from the months of the Dodge Plan in 1949 to the war boom of 1950 to 1951 was so great, and the follow-up orders so large, that, in the words of British economist G. C. Allen, it "swept the economy on to a new plane." He concluded: "It is scarcely possible to exaggerate the importance of these payments to Japan's economic recovery during the critical years after 1951. At a time when the revival of the export trade was in an early stage, they provided her with a fairly steady income which greatly assisted in the re-equipment of her industries and the restoration of prewar levels of consumption." Without American economic aid, he added, "Japan would almost certainly have sunk deeper into economic chaos. The same conclusion applies to the subsequent period when, although her trading enterprise was handicapped by limitations imposed by the United States on her dealings with China, she nevertheless enjoyed the advantage of a vast dollar expenditure at this critical stage of her reconstruction." Shigeto Tsuru described the magnitude of the Korean boom in Japan: "Probably one can find very few examples of mature industrial economies which match the rapidity of general expansion observed here." Finally, it is impossible to underestimate the psychological importance of the cooperation program to Japanese investors against the backdrop of insecurity prior to the Korean War.[3]

The consequences of the "reverse course" and American strategy in Japan were profound. Japan and China were separated, thereby distorting each economy and stunting Chinese technological growth. The cushion of procurement enabled Japan to rebuild a highly competitive economy and, at the same time, to retain the economic "dualism" that continued the subsidization of heavy industry at the expense of the less fortunate workers not employed by the giant corporations. The external stimulation allowed Japanese corporate élites to avoid the social rationalization that would have provided a thriving domestic market to sustain industry. Finally, of course, the imperatives of the Pacific alliance with Japan helped lead the United States to its long and costly intervention in Southeast Asia.[4]

Reference Matter

Appendix

Table 1   United States Balance of Payments (in millions of dollars)

	1939	1945	1946	1947	1948	1949	1950	1951	1952
Exports	4,432	16,273	14,804	19,834	17,237	15,981	14,327	20,183	20,574
Imports	3,366	10,232	6,991	8,208	10,349	9,621	12,028	15,073	15,766
Commercial balance	+1,066	+6,041	+7,813	+11,626	+6,888	+6,360	+2,299	+5,110	+4,808
Foreign economic aid (net)	—	−6,542	−2,274	−1,897	−3,894	−4,997	−3,484	−3,035	−1,960
Military expenditures	46	−2,434	−493	−455	−799	−621	−576	−1,270	−2,054
Net private foreign investment	339	−550	−413	−987	−906	−553	−1,265	−1,048	−1,160

	1953	1954	1955	1956	1957	1958	1959	1960
Exports	21,123	21,121	22,392	26,162	28,899	25,353	25,450	28,778
Imports	16,561	15,931	17,795	19,628	20,752	20,861	23,342	23,188
Commercial balance	+4,562	+5,190	+4,597	+6,534	+8,147	+4,492	+2,108	+5,590
Foreign economic aid (net)	−1,837	−1,647	−1,901	−1,733	−1,616	−1,616	−1,633	−1,664
Military expenditures	−2,615	−2,642	−2,901	−2,949	−3,216	−3,435	−3,107	−3,048
Net private foreign investment	−383	−1,622	−1,255	−3,071	−3,577	−2,936	−2,375	−3,882

Source: Balance of Payments Statistical Supplement, Revised Edition, U.S. Department of Commerce, 1961.

Table 2 Defense Expenditures Abroad for Goods and Services by Major Category, 1953–1960 (in millions of dollars)

Expenditures	1953	1954	1955	1956	1957	1958	1959	1960
Expenditures by troops, civilian personnel, post exchanges, etc.	864	846	862	861	881	890	888	873
Foreign expenditures for construction	301	275	313	369	372	321	215	175
Contributions to the NATO multilateral construction program	91	69	84	68	65	81	58	117
Contractual services	454	370	412	481	640	772	765	774
Offshore procurement under military assistance programs	326	595	640	515	371	212	150	141
Purchases of equipment	71	70	37	42	55	49	39	44
Purchases of other materials and supplies	508	417	553	613	832	1,110	992	924
Total	2,615	2,642	2,901	2,949	3,216	3,435	3,107	3,048

Source: Balance of Payments Statistical Supplement, Revised Edition, U.S. Department of Commerce, 1961.

Table 3   Japan, Indices of Production (1955 = 100)

	All Industries	Utilities	Manufacturing	Machinery	Chemicals
1944	98.2	62.1	101.2	135.6	50.1
1945	43.2	36.9	42.9	57.6	20.8
1946	19.2	47.7	16.1	17.4	12.1
1947	23.9	53.6	20.1	21.0	16.8
1948	231.1	58.5	26.9	32.3	22.0
1949	40.0	66.4	35.7	40.2	30.7
1950	48.6	71.1	44.7	41.6	42.0
1951	66.2	76.1	63.1	67.5	55.6
1952	71.1	81.8	68.0	69.1	61.6
1953	85.8	87.9	84.2	87.7	75.9
1954	93.0	93.5	92.4	98.8	86.5
1955	100.0	100.0	100.0	100.0	100.0
1956	123.3	115.0	123.5	145.2	120.8
1957	143.3	128.2	146.4	202.1	142.0
1958	144.2	136.0	147.0	216.4	147.3
1959	178.2	155.9	185.2	310.1	168.1
1960	224.8	183.3	236.3	442.4	199.7

Source: Ōkurasho Zaisei Shishitsu, ed. (Ministry of Finance, Financial History Section), Shōwa Zaisei Shi: Shusen kara Kowa made (Financial History of the Shōwa Period: From War's End to the Conclusion of the Peace Treaty) Volume 19: Toku (statistics) 1978: Tōyo Zeiza Shimbunsha

Table 4 Japan Exports by Destination (in millions of yen)

	Total	Asia	South East Asia	China	North America	United States	South America	Europe	Africa
1945	388	388	—	372	—	—	—	—	—
1946	2,260	747	—	221	1,472	1,472	—	28	—
1947	10,148	6,814	—	761	1,864	1,791	4	863	337
1948	52,022	24,581	—	287	17,692	16,894	371	5,473	2,714
1949	169,841	84,523	—	928	34,286	30,736	1,061	22,792	19,793
1950	298,021	137,931	102,011	7,068	75,688	64,547	11,166	35,893	26,554
1951	488,777	251,780	159,844	2,098	76,697	66,578	28,866	52,649	40,302
1952	458,243	236,237	166,001	216	94,382	82,504	13,205	64,381	34,003
1953	458,943	235,630	158,290	1,634	105,529	81,663	20,970	42,748	46,361
1954	586,525	286,852	185,975	6,875	125,418	99,628	56,937	52,667	49,857
1955	723,816	303,460	203,270	10,277	191,547	161,732	53,533	74,086	74,009
1956	900,229	367,990	235,173	24,242	234,305	195,594	48,273	90,133	141,300
1957	1,028,887	412,709	271,478	21,774	261,323	214,770	33,777	117,558	179,623
1958	1,035,562	386,756	233,827	18,216	305,444	244,942	41,394	119,988	149,584
1959	1,244,337	419,654	271,532	1,313	448,651	371,032	51,003	134,989	147,561
1960	1,459,633	540,325	359,640	981	477,977	389,837	64,657	178,200	126,637

Source: *Economic Statistics of Japan: 1960*, Statistics Department, The Bank of Japan, Tokyo, 1961

Table 5   Japan, Imports by Commodity Group (in millions of yen)

	Total	Food and Beverages	Textile Materials	Metal Ores	Non-metallic Minerals	Mineral Fuels
1950	348,196	111,863	133,066	6,475	10,948	19,245
1951	737,241	181,081	281,530	33,993	26,721	57,586
1952	730,352	222,384	220,249	52,327	22,145	84,304
1953	867,469	225,014	245,759	62,404	16,276	103,973
1954	863,785	235,363	229,844	61,611	19,544	96,246
1955	889,715	224,992	216,669	66,867	25,367	104,040
1956	1,162,704	200,990	287,401	164,379	34,436	148,553
1957	1,542,091	206,670	297,183	249,414	38,951	244,733
1958	1,091,925	190,517	222,622	92,725	23,704	185,136
1959	2,120,985	1,295,817	236,321	178,684	28,563	200,647
1960	2,664,699	1,616,807	284,263	242,363	37,254	266,974

Japan, Exports by Commodity Group (in millions of yen)

	Total	Food and Beverages	Textiles	Chemicals	Metals/ Metal Products	Machinery
1946	2,260	—	—	—	—	—
1947	10,148	—	—	—	—	—
1948	52,022	—	—	—	—	—
1949	169,841	—	—	—	—	—
1950	298,021	18,727	143,550	5,599	54,573	29,505
1951	488,777	24,866	226,529	13,227	107,924	39,346
1952	458,243	35,786	162,915	14,354	122,634	39,636
1953	458,943	47,302	165,721	22,417	67,148	67,936
1954	586,525	48,481	236,515	28,404	89,939	72,825
1955	723,816	49,007	269,786	33,751	138,942	88,835
1956	900,229	64,757	313,587	38,403	122,369	174,095
1957	1,028,887	65,959	365,430	45,342	116,409	226,644
1958	1,035,562	84,893	321,026	49,601	133,702	225,849
1959	1,244,337	93,913	371,132	59,973	144,226	291,403
1960	1,459,633	96,330	440,407	60,921	202,127	334,174

Source: Economic Statistics of Japan: 1960, Statistics Department, The Bank of Japan, Tokyo, 1961

Table 6 Military Expenditures in Japan (in millions of dollars)

	Special Procurement	International Cooperative Administration Procurement	Total U.S. Military Expenditures
1951	624	—	—
1952	824	—	—
1953	809	—	—
1954	596	—	—
1955	570	—	—
1956	587	—	—
1957	—	126	398
1958	—	110	374
1959	—	109	349
1960	—	147	402

Source: Economic Survey of Japan, Economic Council Board, Government of Japan, Tokyo, 1951–1960.

Table 7   Japan, Exports and Imports by Area (in tens of thousands of dollars)

	Exports				Imports				Balance		
	Total	Dollar Area	Sterling Area	Open Account Area	Total	Dollar Area	Sterling Area	Open Account Area	Total Balance	Dollar Area	Sterling Area
Sept. 1945–Dec. 1946	10,329	8,220	233	1,876	30,561	30,275	35	252	−20,232	−22,054	198
1947	17,357	4,882	5,622	6,853	52,613	49,062	2,475	1,077	−35,256	−44,180	3,148
1948	25,827	8,698	6,165	10,964	68,422	56,278	7,349	4,795	−42,595	−47,580	−1,184
1949	50,970	16,803	22,775	11,393	90,484	68,034	13,961	8,490	−39,514	−51,231	8,814
1950	82,006	29,445	24,408	28,152	97,434	55,886	22,214	19,334	−15,428	−26,440	2,094
1951	135,452	31,681	58,506	45,265	199,504	118,023	45,365	36,116	−64,052	−86,342	13,142
1952	127,292	39,700	53,967	33,625	202,819	122,168	50,160	30,491	−75,528	−82,468	3,806
1953	127,484	49,010	31,750	46,724	240,964	130,478	60,276	50,209	−113,479	−81,469	−28,526
1954	162,924	56,092	49,276	57,556	239,940	141,107	43,319	55,492	−77,017	−85,015	5,957
1955	201,060	81,647	64,908	54,505	247,143	133,203	59,951	53,977	−46,083	−51,556	4,957
1956	250,064	109,528	90,646	49,890	322,973	172,515	105,748	44,702	−72,910	−62,987	−15,002
1957	285,802	131,873	124,723	29,193	428,359	240,370	159,107	28,871	−142,557	−108,497	−34,384
1958	287,656	142,676	124,210	20,749	303,313	171,991	117,303	14,007	−15,657	−29,315	6,908

Source: Ōkurashō Zaisei Shishitsu, ed. (Ministry of Finance, Financial History Section), Shōwa Zaisei Shi: Shusen kara Kowa made (Financial History of the Shōwa Period: From War's End to the Conclusion of the Peace Treaty) Volume 19: Toku (statistics) 1978: Tōyo Zeiza Shimbunsha

Notes

Chapter 1

1 Henry Simons, "Trade and the Peace," in Seymour Harris, ed., *Postwar Economic Problems* (Cambridge: Harvard Univ. Press, 1943), p. 142. For an analysis of the economic advantages of multilateralism for the United States, see Charles Kindleberger, *The Dollar Shortage* (New York: MIT-Wiley, 1950). Kindleberger, who was instrumental in formulating the Marshall Plan while at the State Department, explained that American producers needed exports to realize maximum production. Greater production meant higher profits due to greater efficiency (this is known as the benefits of economies of scale). Whereas formerly domestic producers desiring tariff protection were most influential, by 1947 export cartels had "gained political ascendancy" and demanded free trade. Thus, the "avalanche" of special interest groups which demanded consideration in ECA purchases reflected the "pervasive influence of the profit motive." See pp. 21, 31, 34, 36.

2 Perhaps the most useful survey of pre-1940 international economic relations is Karl Polanyi's insightful *The Great Transformation* (Boston: Beacon, 1944). See especially pp. 194–195. For the American pursuit of multilateralism in the 1920s, see Carl Parrini, *Heir to Empire* (Pittsburgh: Univ. of Pittsburgh Press, 1969). My approach to the primary materials researched for this chapter has, of course, been shaped by other authors. See especially Richard Freeland, *The Truman Doctrine and the Origins of McCarthyism* (New York: Schocken, 1970); Joyce and Gabriel Kolko, *The Limits of Power* (New York: Vantage, 1973); Lloyd C. Gardner, *Architects of Illusion* (Chicago: Quadrangle, 1970); Thomas G. Patterson, *Soviet-American Confrontation* (Baltimore: Johns Hopkins Univ. Press, 1973). These works contain more than ample documentation for the basic thrust of multilateralism and the importance of exports and foreign aid to the American economy. By focusing on the

233

fundamental characteristics of the dollar gap, this chapter attempts to provide a more clear understanding of the economic forces which contributed significantly to the shaping of American foreign policy after 1948 and of the dramatic merger of military and economic policy after 1949.

3 The oral history interviews with John Leddy and Winthrop G. Brown in the Truman Library are extremely informative about U.S. postwar multilateral policy. Indeed, the entire collection of Truman Library oral history interviews reflects the considerable knowledge of the postwar economic situation of interviewer Richard D. McKenzie and constitute an excellent source. For the key role of postwar American policymakers in developing the concept of economic integration, see Fritz Machlup, *A History of Thought on Economic Integration* (New York: Columbia Univ. Press, 1977); see chaps. 6–8 for sketches of proponents of economic integration, including H. Van Buren Cleveland, Kindleberger, Robert Triffin, Acheson, Truman, Marshall, Clayton, and the Harriman, Nourse, Krug, and Herter reports.

4 For Keynes's views, see Kindleberger, *The Dollar Shortage,* pp. 118–119. For the role of the IMF, see the oral history interview with Edward Mason at the Truman Library.

5 Charles Kindleberger, "International Monetary Stabilization," in Harris, ed., *Postwar Economic Problems,* p. 390. For a discussion of structural economic problems, see the *Interim Report of the OEEC* (Paris, 1949), pp. 15–22.

6 Paul Hoffman, "ECA Bulletin: The ECA Program Moves into High Gear," attached to Jones to Elsey, November 17, 1949, George Elsey Papers, Truman Library, Independence, Mo., box 59, "Foreign Economic Policy." Walter S. Salant memo, "International Economic Relations," Walter S. Salant Papers, Truman Library, box 2, "International Relations 1946–1947."

7 Winthrop G. Brown, "U.S. Foreign Economic Policy," Department of State Commercial Policy Series 117, *Building World Trade* (Washington, D.C., November 1948). Kindleberger later defined structural disequilibrium as when a "change in demand or supply of exports or imports alters a previously existing equilibrium or when a change occurs in the basic circumstances under which income is earned or spent abroad, in both cases without the requisite changes elsewhere in the economy" (*The International Economy* [Homewood, Ill.: Erwin, 1958], p. 534).

8 Paul Nitze, "A Sound International Trade Program: Its Meaning for American Business," Department of State Commercial Policy Series 117, *Building World Trade* (Washington, D.C., November 1948). See also

David Eakins, "Business Planners and America's Postwar Expansion," in David Horowitz, ed., *Corporations and the Cold War* (New York: *Monthly Review,* 1969). See also William Appleman Williams, "The Large Corporation and American Foreign Policy," in Horowitz, ibid.

9 R. B. Bryce, "International Aspects of an Investment Program," in Harris, ed., *Postwar Economic Problems.* See other essays here on the theoretical foundations of postwar American multilateral foreign economic policy, especially Haberler and Ellis. For the essence of the Keynesian versus Marshallian view of the world economy, as represented by Harvard economists Alvin Hanson and Gottfried Haberler, see Seymour Harris, ed., *Foreign Economic Policy of the United States* (Cambridge: Harvard Univ. Press, 1948), p. 382. See also Norman S. Buchanon and Frederick A. Lutz, *Rebuilding the World Economy* (New York: Twentieth Century Fund, 1947).

10 UN Economic Commission for Europe, *Report of the Committee on European Economic Cooperation* (Paris, September 1947), p. 34; Organization of European Economic Cooperation (OEEC), *Second Report of the Organization for European Economic Cooperation, 1949* (Paris, February 1950), p. 30; Economic Cooperation Administration (ECA), *Second Report to Congress of the Economic Cooperation Administration,* 1949, p. 11.

11 OEEC, *Second Report,* pp. 141, 169, 16. See also p. 260, for the internal contradiction in the ERP between the policies of increasing credit and investment in order to increase production and debt retirement for fiscal soundness.

12 *New York Times,* March 19, 1949, p. 21. See also Hoffman statement, Senate Foreign Relations Committee Hearings, *Extension of the European Recovery Program, 1949,* p. 528.

13 ECA, *Fifth Report to Congress,* 1949, p. 10; ECA, *Tenth Report to Congress,* 1950, p. 63; Senate Foreign Relations Committee, *Extension of the European Recovery Program,* 1949, 81:1, *Executive Sessions,* Historical Series, pp. 194–195. For American policy for multilateral development of the Third World since 1900, see Thomas J. McCormick, *China Market* (Chicago: Quadrangle, 1967).

14 Oral history interview with Walter Salant, Truman Library. Walter Salant, "The Point IV Program and the Domestic Economy," April 22, 1949, Salant Papers, folder on "International Relations—1949." Nourse commented that Salant was the most astute economist in the Administration; see oral history interview with Edwin Nourse, p. 12, Truman Library. For the long-term nature of colonial development as a solution for the dollar gap, see OEEC, *Second Report, 1949,* p. 18.

15 OEEC, *Interim Report of the OEEC,* vol. 1 (Paris, 1948), p. 193; *Economist,* January 8, 1949, p. 42.

16 *Marshall Plan Letter* (published by the *Army Times* in Washington, D.C.), January 27, 1949 and January 6, 1949. This weekly well captures the mood of ECA officials, Congress, and small business in 1948 and 1949 toward the ERP, especially the fear of the end of aid in 1953 and the resulting shock to the American economy, the resistance of Congress to financing industrial competitors, the pro-European role of the ECA, and the intense conflict between Congress and the Administration. See also ibid., June 9, November 25, December 9, 16, 23, 30, 1948, January 13, 20, February 10, 17, 24, March 3, 17, 31, and April 14, 1949. Walter Salant, "The Point IV Program and the Domestic Economy," Salant oral history interview.

17 *Economist,* July 2, 1949, p. 1; *New York Times,* July 10, 1949, section E, p. 8. M. J. Ghozlan ("The Recession of 1948 and 1949 in the United States," Ph.D., Yale University, 1954) states that the increase in foreign aid and defense spending in late 1948 and early 1949 was of "considerable value" in preventing a more serious recession (p. 459). See also Walter Salant, "Effect of the ERP on the U.S. Economy in 1949," February 28, 1950, Salant Papers, "International Relations—1950"; OEEC, *Second Report, 1949,* p. 141; ECA *Fifth Report to Congress,* p. 3; *Economist,* August 13, 1949, p. 331.

18 See Lloyd C. Gardner, *Architects of Illusion,* pp. 206–209; Thomas G. Patterson, "Presidential Foreign Policy, Public Opinion and Congress: The Truman Years," *Diplomatic History* (Winter 1979), pp. 1–18.

19 For McKellar quote, see Senate Appropriations Committee, *Hearings on FY 50 Foreign Aid Legislation,* 81:2, 1950, pp. 236, 206. Senate Foreign Relations Committee, *Extension of the European Recovery Program,* 81:1, 1949, pp. 2–12 (for the extreme sensitivity of Congress and business to European competition). For fiscal conservatism by elements of the business community, see *First National City Bank Newsletter,* February, June, July, and December 1949, and April 1950.

20 Senate Foreign Relations Committee, *Extension of the European Recovery Program,* 81:1, 1949, pp. 83–87, 196–199. See also Senate Foreign Relations Committee, *Extension of the European Recovery Program,* 81:2, 1950, pp. 7, 23.

21 *New York Times,* May 21, 1950, p. 4; *Economist,* May 7, 1949, p. 828; ECA, *Seventh Report to Congress,* May 1950, p. 15. Robert Tufts warned fellow members of the State Department's Policy Planning staff that if Congress was told that European unity was the solution to the dollar gap, the State Department "would be in trouble later." At the same meet-

ing George Kennan commented that "Congress must get over the idea that everything is over by 1952." Paul Nitze added: "That is true irrespective of whether you get union or not." 152d meeting of the State Department Policy Planning staff, October 18, 1949, records of the Policy Planning staff, Diplomatic Branch, National Archives, Washington, D.C., box 27, folder 3, "Western Europe."

22 ECA, "Bulletin: The ECA Program Moves into High Gear," Washington, D.C., 1949; *New York Times,* October 23, 1949, pp. 1, 38; Walter Salant, "International Transactions and Policies," March 31, 1949, Salant Papers, box 2. For profit remittances exceeding the net outflow of foreign investment dollars, see Evsey Domar, "Foreign Investment and the Balance of Payments, *American Economic Review* (December 1950), p. 805. For "depressed equilibrium," see Wolfgang Stolper, "Notes on the Dollar Shortage," *American Economic Review* (May 1950), p. 288.

23 OEEC, *Interim Report of the OEEC,* p. 59. See also p. 64, which explains that Europe's goal of increased exports to South America to help cover the dollar gap "would mean a reduction of at least one half in the United States market in South America." This analysis was also featured in the *Economist,* January 8, 1949, p. 42. The structural shift in trade patterns that underlay the dollar gap was explained in ECA, *Fourth Report to Congress,* 1949, p. 6; and OEEC, *Second Report, 1949,* p. 18.

24 *Economist,* June 11, 1949, p. 1074.

25 OEEC, *Second Report, 1949,* p. 21. American economic opinion believed, in the main, that the cause of the disequilibrium was European and especially British high consumption policies. Gottfried Haberler was perhaps the strongest proponent of this classical economic view. The *First National City Bank Newsletter* of July 1949 blamed "overambitious capital development programs, unbalanced budget, 'easy money' policies, and inadequate incentives to produce" abroad for the extreme dollar gap. See also ibid., November 1949, p. 128, and December 1949, p. 139, for the "bankruptcy of Keynesianism." British socialism was a particularly appealing target of Congress and much of American business. See the statement by Senator James P. Kem, a Republican from Missouri, in Senate Appropriations Committee, *FY 50 Foreign Aid Hearings,* 81:2, 1950, p. 322. Hoffman also blamed Britain and not the American recession for the sterling crisis of 1949. See Hoffman to Harriman, August 5, 1949, Department of State, *Papers Relating to the Foreign Relations of the United States (FRUS),* 1949, IV, pp. 416–417.

26 The Keynesian view that the strongest "engines" of the capitalist economy should pull their neighbors out of recession through stimulatory domestic policies to increase imports and reduce pressures to export has

become conventional theory since the 1950s and the more widespread acceptance of Keynesian doctrine. For example, a 1958 economics text explains that deflating the nation suffering from a trade deficit to produce a balance leads to a downward spiral of trade and the threat of international depression: "The solution much to be preferred in this situation is the concerted adoption of expansionary monetary and fiscal policies, especially in the economically more important countries. If the larger countries simultaneously generate a recovery of income and employment, their imports will increase, spreading the impulse toward expansion throughout the world. The exports of each will increase as income and imports rise in other countries." P. T. Ellsworth, *The International Economy* (New York: Macmillan, 1958), pp. 354–355. This view was, of course, not universally accepted in the 1940s, and was opposed by the conventional economic thinkers of the day, who blamed socialism and Keynesianism for the disequilibrium. The radical notion of spending more to reach equilibrium was advanced by many in Britain and by Kindleberger and Salant, two of the most intelligent and advanced American economic policymakers. In 1950 Kindleberger explained the need for United States domestic expansion and blamed the propensity of American investment to lag in peacetime (*The Dollar Shortage*, pp. 96–121). Walter Salant's recommendations from 1947 to 1950 reflected his deep understanding of the structural problem and the key role of American demand for foreign goods. See Salant to Stabilization Devices Committee, April 20, 1948, and April 30, 1948, Salant Papers, box 2, "International Relations—1948." See also Salant speech at Harvard, "Some Aspects of the Foreign Aid Program," October 18, 1948, ibid. In 1949 Salant argued that domestic economic expansion was the solution of advancing foreign recovery while cooling protectionism in the United States ("American Policy in Light of Currency Devaluation," ibid., "International Relations—1949"). For British views see R. S. Sayers, "The Instability of the American Economy," *Westminster Bank Review*, August 1949, pp. 1, 2, 5, which states that with the probable end of the postwar boom, public works and defense spending in the United States were the preventative medicine for an international depression. Labor Party economist Thomas Balogh was a most vehement foe of American multilateralism and austerity policies in Europe. See particularly the introduction to his *Dollar Crisis: Causes and Cures* (Oxford: Basil Blackwell, 1950). Balogh also attacked the Administration's militaristic rationale for foreign aid before Congress: "Politically, the reliance on recurrent tension with Russia for obtaining Congressional approval for recovery and aid measures can only end disastrously." The *Times* (London) devoted an entire book to the lively British debates on the dollar gap crisis as they appeared in editorials and letters to the editor (*The Dollar Gap* [London, 1949]).

27 On September 20 and 21, 1949, the State Department invited four influential international economists to discuss "Foreign Aspects of a U.S. Depression." They noted the fear of foreigners that the United States would suffer another depression and discussed devices to stabilize American demand. Salant to Stabilization Devices Committee, October 17, 1949, Edwin Nourse Papers, "Daily Diary—1949," Truman Library, box 6. Such foreign anxiety about American demand represented a major hindrance to American diplomacy in Europe. An American official in Europe warned Acheson that "both the Department and the ECA have felt growing concern over the general psychological outlook of pessimism prevailing in the OEEC, primarily due to growing European awareness of the intractability of the dollar deficit problem" (Perkins to Acheson, *FRUS*, 1949, IV, p. 421). See also the *Economist*, July 9, 1949, p. 59. For European fears of a U.S. slump, see *New York Times*, July 10, 1949, section E, p. 5. In October, the secretary general of the OEEC said the OEEC had no solution for the dollar gap, and the *Economist* described the OEEC as "moribund" (*Economist*, October 29, 1949, pp. 932–933). American officials became increasingly concerned about the health of the OEEC, and tried vigorously to obtain a stronger leader during that "critical time." See Acheson to Douglass, November 16, 1949, *FRUS*, 1949, IV, pp. 448–450; secretary of state to diplomatic officers, December 13, 1949, ibid., p. 459; Harriman to secretary of state, November 6, 1949, ibid., pp. 440–442.

28 Truman to Sidney Souers, August 23, 1949, and attached letter from Truman to Nourse, president's confidential file, Truman Library, box 27, folder on "NSC"; Nourse to Truman, August 26, 1949, "Daily Diary—1949"; oral history interview with Edwin Nourse, p. 96, Truman Library. Nourse claimed his fellow council members offered "nonprofessional" politically oriented advice to Truman by not warning of the dangers of budget deficits. Nourse opposed Keyserling's appointment as Council of Economic Advisors chairman and told Truman that Keyserling did not know how an economy works. See entries of August 15, September 26, October 6, 1949, "Daily Diary—1949." For other attacks on Keyserling's ideas, see *First National City Bank Newsletter*, January, February, June, and July 1949. See also Edward S. Flash, *Economic Advice and Presidential Leadership: The Council of Economic Advisors* (New York: Columbia Univ. Press, 1965), p. 37. For an analysis of the growing influence of Keynesian theory in the United States,

see Herbert Stein, *The Fiscal Revolution in America* (Chicago: Univ. of Chicago Press, 1969), pp. 154–169.

29 *Public Papers of the Presidents: Harry S. Truman, 1949* (Washington: GPO, 1964), July 11, 1949, p. 366; draft memo of conversation between U.S. and British officials, June 9, 1949, *FRUS, 1949*, IV, p. 783; Hoffman to Katz, August 3, 1949, ibid., p. 413; Acheson to Douglass, June 30, 1949, ibid., pp. 797–798. Ambassador Douglass advised Acheson that the British wanted to cut purchases from the United States and that one solution for Britain was a "protected autarchic trading area. We fully appreciate what this would entail in damage to the U.S. economy" and objectives in Europe (Douglass to Acheson, June 22, 1949, ibid., p. 787). See also United States Embassy in the United Kingdom, "Implications of the Sterling Area Crisis to the United Kingdom and the United States," August 18, 1949, ibid., pp. 806–820. The embassy paper frankly admitted that American ideals were directly related to American economic gain: "Sheer intellectual honesty compels us to say that the U.S. favors multilateralism and non-discrimination in areas of trade where we are in a strong competitive position; but resorts to subsidies, protectionism and discrimination in those areas where we are competitively weak," especially shipping and shipbuilding (p. 818). See also decisions by the National Advisory Council on International Monetary and Financial Affairs (NAC), the interdepartmental, economic counterpart to the National Security Council, chaired by the secretary of the treasury. The NAC feared that a permanent European payments union (the organ of European integration) would imperil dollar exports. It did say that incidental discrimination would be tolerated in the transition period, but not deliberate discrimination. See NAC meeting of January 16, 1950, *FRUS, 1950*, I, pp. 815–819.

30 For White House policy, see Stephen Springarn to Clark Clifford, October 3, 1949, Elsey Papers, box 59, "Foreign Economic Policy." For concern on the part of agricultural interests, see Read Dunn, "After the Marshall Plan, What?" (National Cotton Council, December 29, 1949), Stanley Andrews Papers, Truman Library, box 2, "Marshall Plan." Dunn suggested ways to cover the dollar gap and sustain the flow of surplus agricultural commodities abroad. For a British view of the American problem of disposing of its vast agricultural surplus, and the inevitability of the United States' increasing its imports to sustain the exports, see *Times* (London), *The Dollar Gap,* letter to the editor, July 18, 1949, p. 25.

31 For Thorp, see Elsey memo, November 29, 1949, Elsey Papers, box 59, "Foreign Economic Policy." Elsey, memorandum for the president, "Attached Memorandum from the Secretary of State," n.d., ibid. For

Division of Economic Affairs estimates, see Hollis Peter to Joseph D. Coppock, December 6, 1949, ibid. For December 12 meeting, see Battle to secretary of state, December 12, 1949, Acheson memos of conversations, Truman Library, box 64, "December, 1949." See also cabinet meeting of December 22, 1949, ibid.; "Background Memo on the Dollar Gap," February 21, 1950, *FRUS*, 1950, I, p. 831.

32 Elsey memo of conversation, January 17, 1950, Elsey Papers, box 59, "Foreign Economic Policy"; draft of "Memorandum for Discussion: Foreign Economic Policy," ibid.

33 Memorandum to the president from the secretary of state, "Development of Policy for Adjusting the Balance of Payments of the United States," January 26, 1950, Elsey Papers, box 59, "Foreign Economic Policy."

34 Ibid.

35 Ibid.

36 January 27, 1950, version of memorandum to the president, ibid. "Background Memo on the Dollar Gap," February 21, 1950, *FRUS*, 1950, I, pp. 831–833.

37 "Background Memo on the Dollar Gap"; Elsey, memorandum for the president, "Attached Memorandum from the Secretary of State," Elsey Papers, box 59, "Foreign Economic Policy"; Acheson, memorandum for the president, February 16, 1950, attached to McWilliams to Elsey, February 24, 1950, which transmits Department of State, "The Problem of the Future Balance of Payments of the United States," ibid.

38 Acheson memo, meeting with Frank Pace, March 9, 1950, Acheson memos of conversations, Truman Library, box 65; "Background Memo on the Dollar Gap"; Elsey to Murphy, April 26, 1950, Elsey Papers, box 59, "Foreign Economic Policy." See also Department of State, memorandum of conversation, "Dollar Gap Program," April 10, 1950, ibid.

39 Elsey, memorandum for the president, "Appointment of a Public Advisory Commission to Assist Gordon Gray on the Dollar Gap Problem," April 12, 1950, Elsey Papers, box 59, "Foreign Economic Policy."

40 Salant to Thorp, "Balance of Payments Goals Envisioned by the Department of State," and attached, "Possibility of Attaining Revised Import Targets for 1953," Salant Papers, box 2, "International Relations—1950."

41 Ibid.

42 Salant to Thorp, April 27, 1950, "Policy Implications of Revised State Department Import Targets," ibid.

43 Elsey to David Bell, May 1, 1950, Elsey Papers, box 59, "Foreign Economic Policy"; Elsey to Gray, May 1, 1950, ibid.

44 Salant to Gray and Mason, "Comments and Suggestions on ECA's Trade

and Payments Projections for a Post-ERP Year," Salant Papers, box 2, "International Relations—1950."

45 Salant, "Basic Foreign and Domestic Economic Problems Involved in Adjusting the Balance of Payments of the United States," April 14, 1950 (draft), Salant Papers, box 2, "International Relations—1950"; "Basic Studies Required to Determine Needed United States Foreign Policy Programs," April 5, 1950 (draft for discussion), Elsey Papers, box 59, "Foreign Economic Policy."

46 House Appropriations Committee, *FY 51 Foreign Aid Appropriations,* 81:2, February 1950, pp. 60–63, 131; Senate Appropriations Committee, *Foreign Aid Appropriations for 1951,* 82:1, pp. 297–299, 291, 293, 214–215.

47 Paul Nitze memo, December 19, 1949, records of the State Department Policy Planning staff, box 50, "Atomic Energy." Acheson believed that Soviet ideology and not military might was the most direct threat to American security (Acheson Memo, December 20, 1949, ibid.): "He was aware of the Marxist view of the inevitable decay of and conflict within international capitalism, which, more than military conquest, lay at the heart of Soviet ideology." Acheson also said the Soviets had an interest in avoiding a real war over Europe, which would leave them little to gain except a devastated continent.

48 For examples of officials citing the military assistance program as a device to boost investor confidence in European industry, see Katz (special representative to Europe for ECA) to Hoffman, March 31, 1949, *FRUS,* 1949, IV, p. 257; Acheson to Lewis Douglass, ibid., p. 111; Acheson statement before Senate Foreign Relations Committee, *Hearings on the North Atlantic Treaty,* 81:1, 1949, p. 12. See also *New York Times,* May 22, 1949, section F, p. 7.

49 David McClellan, *Dean Acheson* (New York: Dodd Mead, 1976), pp. 30, 38, 45, 48, 124–125. By exploiting the Communist threat, Acheson could motivate the Americans to "gird up as if they were actually at war without the catharsis of war itself." McClellan explains that the public needed an explanation for America's mushrooming involvement in world affairs: "Something or someone had to be blamed for all the pain it was causing." The public had a "natural tendency" to simplify complex world affairs into a Manichean struggle, and the Administration encouraged this distortion in its efforts to "overcome isolationism and partisanship." Acheson believed in rigid formulas and explanations clearer than truth; he disdained reflection or self-doubt. He was perfectly suited to knowingly arousing "an emotional storm in people by demagogic means," to save Western civilization (pp. 133–134, 328). See also Gaddis Smith,

Dean Acheson, American Secretaries of State Series (New York: Cooper Square, 1972), pp. 143, 189, 296.

50 Nitze to Foreign Assistance Steering Committee, January 31, 1949, *FRUS,* 1949, IV, pp. 56–57. Nitze said that providing dollar aid to build arms would pay for Europe's raw materials and make up for any decrease in exports that resulted from arms production.

51 Smith, *Dean Acheson,* p. 190; Dean Acheson, *Present at the Creation* (New York: W. W. Norton, 1969), pp. 373–378. Warner Schilling, Paul Y. Hammond and Glenn H. Snyder, *Strategy, Politics and Defense Budgets* (New York: Columbia Univ. Press, 1962), pp. 309–330.

52 NSC 68, *FRUS,* 1950, I, pp. 235–292.

53 Bureau of the Budget memo on NSC 68, by William F. Schaub, *FRUS,* 1950, I, pp. 298–306. The memo commented on the simplistic nature of NSC 68, which ignored the social roots of the Chinese revolution and the many serious problems in the "free world" which were not caused by Communism. See also Smith, *Dean Acheson,* p. 189.

54 Thorp to secretary of state, April 5, 1950, *FRUS,* 1950, I, pp. 218, 219. Lovett statement, "State-Defense Department Meeting," March 16, 1950, ibid., p. 199; Senate Foreign Relations Committee, *Hearings on the Mutual Security Act of 1951,* 82:1, pp. 29–30.

55 NSC 68, *FRUS,* 1950, I, pp. 261, 278.

56 *New York Times,* April 30, 1950, section E, p. 3.

57 Ibid.

58 Tracy S. Voorhees, "Outline of Work as Under Secretary of the Army, August 1949 to April 1950," March 22, 1967, pp. 62–68, Tracy S. Voorhees Papers, Alexander Library, Rutgers University, New Brunswick, N.J.; Voorhees, "Proposal to Correlate Economic Aid to Europe with Military Defense," May 29, 1950, ibid; Voorhees, "A Proposal for Strengthening Defense without Increasing Appropriations," April 5, 1950, ibid.

59 Voorhees, "A Proposal for Strengthening Defense without Increasing Appropriations," Voorhees Papers.

60 Voorhees, "Proposal to Correlate Economic Aid to Europe with Military Defense," Voorhees Papers.

61 Voorhees, "A Proposal to Correlate Economic Aid to Europe with Military Defense," October 20, 1950, Voorhees Papers.

62 Ibid.; Bureau of the Budget, "Suggestions for the Discussion with Gordon Gray," April 14, 1950, Elsey Papers, box 59, "Foreign Economic Policy."

63 Senate Foreign Relations and Armed Services Committees, *Joint Hearings on the Military Assistance Program,* August and September 1949,

Senate Foreign Relations Committee, *Executive Sessions,* Historical Series, pp. 101–102, 173–175, 351–361, 391, 434–435. Senators were disturbed by the violation of traditional noninvolvement policies inherent in launching arms production in Europe. Administration officials replied that by not financing arms production in Europe, the Congress would be banning all arms production in Europe because no one else would finance it.

64 "For some weeks American officials could be found, in Europe as well as the United States, suggesting that one solution to the problem was for Britain and other west European industrial nations to produce on a substantial scale armaments needed by the European members of the Atlantic Pact. These arms would be paid for with dollars provided by the United States under the Military Aid Programme." The rationale for the new policy was that it would relieve defense burdens on European budgets and "go a long way towards solving Europe's dollar deficit." The Economist Intelligence Unit, "Foreign Report, America's Changing Policy for Europe," July 6, 1950, Tracy S. Voorhees Papers.

65 Smith, *Dean Acheson,* pp. 179, 186; McClellan, *Dean Acheson,* pp. 279–281. In March 1950 Congressman Christian Herter asked Acheson "whether it would be possible to bring about among the American people a realization of the seriousness of the situation without some domestic crisis, something concrete to which your appeal could be tied, such as a break in diplomatic relations. I replied that I do not believe it will be necessary to create such a situation, the chances are too good the Russians will do so themselves." Acheson mentioned Berlin, Austria, and Formosa as likely Soviet targets (memo of conversation, March 24, 1950, *FRUS,* 1950, I, p. 208).

66 V. L. Horoth, "Korea—Its Impact on Foreign Trade," *Magazine of Wall Street,* August 12, 1950; *Business Week,* September 9, 1950, p. 126; OEEC, *Third Report* (Paris, 1951), p. 114. For the slow recovery of European production and employment in 1950, see Economic Cooperation Administration, *Eighth Report to Congress of the Economic Cooperation Administration,* 1950, p. 22, and *Ninth Report to Congress of the Economic Cooperation Administration,* 1950, pp. 5, 12, 17.

67 *Business Week,* Editorial: "Korea and the Dollar Gap," August 19, 1950, p. 10.

68 Edward Mason, "Problem of Presenting Dollar Gap Information to Community Leaders," July 14, 1950, records of SCAP, Record Group 331, Washington National Archives, Suitland, Md., box 7692, "Dollar Gap." Salant memo, August 4, 1950, "Proposed Recommendations for Gray Report," Salant Papers, box 2, "International Economic Relations—1950."

69 Salant memo, "Pattern of International Trade and Payments," July 28, 1950, Salant Papers, box 2, "International Relations—1950."

70 Keyserling statement, Joint Congressional Economic Committee, *Economic Report of the President,* 82:1, 1951, pp. 6, 8.

71 *First National City Bank Newsletter,* December 1950, February 1951.

72 *Magazine of Wall Street,* July 28, 1951, pp. 436–437.

73 Department of State memorandum, "Legislation for Foreign Aid Programs," n.d., *FRUS, 1950,* I, p. 409. Memo of phone conversation between Acheson and Foster, June 27, 1951, *FRUS, 1951,* I, pp. 334–335. Bell to Murphy, August 7, 1952, president's confidential file, Truman Library, box 25, mutual defense folder 7.

74 Averell Harriman statement, House Foreign Affairs Committee, *Mutual Security Act of 1952,* p. 55; Acheson said the solution to the dollar gap "was pretty well accomplished under the Marshall Plan, and we were going along in fine shape when we got to the Korean hostilities and the rearmament program which came out of there" (House Foreign Affairs Committee, *Mutual Security Act of 1954,* p. 139).

75 The key question concerns the effect of the war boom on stimulating world trade and European production and exports. Robert Marjolin, head of the OEEC, wrote that "in the spring of 1950 in Europe, not to mention the United States, the rise in production was not very rapid and we seemed to be approaching a ceiling imposed not by lack of capacity or lack of real needs but by inadequacy of demand" (*Europe and the United States in the World Economy* [Durham: Duke Univ. Press, 1953], p. 30); Fulbright noted Europe's lack of markets in June 1950 (Senate Foreign Relations Committee, *Hearings on the Military Assistance Program,* 1950, p. 62). Europe suffered from structural unemployment because of the lack of markets. See Kindleberger, *Europe and the Dollar* (Boston: MIT Press, 1960), p. 244; statement of the Committee on Economic Development, Senate Foreign Relations Committee, *Mutual Security Act of 1951,* 1951, p. 793; Salant memo, "Foreign Aid and the United States Balance of Payments," May 29, 1951, Salant Papers, box 12, "International Relations—1951." Military-induced demand solved the problem by stimulating triangular trade: "Rearmament has played a large part in the increase in world trade directly after Korea and remains one of the basic elements in the future of world business. No better illustration could be had than the effects of the U.S. withdrawal from the primary markets when it had about completed its stockpiling program. When this occurred the primary markets practically fell apart. It is obvious that foreign economies as well as our own are now mainly dependent on the scope of continued arms spending in this country" (Ward Gates, "Approaching Recession in American Business," *Maga-*

zine of Wall Street, May 31, 1952). See also Gordon Gray to the president, July 20, 1950, president's official file, Truman Library, folder 426N, "Dollar Gap."

This debate also raises a historiographical issue. In his important study *The Truman Doctrine and the Origins of McCarthyism,* Richard Freeland argues that the United States imposed rearmament on Europe to "recreate the dollar gap" and avoid the fear of the Policy Planning staff in December 1949 that conventional solutions to the gap—increased imports and decreased exports—would limit American trade and influence in Europe. The Policy Planning staff argued that instability would erupt in Europe as well as a dangerous vulnerability to Soviet economic overtures. Freeland argues that Europe would have recovered independently of American trade and domination without the rearmament scheme, which gave the United States formal control through NATO and continued the economic dependence of Europe on American aid and trade. I agree to an extent with Freeland's thesis, but my reading of the evidence indicates that Europe would have had a continuing dollar gap without rearmament, and thus the crux of American policy was to continue to finance the gap for reasons of control in Europe and American domestic prosperity. Rearmament was essentially a boon to European recovery and was not primarily a means of re-creating a dependence that would have continued in the absence of rearmament to a greater degree. Joyce and Gabriel Kolko, in their seminal *Limits of Power,* agree with the thesis of this work—that military aid was the "only means" of financing the dollar gap. See Freeland, p. 332, and Kolko and Kolko, p. 630.

76 *New York Times,* November 4, 1951; for Connally, see Senate Foreign Relations Committee, *Mutual Security Act of 1952,* p. 30. Senator Guy M. Gillette, Democrat from Iowa, said: "A man is naive indeed who does not realize that the effect of these cumulative expenditures at home and abroad is having a very serious effect on American economic stability now and in the future" (ibid., p. 311). Republican Senator from Iowa Bourke B. Hickenlooper shared his colleague's fears: "Year by year this contribution to foreign economies has been growing, and we have no prospect in the next two years of any diminishing claims. If I could have at all reasonable assurance that there was any end in sight except just a continually widening hole into which we throw the savings of the American people, and the earnings, not only here but abroad, I would be much happier. But I don't know where we are going. We are just walking into a dark room" (ibid., p. 308). For Smith, see Senate Foreign Relations Committee, *Executive Sessions,* vol. 4, p. 333; for transfer of funds, see ibid., pp. 223, 265, and *New York Times,* November 19, 1951.

77 *New York Times,* September 18, 1951; Senate Foreign Relations Committee, *Executive Sessions,* vol. 4, pp. 338–339.

78 House Foreign Affairs Committee, *Mutual Security Act of 1954,* p. 41; Senate Foreign Relations Committee, *Mutual Security Act of 1952,* p. 413; ibid., pp. 530, 534.

79 For Acheson conversation with Erhart, see Acheson Papers, memos of conversations, 1951, Truman Library, box 66, "July 1951." For Draper, see *New York Times,* April 28, 1952, April 29, 1952, and June 6, 1953. For Voorhees, see House Foreign Affairs Committee, *Mutual Security Act of 1954,* p. 297. For the economics of offshore procurement, see also House Foreign Affairs Committee, *Mutual Security Act of 1957,* 84:2, pp. 872–873; Senate Foreign Relations Committee, *Mutual Security Act of 1958,* 85:1, pp. 419–420; Thomas Blaisdell memo, August 7, 1951, Blaisdell Papers, Truman Library, box 8, "ECA 1951."

The Senate Appropriations Committee forced the Mutual Security Agency to stop the informal purchasing of arms produced in Europe without congressional approval and charged that there was too much emphasis on "balance of payments criteria" in awarding contracts for offshore procurement (*New York Times,* July 28, 1953, p. 9). Defense Secretary Lovett and the Joint Chiefs officially requested offshore procurement to speed the delivery of military material for the Mutual Defense Assistance Program, put Japanese and German labor to work, and aid in alleviating the "critical dollar shortage presently experienced by some of our major allies, such as England and France" (Joint Chiefs to secretary of defense, October 12, 1951, attached to Lovett to Truman, October 23, 1951, *FRUS,* 1951, I, p. 436). On the manipulation of military contracts to replace economic aid, see Cabot to Harriman, October 25, 1951, ibid., pp. 438–439.

The United States Chamber of Commerce called for replacing economic aid with offshore procurement (House Foreign Affairs Committee, Subcommittee on Foreign Economic Policy, 1953, p. 166). For offshore procurement as "balance of payments aid," see Harold Stassen statement, Senate Foreign Relations Committee, 1953, *Executive Sessions,* Historical Series, vol. 5, p. 338. H. Struve Hensel told the House Foreign Affairs Committee in 1954 that "it is perfectly true that when offshore procurement was first suggested, that people thought of it as a lot of economic aid" (House Foreign Affairs Committee, *Mutual Security Act of 1955,* p. 233).

For an analysis of the effect of military expenditures on the ending of the dollar gap in the 1950s and the beginning of the dollar glut of the 1960s, see Fred L. Block, *The Origins of International Economic Disorder* (Berkeley: Univ. of California Press, 1977), pp. 107, 109. Block supports the theme of this work that international rearmament keyed the domestic expansion of the 1950s and subsidized the dollar gap, and that NSC 68 represented "military Keynesianism."

80 United Nations, Economic Commission for Europe, Economic Survey of Europe since the War (Geneva: United Nations, 1953), pp. 85–121.

81 Commission on Foreign Economic Policy, staff memo, "The Nature and Magnitude of the World Dollar Problem," November 20, 1953, Eisenhower Library, Abilene, Kansas, Records of the Commission on Foreign Economic Policy, box 45, "Area 1, No. 3." This report discusses foreign fears of American expenditure cuts or recession and the resulting continuation of discrimination against dollar-area goods to preserve gold and dollar reserves. The Randall Commission included heads of the Bank of America, J. H. Whitney Co., Kimberley-Clark, and Anderson, Clayton, and was appointed August 14, 1953. For the conversion of major exporting corporations from tariff policies to free trade, see *Congressional Quarterly Almanac*, 1953, p. 217. The Randall Commission staff reported that "current and prospective levels of so-called "extraordinary" U.S. disbursements abroad should exercise a strong stabilizing influence on the world's balance of payments in the event of a U.S. recession" and "provide a most favorable environment for rapid progress toward trade liberalization and currency convertibility." Planned foreign spending eliminated the fear that a deep U.S. recession would re-create a huge dollar gap and shatter the industrial alliance system. Japan was by far the worst problem, along with some underdeveloped nations, while Europe had ample dollar reserves ("The International Impact of a U.S. Recession," May 5, 1954, Clarence Jacoby Papers, box 6, "International Economic Policy"). See also "The Foreign Economic Impact of a U.S. Recession," ibid.

82 Commission on Foreign Economic Policy, staff memo, "The Nature and Magnitude of the World Dollar Problem."

83 Department of State, Office of Intelligence and Research, "A Critique of the Randall Report's Analysis of the World Dollar Problem, "February 8, 1954, Eisenhower Library, Clarence Jacoby Papers, box 6, "International Economic Policy"; "The International Impact of a U.S. Recession," May 5, 1954, ibid. As international economist Raymond Mikesell explained, the Randall Commission staff was correct. "Covering defense expenditures with dollar aid is equivalent to providing a dollar market for defense production," which was an "additional dollar market." Thus, offshore procurement "is improving the dollar position of these countries by providing an additional dollar market for their products. The only case where this would not be true is that of a country

which could fully utilize for the output of dollar-earning or dollar-saving commoditics the resources it directed to defense production." He mentioned that American officials "were strongly in favor of expanding this form of U.S. military assistance to contribute both to Europe's defense and to the solution of the dollar problem." He said "balance of payments criteria have loomed large in the determination of offshore procurement policy." Offshore procurement "can and should contribute to the permanent solution of Europe's dollar problem," and thereby usher in a new era of convertibility (Raymond F. Mikesell, *Foreign Exchange in the Postwar World* [New York: Twentieth Century Fund, 1954], pp. 526–528).

84 See Hagerty diary of White House meetings, February 26, 1954, March 26, 1954, and April 26, 1954, and Whitman file minutes of the March 26, 1954 meeting, Truman Library. On the stretch-out of rearmament, see Edward S. Flash, *Economic Advice and Presidential Leadership: The Council of Economic Advisors* (New York: Columbia University Press, 1965), pp. 96–97. Economists were confused about the dollar gap through 1958; for example, see Kindleberger, *The Dollar Shortage,* pp. 166–169.

85 Richard N. Cooper, "The Competitive Position of the United States," in Seymour Harris, ed., *The Dollar in Crisis* (New York: Harcourt Brace and World, 1961), pp. 137–150.

86 See Ernest Mandel, *Decline of the Dollar* (New York: Monad Press, 1972), for analysis of American policy in the 1960s.

87 Charles Kindleberger, "Cause and Cure of Disequilibrium," in *Europe and the Dollar,* pp. 143, 144, 146, 154.

Chapter 2

1 Herbert Feis, *Contest over Japan* (New York: W. W. Norton, 1967). See also John W. Dower, "Occupied Japan and the American Lake," in Mark Selden and Edward Friedman, eds., *America's Asia* (New York: Random House, 1971), pp. 146–206.

2 Mason to Collado, January 22, 1945, Department of State, decimal file 894.50, Diplomatic Branch, National Archives, Washington, D.C., hereafter DOS and file number; Collado to Clayton, April 25, 1945, ibid.

3 Foreign Economic Administration, Enemy Branch, memo, Records of SCAP, box 6799, "FEA Documents"; Dunn to Wilcox, September 12, 1945, DOS, 894.50; State-War-Navy Coordinating Committee, SWNCC

150/4, "Policy with Respect to Japan," approved September 6, 1945, by Truman; see SCAP Monographs, vol. IX, "Reparations and Property Administration," pt. 1, pp. 2–3.

4 Walter Millis, ed., *The Forrestal Diaries* (New York: Viking, 1951), p. 105. For earlier Harriman-Forrestal thinking, see ibid, p. 56.

5 Pauley to Truman, April 15, 1947, president's official file, folder 383, Truman Library.

6 H. D. Maxwell, chief of staff, to Pauley, December 26, 1945, in the collection of Dick K. Nanto.

7 Ibid.; Pauley, "Interim Report to the President," December 7, 1945, Nanto Collection; SCAP, "Reparations."

8 Pauley to the secretary of state, December 28, 1946, on SCAP's "Comments on Ambassador Pauley's Report to the President," of September 20, 1946, Nanto Collection.

9 Ibid.

10 Fearey et al. (from POLAD's office) to secretary of state, April 17, 1946, Nanto Collection. The political advisor's office (POLAD) was a compromise between State and SCAP on State Department representation under the Occupation. MacArthur originally wanted the State Department to run the government section under SCAP control, but State insisted on an independent presence. SCAP then set up its own government section and left the diplomatic section to the POLAD. The first POLAD was George Atcheson, who died in a plane crash in 1947 and was replaced by William Sebald. Max Bishop was the original State Department representative to Japan in 1947. See Bishop memo, April 4, 1946, *FRUS*, 1946, VIII, pp. 188–190.

11 Emmerson memo, August 10, 1946, *FRUS*, 1946, VIII, pp. 337–339. For the zealousness of the Japanese public embracement of reform policies, see "State Department Foreign Policy Reports: Daily Summary of Opinion Development," September 4–5, 1945, and October 10, 1945, president's confidential file, Truman Library, folder 55.

12 Department of State, Division of Research for the Far East, memo on "Far East Economic Prospects," DOS, DRF 4256.1, January 1, 1949.

13 Hamilton to Nitze, November 14, 1946, DOS, 890.50.

14 Warren Hunsberger, "The Place of Foreign Trade in the Japanese Economy," Department of State Office of Intelligence and Research, August 29, 1946, records of SCAP, 6670.

15 Ibid.

16 Harriman to W. L. Batt, December 20, 1946, cited in Kolko and Kolko, *The Limits of Power*, p. 751.

17 Dick K. Nanto, "The United States Role in Japan's Economic Recovery," Ph.D. diss., Harvard University, 1977, pp. 207–211.

18 Ibid., pp. 208–209.
19 Ibid., pp. 209–211.
20 Atcheson to Truman, January 5, 1947, *FRUS,* 1947, VI, pp. 157–159.
21 Martin to Hilldring, "A Positive Economic Program for Japan," March 12, 1947, *FRUS,* 1947, VI, pp. 184–185.
22 Walker to Hess, July 10, 1947, DOS, 894.50.
23 Forrestal to Snyder, March 3, 1947, *Forrestal Diaries,* p. 248. For Acheson, see Joseph M. Jones, *The Fifteen Weeks* (New York: Harcourt Brace and World, 1955), pp. 205–210.
24 SCAP to Department of the Army, "A Possible Program for a Balanced Japanese Economy," March 27, 1947, records of SCAP, 6670.
25 For Strike Report, see SCAP, "Reparations." Cheseldine to MacArthur, February 17, 1947, MacArthur Papers, MacArthur Memorial Library, Norfolk, Virginia, Record Group 5; Hoover to Patterson, May 7, 1947, Voorhees Papers, "Food."
26 See Frederick S. Dunn, *Peace-Making and the Settlement with Japan* (Princeton: Princeton Univ. Press, 1963), pp. 59–62. For origins of peace planning, see Bacon to Vincent, October 25, 1946, *FRUS,* 1946, VIII, pp. 348–349; for Policy Planning staff rejection of peace plans, see PPS 10, "Results of Planning Staff Study Questions Involved in the Japanese Peace Settlement," State Department Policy Planning staff files, box 1.
27 SCAP, Selected Data on the Occupation of Japan 1950, p. 66; House Appropriation Committee Hearings, *Foreign Aid for 1949,* pt. 2, 80:2, May 1948, pp. 87–97.
28 House Appropriations Committee Hearings, *Foreign Aid for 1949,* pt. 2, 80:2, May 1948, p. 162.
29 Nanto, "The United States Role"; *FRUS,* 1946, VIII, pp. 197–198, 298–299, 339–340, 389–390.
30 United Kingdom to MacArthur, June 1, 1948, records of SCAP, 6323, "Sterling Area Trade Arrangements," tab B. See also SCAP Monographs, "Commerce," vol. XVII, pt. 1, on Foreign Trade.
31 Nanto, "The United States Role."
32 Saltzman to Draper, November 12, 1947, *FRUS,* 1947, VI, pp. 313–314; Saltzman to State-War-Navy Coordinating Committee secretary, October 9, 1947, DOS, 894.50.
33 Saltzman to State-War-Navy Coordinating Committee secretary, October 9, 1947, DOS, 894.50. Howard Schonberger, "General William S. Draper, the 80th Congress and the Origins of Japan's Reverse Course," 1980, in author's possession.
34 McCoy to Hilldring, June 20, 1947, DOS, "FEAC"; McCoy to Hill-

dring, August 11, 1947, DOS, 894.50. For McCoy's dilemma, see George Blakeslee, *The Far Eastern Commission,* Department of State Publication 5138, Far East Series 60, 1953. McCoy was especially embarrassed by the subsequent Draper mission. See Saltzman and Butterworth to Marshall, May 17, 1948, DOS, "FEAC." American policy was expressed by Kennan, who said of the FEC: "We could easily render it quiescent, and permit it to languish as long as we please" (Kennan to MacArthur, March 25, 1948, *FRUS,* 1948, VI, p. 704).

35 Blakeslee, *The Far Eastern Commission.*

36 Barnett to Martin, September 30, 1947, DOS, 894.50; McCoy to Hilldring, June 20, 1947, DOS, "FEAC." For Evatt (Australian foreign minister), see "SWNCC Corrigendum to SANACC 381/1," records of SCAP, 5976, "CAD-1947"; W. MacMahon Ball, *Japan: Enemy or Ally* (New York: John Day, 1949).

37 Sebald memo, October 26, 1947, *FRUS,* 1947, VI, pp. 547–548; for Philippine reaction, see Ely memo, March 15, 1948, *FRUS,* 1948, VI, p. 683. See also ibid., pp. 799–800, 812–813, 854–855.

38 For Strike, see Ross to Marquat, December 5, 1947, records of the civil affairs division, Department of the Army, Modern Military Branch, National Archives, box 48. SCAP to Department of Army, December 15, 1947, ibid.

39 Martin Bennett, "Japanese Reparations: Fact or Fantasy," *Pacific Affairs* (June 1948), pp. 185–193.

40 Ibid.; Draper copy of FEC committee report on "Strike and Johnston Reports," June 9, 1948, records of the office of the under secretary of the Army, Modern Military Branch, National Archives, box 54.

41 Kennan conversation with MacArthur and Draper, PPS 28, "Recommendations with Respect to U.S. Policy toward Japan," conversations of March 1, 5, 28, 1948, *FRUS,* 1948, VI, pp. 697–719 (also in records of State Department Policy Planning staff, box 1).

42 Johnston Report, records of SCAP, 5977, "Draper Mission." See also oral history interview with William Draper, Truman Library.

43 Marshall to Royall, September 17, 1948, Draper/Voorhees project file, 1947–1950, Modern Military Branch, National Archives, RG 335, box 18; Bishop to Butterworth, December 17, 1948, *FRUS,* 1948, VI, p. 1065.

44 Gross to Saltzman, "Legal Obligations of the United States with Respect to Japanese Reparations," December 27, 1948, *FRUS,* 1948, VI, pp. 1068–1073; Tate to Acheson, January 27, 1949, *FRUS,* 1949, VII, p. 632.

45 Nitze to Thorp, January 27, 1949, *FRUS,* 1949, VII, pp. 609–614.

46 Sebald to Butterworth, July 26, 1949, *FRUS,* 1949, VII, p. 809; Webb to Acheson, May 27, 1949, ibid., p. 759.

47 Saltzman to Acheson, January 27, 1949, *FRUS,* 1949, VII, pp. 639–640; for the views of the Far East division, see Butterworth to Acheson, January 27, 1949, ibid., pp. 633–639.

48 Acheson memo of conversation with McCoy, February 28, 1949, Acheson Papers, Truman Library, box 64; Acheson memo, February 1, 1949, *FRUS,* 1949, VII, pp. 640–642. NSC 13/3, "Recommendations with Respect to United States Policy toward Japan," May 6, 1949, ibid., pp. 730–736.

49 For McCoy speech, see Acheson to diplomatic officers, April 27, 1949, *FRUS,* 1949, VII, pp. 716–720; for protests, see ibid., p. 813 (Canada), Acheson to Sebald, March 24, 1949, ibid., pp. 689–690 (Romulo); chargé in Australia to Acheson, May 13, 1949, DOS, 711.90, "Control Japan"; New Zealand protests of May 17, 1949, and April 22, 1948, DOS, FEAC; *Economist,* November 20, 1948, p. 828. See also "United States Repudiates Philippine and Chinese Complaints on Japanese Reparations Removals," *Department of State Bulletin* 20 (June 26, 1949): 831–833.

50 Asahi Shimbun, *The Pacific Rivals* (New York: Weatherill Asahi, 1976), pp. 191–192. Mark Gayn, *Japan Diary* (New York: William Sloane, 1948).

51 The best source on the Japan Lobby is Howard Schonberger, "The Japan Lobby in American Diplomacy," *Pacific Historical Review,* January 1977.

52 Memo of conversation with the National Foreign Trade Council, "Economic Aspects of the Japanese Occupation," July 27, 1948, DOS, 894.50. For corporate concern over affiliates in Japan, see Draper memo of July 26, 1948, meeting with National Foreign Trade Council, office of the under secretary of the Army files, National Archives, 51, SAOUS, 004, Japan.

53 Kennan conversations with MacArthur and Draper, PPS 28, records of Department of State Policy Planning staff, box 1; George F. Kennan, *Memoirs, 1925–1950* (Boston: Little, Brown, 1967), pp. 386–387; MacArthur to civil affairs division, records of the civil affairs division, Department of Army, box 248, p. 8; MacArthur letter, January 9, 1948, ibid., box 249.

54 Edward Welsh, "Democratization of Business Program," August 28, 1949, records of SCAP, 5981, "Voorhees trip." Welsh blasted the reverse course, attributing the gutting of the deconcentration program to "(1) Growing resistance on the part of the present Japanese Government to having the special privileges and control of their powerful friends diminished; (2)

Support of this undemocratic movement by non-Japanese who also oppose freedom of competition—freedom of enterprise outside Japan; (3) Misunderstanding on the part of some and payment of lip service on the part of others to the idea that economic recovery in Japan is in conflict with the development of democratic capitalism; (4) Misunderstanding by some and deliberate compounding of the confused idea on the part of others that the program has been about completed and that Japan has practically overnight become free of cartels and combines and Zaibatsu influences and restraints of trade and government ownership in and control over private business." See also Kennan conversations with MacArthur, PPS 28.

55 For Butterworth, see conversation with National Foreign Trade Council; for Draper, see oral history interview with William Draper, Truman Library.

56 Feary to Penfield, January 1, 1948, DOS, 894.50. Army Secretary Royall complained to the NAC in December 1948 that the Army Department was criticized both for interfering too much in the Japanese economy and for not sufficiently controlling and stabilizing the Japanese economy (NAC meeting, December 3, 1948, records of the National Advisory Council, National Archives). At this meeting the NAC decided to order a stabilization program to control wages before approving EROA aid.

57 Saltzman to Draper, September 13, 1948, DOS, 894.50; Lincoln to Saltzman, October 15, 1948, ibid. These memos discuss the "pay-as-you-go" suggestion and the decontrol of the Japanese economy. For the ECA, see Butterworth to Allison, "Possible Inclusion of Japan within the Orbit of ECA Operations," October 23, 1948, DOS, 894.50; Allison to Butterworth, October 29, 1948, ibid.; Butterworth and Thorp to Webb, September 27, 1949, ibid.; Fearey and Hemmindinger to Allison, October 21, 1949, ibid.

58 For "Standby SCAP" idea, see Howard to Merchant, February 6, 1949, DOS, 894.50, and Hemmindinger and Fearey to Allison, October 21, 1949, ibid.

59 PPS 28, March 25, 1948, *FRUS, 1948,* VI, pp. 693–695; Sebald memo, July 26, 1949, *FRUS, 1949,* VII, p. 809; Bishop to Butterworth, February 18, 1949, ibid., p. 660; Webb to Acheson, May 27, 1949, ibid., p. 759; NSC 13/3, May 6, 1949, ibid., pp. 733–737.

60 Acheson to diplomatic officers, December 27, 1949, *FRUS, 1949,* VII, p. 932.

61 Kurusu to Draper, March 26, 1949 (cited in Nanto, "The American Role," p. 54). Draper oral history interview, Truman Library; Lincoln to Draper, November 18, 1948, Draper/Voorhees file, box 19, "Stabilization Program, 091.3."

62 Ralph Young et al., "Report of the Special Mission on Yen Foreign Exchange Rate Policy," June 12, 1948, pp. 9, 22, 23, 42, Nanto Collection.

63 C.J. Hynning memo, "Some Issues on the Financial Agenda for Planning Aid for Asia and Post-ECA Europe," April 11, 1950, Department of Treasury, 67-A-245, box 14, "Far East General"; "NAC Proposed Cable to Young Mission," n.d., Department of Treasury 67-A-245, box 22, "Japan: Missions, Young, 1948." For Treasury opposition to aid, see Stuart to Willis, November 22, 1949, 67-A-245, Department of Treasury, box 20; "Japan Aid Program."

64 Ralph Young et al., "Report of the Special Mission . . ."

65 Treasury Department memo, "Basic Differences of Judgement between Washington and SCAP," July 1, 1948, Department of Treasury, 67-A-245, box 22. NAC meeting, December 2, 1948, records of the National Advisory Council, National Archives.

66 NAC meeting, December 3, 1948, records of the National Advisory Council, National Archives; NAC meeting, December 2, 1948, ibid. SCAP told the Army that another year of inflation was preferred to the impact of the stabilization program on recovery.

67 Sherwood Fine, "Japan's Postwar Industrial Recovery" (Tokyo: Foreign Affairs Association of Japan, 1953), pp. 31, 36, 37; Economic Stabilization Board, "Five Year Plan for Japanese Economic Rehabilitation," records of SCAP, 8354; Ross to Marquat, April 28, 1948, ibid.

68 "Program for a Self-Supporting Japanese Economy," November, 1948, records of SCAP, 8361.

69 Eberle to Draper, November 29, 1948, and MacArthur to SAOUS, December 12, 1948, records of the office of the under secretary of the Army, 50, "Japan SAOUS"; Lincoln to Draper, November 18, 1948; Dodge memo, December 13, 1948, Dodge Papers, Nanto Collection.

70 Dodge memo, "Notes on the Inflation Problem," n.d., Dodge Papers, in the collection of John W. Dower. Dodge wrote that there were "three simple truths. The first is that the standard of living can only be improved by increased production—one cannot consume more than one produces. The second is that saving is a necessary prerequisite for progress. And the third is the necessity for the state economy to balance and the state expenses not to exceed the economic possibilities of the country" ("Notes for the Dodge File," n.d., Dodge Papers, Nanto Collection). Dodge to Martin Bronfenbrenner, June 12, 1950, ibid.

71 Dodge memo, "Notes on the Inflation Problem," n.d., Dodge Papers, Nanto Collection.

72 For stabilization directive, see Fine, "Japan's Postwar Industrial Recov-

ery," pp. 36–37; Dodge to Ikeda, August 9, 1949, Dodge Papers, Nanto Collection.

73 Dodge to Ikeda, August 9, 1949, Dodge Papers, Nanto Collection.

74 For the benefits of the Reconstruction Finance Bank, see George C. Allen, *Japan's Economic Recovery* (London: Oxford Univ. Press, 1958), p. 33. Dodge memo, April 7, 1949, "Counterpart Fund and Credit Policy," Dodge Papers, Nanto Collection; Dodge to Japanese government, April 1, 1949, ibid.

75 Dodge memo, March 30, 1949, Dodge Papers, Dower Collection. For debate on the impact of the Dodge Plan, see Nanto, "The United States Role," pp. 280–281.

76 Dodge to Bronfenbrenner, June 12, 1950, Dodge Papers, Nanto Collection; Robert W. Barnett, "Problems in Japan's Economic Recovery," *Far Eastern Survey,* May 4, 1949, p. 103.

77 For economic events in Japan in 1949, see *Bank of Japan Quarterly Review,* January through December 1949.

78 Ormond Freile et al., "Report of the Advisory Mission for International Trade" (Tokyo, 1949), Dower Collection. For an examination of Japan and the British Empire, see Chapter 6.

79 Freile et al., "Report of the Advisory Mission for International Trade"; Jan V. Mladek and Ernest A. Wichin, "Confidential Supplement to the Report on Exchange and Trade Controls in Japan," November, 1949, Nanto Collection. For Logan Plan, see memo on programs and statistics division staff meeting, February 27, 1950, records of SCAP, 8034, "Staff Meetings."

80 For MacArthur's complaint on aid cuts, see "NAC Weekly Group," December 15, 1949, Department of Treasury, 67-A-245, box 21, "Japan— Economic and Financial"; Marquat to Department of Army, March 17, 1949, records of SCAP, 6329, "FY 50 GARIOA-EROA"; Marquat to Voorhees, May 25, 1949, ibid., NAC, "Economic Summary for Japan," November 1949, DOS, 894.50, December 21, 1949; Stuart to Willis, November 22, 1949, Department of Treasury, 67-A-245, box 20, "Japan: Aid Program"; Acheson memos of conversations, December 15, 1949, meeting with Voorhees, Acheson Papers, box 64, "December 1949."

81 United Kingdom memo to MacArthur, June 1, 1948, records of SCAP, 6323, "Sterling Area Trade Arrangements," tab B; Sebald to Department of State, July 22, 1949, records of POLAD, Washington National Records Center, 2293, "500—Economic Affairs."

82 *Bank of Japan Quarterly Review,* January–March 1950, p. 6.

83 Acheson memos of conversations, January and February, 1950, have

discussions about the International Wheat Agreement and Japan. Department of Army memo, March 8, 1950, the International Wheat Agreement. All in Acheson Papers, box 65.

84 See Japan Management Association (Keizai Doyu Kai), "Recent Conditions of Japan's Economy," December 7, 1949, DOS, 894.50; Economic Stabilization Board, "Items of Solicitation in Connection with Enforcement of Economic Stabilization Program," November 9, 1949, records of SCAP, 8105, "ESB." The Bank of Japan issued the following analysis of the problems facing the Dodge Plan: "The Dodge Plan was designed to achieve compulsory accumulation of capital through public finance, to increase production and to cover the resultant imbalance between domestic production and consumption with promoted exports. The setting up of the single foreign exchange rate aimed also at indirectly supporting the promotion of exports. A review of the export developments after the enforcement of the Dodge Plan, however, shows that business failed to expand as expected, due to an unusual combination of adverse factors. It was quite natural that the establishment of the single exchange rate dealt a serious blow to those enterprises which were not able to operate profitably at a high yen rate. It must be pointed out, however, that various unfavorable factors coincided with the enforcement of the Dodge Plan, such as a downward tendency of commodity prices abroad, the U.S. in particular, the continued shortage of dollar funds in the non-dollars areas, difficulties in the convertibility between the dollar and pound sterling, an expansion in the scope of internecine warfare in China, the devaluation of the pound-sterling, and difficulties in the thorough rationalization of Japanese industrial enterprises" (*Bank of Japan Quarterly Review,* January–March 1950, p. 41). Economic Stabilization Board, "Analysis of Economy in Transition," August, 1, 1949, Dower Collection. The *Oriental Economist* attacked the Dodge Plan throughout 1949 and early 1950.

85 *Asahi Shimbun,* February 13, 1950, cited in *Nippon Times,* February 14, 1950. For discussion about the high costs of American imports, see *Nippon Times,* January 1, 1950, p. 3.

86 Morrow to Marquat, June 29, 1950 (on unemployment figures), records of SCAP, 5980. For criticisms of Ikeda, see *Nippon Times,* March 3, 1950, p. 1. Ikeda pleaded with Dodge to release counterpart funds (Dodge meeting with Ikeda, December 8, 1949, records of SCAP, 5977, "Dodge Mission"). For Yoshida's plan to send Ikeda to the United States, see Marquat to Yoshida, March 22, 1950, and MacArthur to Yoshida, May 24, 1950, records of SCAP, 5980, "Prime Minister" (MacArthur said that "the present difficult economic situation in Japan is the direct result

of Dodge's recommendations," and that Dodge should stay in Japan to oversee his program). Sebald to Butterworth, July 26, 1949, *FRUS, 1949*, VII, p. 810. For meeting of Dodge and Ikeda in the United States, see May 3, 1950, memo on meetings of April 30 and May 2, 1950, Department of Treasury, 67-A-245, box 22, "Japan: Missions to United States."

87 *U.S. News and World Report,* April 28, 1950; "ESS/LAB Comments on the Dodge Plan," n.d., Dodge Papers, Dower Collection; Morrow to Marquat, "The Deflationary Crisis and the Counterpart Fund," January 14, 1950, records of SCAP, 8355, "Misc."

88 Dodge to Marquat, July 22, 1949. Dodge wrote that "the *Oriental Economist* appears part of propaganda directed to reversing the stabilization program, or failing that, create fears which stimulate plunging the economy into disaster if possible" (records of SCAP, 8348, "Dodge"). See also Fine to Morrow, June 3, 1950, with excerpts from Dodge memo of May 18, 1950, records of SCAP, 8033, "Corporate Stats"; Diehl blasted the Bank of Japan article on the Dodge Plan (see note 84) and argued that the Japanese were too pessimistic despite high inventories; Diehl praised the efficiency generated by layoffs. (Diehl to Dodge, April 27, 1950, Department of Treasury, 67-A-245, box 22, "Japan: Missions— Dodge, 1949–1952").

89 Nanto, "The United States Role." Nanto confirms the argument of the *Oriental Economist* (January 7, 1950) that prices were due to fall in 1949 and 1950 even without the Dodge Plan, as inflationary forces had largely been exhausted by 1949. There are two critical facts about the Japanese economy on the eve of the Korean War: the first was that investment was not yet sufficient to finance industrial modernization; the second was that foreign trade obstacles associated with the world dollar gap and postwar trade dislocations prevented export demand from compensating for limited domestic demand. Two experts testified before the Diet that there was a contradiction between austerity and the need for investment; Japanese business was starved for capital (*Nippon Times,* February 15, 1950, p. 1). Japanese business sought to import massive amounts of capital to finance industrial modernization. This was a central theme of their economic policy because they realized trade recovery depended on more modern production methods. See Economic Stabilization Board, "Private Foreign Investment," December 19, 1949, Dower Collection. Although Nanto concludes that the Dodge Plan did not lengthen the recovery process significantly, he does recognize that world trade conditions held the key to recovery: "Japanese export elasticity vis-à-vis world trade was high." He adds that American and Japanese

policymakers were "lucky that the Korean War rescued them from this predicament" ("The United States Role," pp. 156, 288). Dodge to Bronfenbrenner, June 12, 1950, Nanto Collection. Allen, *Japan's Economic Recovery,* p. 34, discusses the efforts of the Japanese to weaken the Dodge Plan. Marquat to Garvin, June 13, 1950, Nanto Collection.

90 Chalmers Johnson, *Conspiracy at Matsukawa* (Berkeley: Univ. of California Press, 1972), pp. 23–24.

Chapter 3

1 Grew to Arita, June 19, 1940, *FRUS,* Japan 1931–41, II, pp. 84, 85.

2 Ibid. Matsuoka address, December 19, 1940, *FRUS,* Japan 1931–41, II, pp. 125–126; Grew to secretary of state, January 27, 1941, ibid., p. 134; Ballantine memo, December 1, 1941, ibid., p. 774; Nomura to secretary of state, December 7, 1941, pp. 787–793.

3 Hull memos, April 14, 1941, *FRUS,* Japan 1931–41, II, p. 404, and May 11, 1941, ibid., p. 417; Ballantine memo of November 7, 1941, ibid., p. 708; Welles memo of October 24, 1941, ibid., p. 695.

4 State Department memo on "Informal Japanese-American Conversations: 1941," May 19, 1942, *FRUS,* Japan 1931–41, II, pp. 328–329. See also Grew memo of November 11, 1941, on Japanese rights in Asia, ibid., pp. 711, 713.

5 "Joint Declaration by the United States and Japan on Economic Policy," November 15, 1941, *FRUS,* Japan 1931–41, II, pp. 734–737.

6 Hull memo, March 8, 1941, *FRUS,* Japan 1931–41, II, pp. 389–395.

7 For American open-door diplomacy, see Thomas McCormick, *China Market* (Chicago: Quadrangle, 1967). For American-Japanese relations in the New Deal era, see Lloyd C. Gardner, *Economic Aspects of New Deal Diplomacy* (Boston: Beacon, 1964), pp. 133–152.

8 Max Bishop memo, November 11, 1945, Nanto Collection.

9 Singapore Consul General Josselyn to secretary of state, January 7, 1947, *FRUS,* 1947, VI, pp. 54–55.

10 Byrnes to embassy in Paris, January 8, 1947, *FRUS,* 1947, VI, p. 58, and Stanton, minister in Siam, to secretary of state, January 7, 1947, ibid., pp. 56–57. American multilateral policy did not envision eliminating European influence in Asia, just sharing control with the United States and Japan. Russell Fifield has noted that battle between the European and Far Eastern desks of the State Department over colonialism in Asia: while all officials sought an "open door" policy, they agreed colonialism was preferable to Communism (*Americans in Southeast Asia* [New York: Crowell, 1973], pp. 68–71).

11 There are three particularly useful studies of Asian development. Clifford Geertz, *Agricultural Involution* (Berkeley: Univ. of California Press, 1968), is a brilliant study of development retarded by colonialism. It is one of the best analyses of dualistic development, where the modern sector, with its advanced technology and high wages, causes the decay of the traditional sector, upon which most of the population depends. Mark Selden edited *Remaking Asia: Essays on the American Uses of Power* (New York: Pantheon, 1974), containing useful essays on the Western economic impact on Southeast Asian development. Especially valuable are studies of Western and Japanese institutions, such as the IMF and Asian Development Bank, and their control over Asian development policies. Finally, the Asian Development Bank's *Southeast Asia's Economy in the 1970s* (London: Longman, 1972) lays out the Western/Japanese approach to development: encouragement of favorable conditions for foreign investment, industries limited to first-stage processing of local raw materials, and emphasis on increasing primary exports. This study reveals the lack of progress in Western development theory, which is based on the needs of the industrial nations and which ignores the empirical and theoretical arguments for economic diversity as the key to development within a global trading system.

12 Sumner to Lockhart, on Coppock's memo, July 2 and August 25, 1945, "Basic Policies and Objectives of the U.S. in the Pacific and the Far East," DOS, 890.50.

13 Translations of Japanese article of February 15, 1946, "Loss of Overseas Territories and Effect on Japan's Economy," records of POLAD, 2279, "850"; "Trade and Financial Arrangements," n.d., records of SCAP, 6712. See also SCAP Monograph on "Foreign Trade," p. 153.

14 Penfield to Bennett, November 29, 1946, DOS, 890. 50; Hamilton to Nitze, November 14, 1946, ibid.

15 See Martin memo, March 12, 1947, *FRUS*, 1947, VI, pp. 184–186; SWNCC 381, July 22, 1947, records of SCAP, 7689; Kennan memo, PPS 10, October 14, 1947, *FRUS*, 1947, VI, p. 541. See also Sebald to secretary of state, September 16 and 27, 1947, ibid., pp. 290–295. Before the Communist victory in China, the preferred trade area for Japan was termed "Mainland Asia," referring to China, Korea, and Southeast Asia. After 1948, the most common term used was "Southeast Asia," i.e., Burma, Thailand, Indochina, Malaya, the Philippines, and Indonesia. The term "South and Southeast Asia," which included India and Pakistan, was also common. Recall from Chapter 2 that the disagreement between the Army and State departments over recovery policy stemmed from conflicting views on the need for tact to obtain Southeast Asian cooperation in Japanese trade revival.

16 Allison memo, December 17, 1947, DOS, 894.50. SWNCC 381 did consider Japan's need to trade with Southeast Asia, but did not consider using incentives to induce cooperation with Japan.

17 Department of Research for the Far East, "Economic Recovery in Japan" (DRF 59A), May 3, 1948, records of SCAP, 7688, "Economic Recovery Plan."

18 Sebald to secretary of state, October 24, 1947, *FRUS, 1947,* VI, pp. 308–310. Sherwood Fine represented SCAP at the ECAFE conference in the Philippines in December 1947.

19 *New York Herald Tribune,* December 4, 1947, DOS, 501 BD Asia; *Manila Evening News,* December 15, 1947, ibid.; Lovett to Davis, December 1, 1947, ibid.

20 Whitman to Gilpatrick, August 1, 1947, DOS, 894.50.

21 U.S. consul general in Shanghai to POLAD, July 15, 1947, in State-War-Navy Coordinating Committee corrigendum to SANACC 381/1, records of SCAP, 5976, "CAD, 1947"; Barnett to Martin, May 13, 1947, DOS, 894.50. See also John W. Dower, "Occupied Japan in an American Lake," in Mark Selden and Edward Friedman, eds., *America's Asia* (New York: Vantage, 1971), p. 189.

22 Lacy and Ogburn to Reed, November 19, 1948, DOS, FW 501 BD Asia.

23 Ibid. For analysis of Asian opposition and the necessity of focusing on Japan, see Edward P. Reubens, "Asia and Truman's 4th Point," *Far Eastern Survey,* March 23, 1949, pp. 61–67.

24 Brown to Gay, "CP Comments on Japanese Economic Policy," December 27, 1948, DOS, 890.50. This memo pleads for the United States to focus on China instead of unreliable Southeast Asia. It maintains that there is no evidence that Soviet-dominated forces will win in China. Not clear is whether the author means that Chiang will win or that Mao is not dominated by the Soviets.

25 Cowen to secretary of state, December 3, 1948, DOS, 501 BD Asia; Marshall to Cowen, November 26, 1948, ibid.

26 Sydney to secretary of state, December 6, 1948, DOS, 501 BD Asia; Lovett to Lapstone, December 6, 1948, ibid.; Durward V. Sandifer to Cowen, October 7, 1949, ibid.

27 Sebald to Acheson (relating Fine report), November 12, 1949, DOS, 894.50. "U.S. Position Paper on ECAFE Committee Meetings," October 7, 1949, DOS, 501 BD Asia. See also David Wightman, *Toward Economic Cooperation in Asia: The ECAFE* (New Haven: Yale Univ. Press, 1963), p. 275.

28 "U.S. Position Paper on ECAFE Committee Meetings," October 7, 1949, DOS, 501 BD Asia.

29 Institute for Pacific Relations, *Problems of Reconstruction in the Far East* (New York, 1949), p. 82.

30 Sebald to the State Department, March 29, 1948, and October 7, 1949, DOS, 894.50. Economic Stabilization Board, "Five Year Plan for Japanese Economic Rehabilitation," 1948, records of SCAP, 8354. The Economic Stabilization Board declared that Japan could not "consider Japan's resuscitation independently of the resuscitation of East Asia as a whole" because of the need for raw materials.

31 Civil affairs division, Department of Army, "Japan and the Ryukus: Problems of the U.S. Army in Occupation," January 1, 1948, pp. 23–25, records of SCAP, 8354; Department of Army, "Economic Rehabilitation of Japan, South Korea, and the Ryukus, April 1, 1948, to June 30, 1949," records of SCAP, 6727. SCAP advised that "Japan is actively gearing its productive capacities to meet these new productive demands of the ECAFE countries." "ECAFE Regional Capital Requirements and Japan's Potential Contribution," n.d., records of SCAP, 8031, "Foreign Trade, ECAFE Region." This was most likely a study in response to an Army request for SCAP to plan the "role and contribution of Japan in increasing production in Southeast Asia." CSCAD to SCAP, July 23, 1948, records of SCAP, 6709, "Trade Program."

32 ESS, "Program for a Self-Supporting Japanese Economy," November, 1948, records of SCAP, 8361; Daniel Cox Flaherty, National Security Resources Board, to Admiral Souers on NSC 13 revision, August 10, 1948, DOS, 894.50; Draper to Lovett, December 14, 1948, records of SCAP, 7688, "Program for a Self-Supporting Japanese Economy."

33 Lovett to Draper, December 28, 1948, records of SCAP, 7688 (also in *FRUS,* 1948, VI, pp. 1073–1075). State Department Policy Planning staff, PPS 28, "Policy with respect to Japan," records of the State Department Policy Planning Staff, RG 59, box 1, NARS. See "Conversations with MacArthur PPS 28," p. 4.

34 "Meeting of Economic Consultants," John A. Loftus, Jacob Viner, Edward S. Mason, Clair Wilcox, December 3, 1948, DOS, 890.50.

35 Edwin Martin memo, March 12, 1947, *FRUS,* 1947, VI, pp. 184–186.

36 Butterworth to Lovett, October 27, 1948, DOS, 890.50.

37 Ibid.; Magill to Butterworth, June 2, 1949, DOS, 890.50. Magill notes the extreme sensitivity of the economic affairs division's plan to integrate Japan and Southeast Asia. This study cannot undertake to analyze comparative Asian economic development in the postwar period, specifically, the question of the economic "miracle" of South Korea and Taiwan, in contrast to the six Southeast Asian states. Suffice it to say

that such an analysis would have to go beyond gross national product growth.

38 Jerome Cohen, "Japan's Economy on the Road Back," *Pacific Affairs* (September 1948), p. 279; Robert V. Barnett, "Problems in Japan's Economic Recovery," *Far Eastern Survey,* May 4, 1949, p. 103. See Yole Granada, "Should We Rebuild Japan," *Nation,* August 14, 1948, pp. 180–182, and reply by Harold Strauss, August 21, p. 214; W. MacMahon Ball, *Japan: Enemy or Ally* (New York: John Day, 1949), p. 186.

39 Joseph Z. Reday, "Reparations from Japan," *Far Eastern Survey,* June 29, 1949, pp. 146–149. See also Tokyo dispatch of September 13, 1949, to State Department (DOS, 894.50), which contains Tokyo speeches by Brooks Emeny and Sherwood Fine of August 30, 1949, calling for U.S. technical assistance to increase raw material production in Southeast Asia.

40 Dodge statement for the NAC, "FY 51 Appropriation for Economic Aid to Japan," January 19, 1950, Dodge Papers, Nanto Collection.

41 Acheson to state department officers, July 11, 1949, DOS, 894.50.

42 Ibid.

43 For ESS thinking on China trade, see Sebald memo of January 7, 1949, records of POLAD, 2293, "500 Economic Affairs." Dulles warned Acheson that Japan was extremely vulnerable to Communist influence because of its proximity to Communist Asia, its economic dependence on China, its history of totalitarian government, its pacifism, and its non-Western, noncapitalist proclivity for collectivism (Dulles to Acheson, June 7, 1950, *FRUS,* 1950, VI, pp. 1207–1212). For the great ambivalence on China trade, see mèeting between Butterworth and the Department of Army, January 10, 1949, office of the under secretary of the Army, box 53, "123.7 Japan"; Lincoln memo, January 8, 1949, Draper/Voorhees file, box 18. For SCAP pressure for trade with China to help Japan's dollar problem, see Department of Army to SCAP, March 10, 1949, C. C. Campbell memo of August 13, 1949, and Marquat to Voorhees, December 6, 1949, all in records of SCAP, 6288, "Secret and Other Classified Material Pertaining to General Subjects," vols. 1 and 2; and Hale to Marquat, April 18, 1950, records of SCAP, 6810, "Reports of Special Committees." For dealing with Mao, see Bangkok conference conclusion that "recognition by U.S. of Chinese Communists would be a severe blow to U.S. interests in Asia" (office of under secretary of the Army to SCAP, February 22, 1950, Draper/Voorhees file, box 18). An excellent treatment of this subject is Nancy Bernkopf Tucker, "Sino-Japanese Trade in the Postwar Years: Politics and Pros-

perity," 1982, unpublished manuscript in the author's possession. This paper explores the insoluble contradictions between American desires to ostracize Mao and Western desire to trade with China. See especially pp. 20–21.

44 Acheson to State Department officers, May 8, 1949, *FRUS,* 1949, VII, p. 736.

45 NSC 41, "U.S. Policy with Respect to Asia," February 8, 1949, records of the National Security Council, Modern Military Branch, National Archives. See also Nancy Bernkopf Tucker, "Sino-Japanese Trade," pp. 20–29.

46 Marshall Green, memo of conversation with British representatives, September 9, 1949, DOS, 711.90 (and *FRUS,* 1949, VII, pp. 853–855). It is impossible to determine what decision would have emerged on Japanese-Chinese trade had the Korean War not broken out in 1950. Yet the rigid ideological policy of NSC 68 to create extreme global polarization and increase tensions between East and West led to Korean intervention and would likely have prevented any meaningful rapprochement between China and Japan, despite the awareness of Japan's trade needs. See Lacy to Rusk, September 5, 1950, *FRUS,* 1950, VI, pp. 140–141.

47 PPS 51, "U.S. Policy towards Southeast Asia," *FRUS,* 1949, VII, pp. 1128–1130.

48 Bishop to Rusk, August 24, 1949, DOS, 890.20 (and *FRUS,* 1949, VII, p. 1192).

49 *Nippon Times,* January 13, 1950, p. 1; Reed memo of conversation with British representatives, February 23, 1949, *FRUS,* 1949, VII, pp. 118–119; Butterworth memo, December 24, 1949, ibid., p. 931; Butterworth memo, September 12, 1949, DOS, 890.20 (and *FRUS,* 1949, VII, pp. 1197–1200).

50 Hale memo, May 20, 1950, records of SCAP, 5977; *Nippon Times,* January 23, 1950, p. 6.

51 Japan Management Association, "The Present Condition of the Japanese Economy," December 7, 1949, p. 23, DOS, 894.50; Economic Stabilization Board, "Japan's Share in the Economic Development of Southeast Asia," January 28, 1950, records of SCAP, 8105; Economic Stabilization Board, "On the Promotion of Trade Between Japan and Asia," April 18, 1950, ibid. See also Economic Stabilization Board, "Potential Capacity of Japan to Export Capital Goods to Southeast Asian Countries," ibid.; and Japanese Ministry of International Trade and Industry (MITI), "The Present Condition of Japanese Foreign Trade," May 29, 1950, records of SCAP, 6329; Hisato Ichimada to Robert West, March

23, 1950, Dower Collection; Inagaki statement in *Nippon Times,* January 10, 1950, p.3; SCAP, Monograph on "Foreign Trade," p. 246.

52 Reid to West, June 22, 1949, Dower Collection. Bishop to Butterworth, February 18, 1949, DOS, 894.00.

53 Tracy S. Voorhees, "Outline of Work as Under Secretary of the Army, August 1949 to April 1950," March 22, 1967, pp. 62–68, Tracy S. Voorhees Papers.

54 Tracy S. Voorhees, "Coordination of American Economic Aid to the Far East," attachment to NSC 61, January 10, 1950, Voorhees Papers and records of National Security Council; Stuart to Willis, February 10, 1950, Department of Treasury, 67-A-245, box 22, "Far East General."

55 Department of Army to SCAP, December 24, 1949, records of SCAP, 6726, "Confidential #2." See also secretary of the Army, Office of the under secretary to SCAP, December 31, 1949, Stanley Andrews Papers, Truman Library, box 2, "1949 General."

56 Andrews and West, "Report of the Southeast Asian and South Asian Food and Trade Mission," March 13, 1950, records of SCAP, 6365, "Andrews-West"; secretary of the Army, Office of Occupation Affairs, Budget Group (Wilfred Garvin) to Marquat, "Foreign Trade and Economic Aid Requirements," July 6, 1950, Dodge Papers, Nanto Collection. Garvin reported that of $176 million saved, $114 million derived from triangular trade earnings from nondollar areas, and only $6 million derived from increased sales to the dollar area. See also Andrews and West, "Coordination of American Economic Aid in South and Southeast Asia," Stanley Andrews Papers, box 2, "Trip to Thailand 1949"; Andrews and West to Voorhees, April 22, 1950, "Attachment A, Necessity for Authoritative Coordination of U.S. Aid Programs in the Far East," Stanley Andrews Papers, box 3, "Foreign Aid Memoranda."

57 Andrews and West to Voorhees, April 22, 1950, "Attachment A" and "Attachment B, Illustrative Potential Savings in Appropriated Funds Which Might Be Possible Through Effective Coordination of Far Eastern Aid Programs," Stanley Andrews Papers, box 3, "Foreign Aid Memoranda."

58 Andrews and West to Voorhees, April 22, 1950, Attachment B.

59 Marquat to Voorhees, March 22, 1950, MacArthur Papers, RG 9, DA CX C 55523; William Draper, "The Rising Sun of Japan," October 31, 1950, Dodge Papers, Dower Collection.

60 Voorhees to MacArthur, April 6, 1950, MacArthur Papers, RG 5.

61 Tracy S. Voorhees, "Outline of Work as Under Secretary of the Army." See also Voorhees's testimony before the Senate Appropriations Committee, *Foreign Aid Appropriations,* FY 51, May 1950, p. 532.

62 Statement by Senator Maybank, Senate Appropriations Committee, *Foreign Aid Appropriations,* FY 51, May 1950, p. 526. For textiles, see complaint of United Textile Workers, president's official file, Truman Library, box 27, "x197 misc." For Export-Import Bank credit restrictions, see statement by Senator McKellar, Senate Appropriations Committee, *Foreign Aid Appropriations,* FY 51, May 1950, p. 564. The senator specifically refers to the $100 million credit for Indonesia and insists it be spent in the United States. For Voorhees, see Tracy S. Voorhees, "Outline of Work as Under Secretary of the Army."

63 ECA, "Coordination of U.S. Assistance in the Far East," June 22, 1950, records of the Council on Foreign Economic Policy, 1953–54, Eisenhower Library, box 60, "Gray Report (2)."

64 Ibid.

65 Ibid. The British and Japanese both requested untied aid to Southeast Asia. For British request, see Acheson to embassy in France, August 30, 1950, *FRUS,* 1950, VI, p. 135; for Japanese request, see Economic Stabilization Board paper of November 11, 1949, Dower Collection.

66 These Japan-centric attitudes emerge strongly from the SCAP and Army records. The primary function of the ESS and the main concern of the Army were Japanese trade recovery and a reduction in the aid burden on the United States. Harlan Cleveland, head of the ECA's program in Asia, wrote that aid to Southeast Asia coordinated to help Japan "has very strong support within State" because it was an "obviously attractive proposition in terms of economizing on the expenditure of American Assistance funds. . . . At the same time it seems to me to possess grave dangers along both economic and political lines." Offering yen credits to finance Japanese trade would give "Japan a terrific bargaining advantage. . . . Certain difficulties that would be encountered in endeavoring to prevent an exploitation of essentially monopolistic advantages by Japan are fairly obvious. They include the natural tendency of American groups increasingly to sympathize with the country in which they are stationed as against other foreign countries, as well as the greater familiarity of such Americans with the necessities confronting Japan." He warned that the United States would be "accused of assisting Japan to restore a pre-war trading position by means of procedures associated therewith." Cleveland's memo reveals the Japan-oriented policies of SCAP, but does not recognize that the ECA, of course, was more familiar with Europe's necessities and that Europe had similar "terrific bargaining advantages" based on colonial ties, superior ability to offer credits to purchasers of capital goods, and American aid to European dependencies. Cleveland to Sumner, "Rumored State Department Staff

Ideas Re: Japanese Economy," April 22, 1950, John D. Sumner Papers, Truman Library.

67 Marquat to Department of the Army, February 13, 1950, records of SCAP, 6726, "GATT"; Department of Army to SCAP, February 10, 1950, ibid; "U.S. Position Paper on GATT," February 21, 1950, ibid; Fine memo of April 25, 1950, ibid.

68 Sebald to Acheson, July 17, 1948, DOS, 890.50. See also Butterworth to Smith, August 2, 1948, ibid. Butterworth warned that the conference should be small to avoid attracting attention to American aims to reintegrate Japan and Southeast Asia. Acheson to Sebald, December 22, 1949, DOS, 890.20.

69 Statements by Thomas Blaisdell, April 17, 10:30 AM and April 18, 1950, "Minutes of Department of State Tokyo Economic-Commercial Conference," records of SCAP, 6721.

70 Statement by Thomas Blaisdell, April 18, 1950, pp. 7–8. Statement by Mr. White, April 17, 1950, afternoon sessions, "Minutes of Department of State . . . Conference."

71 C. J. Hynning memo, "Some Issues on the Financial Agenda for Planning Aid for Asia and Post-ECA Europe," April 11, 1950, Department of Treasury, 67-A-245, box 14, "Far East General."

72 Stibravy statement, April 18, 8:30 AM session, "Minutes of Department of State . . . Conference," p. 14.

73 "Report of Committee II-C on Exchange Convertibility," "Minutes of Department of State . . . Conference"; Hale statement, ibid.

74 "Report of Committee I-A," "Minutes of Department of State . . . Conference."

75 Ibid.; Shohan to Merchant, March 16, 1950, *FRUS,* 1950, VI, p. 62.

76 April 18, 10:30 AM session, "Minutes of Department of State . . . Conference," p. 10; statement of Dr. Stevens, April 21, 9:00 AM session, p. 25, with Sebald statement following, ibid. The Griffin mission reported to Washington after a trip to Southeast Asia that "some Southeast Asian Governments had developed peculiar attitudes toward Westerners." Given the history of European colonization in Asia and the American effort to favor Japanese revival after a bitter war, the attitudes of Southeast Asian governments are not surprising. "Interdepartmental Meeting on the Far East," May 2, 1950, *FRUS,* 1950, VI, p. 90.

77 April 18, 8:30 AM session, "Minutes of the Department of State . . . Conference", p. 6; Ogburn memo, April 3, 1950, *FRUS,* 1950, VI, p. 73; C. J. Hynning memo, "Some Issues on the Financial Agenda. . . ."

78 Cleveland to Sumner, "Rumored State Department Staff Ideas Re: Jap-

anese Economy"; Shohan to Merchant, March 16, 1950, *FRUS,* 1950, VI, pp. 61–62 and note p. 1223. See C. J. Shohan memos to Merchant, March 8 and 9, 1950, records of the Philippines, Southeast Asia section, Far East division, DOS, box 1. Shohan mentioned the awkward domestic problem of keeping American exports out of Southeast Asia to favor Japan. Doherty to Allison, March 20, 1950, ibid., box 2.

79 Diehl to Sebald, June 20, 1950, *FRUS,* 1950, VI, pp. 1223–1227; Garvin to Marquat, May 29, 1950, records of SCAP, 8355. "Foreign Trade and Economic Aid Requirements," July 6, 1950, Dodge Papers, Nanto Collection.

80 See French to Morrow, attached to Morrow to Marquat, June 21, 1950, "Proposal to Change U.S. Aid Program Approach," Dodge Papers, Nanto Collection.

81 Stuart to Willis, May 18, 1950, Department of Treasury, 67-A-245, box 23, "Trade, Vol. I"; Diehl to Sebald, June 20, 1950, *FRUS,* 1950, VI, pp. 1223–1227.

82 Stuart to Willis, May 18, 1950, Department of Treasury, 67-A-245, box 23, "Trade, Vol. I"; Diehl to Sebald, June 20, 1950, *FRUS,* 1950, VI, pp. 1223–1227.

83 Shigeru Yoshida, *The Yoshida Memoirs* (London: Heineman, 1961), p. 192; Ohly to Lemnitzer, August 15, 1950, citing Ohly memo of June 9, 1950, on "Possible Contribution by SCAP to MDAP in South and Southeast Asia," *FRUS,* 1950, VI, p. 1275; Dodge Memo of May 8, 1950, Dodge Papers, Nanto Collection.

84 See NSC 64 and NSC 124/1, records of the National Security Council, National Archives. Memos relating to State Department thinking on Indochina are found in *FRUS,* 1950, VI, pp. 711–751. Johnson to Acheson, April 14, 1950, ibid., p. 784.

85 Samuel P. Hayes, *The Beginning of American Aid to Southeast Asia: The Griffin Mission of 1950* (Lexington, Mass.: D.C. Heath, 1971), p. 22; Marquat to Griffin, March 10, 1950, and Griffin to Marquat, records of SCAP, 5978, "Griffin Mission." Russell Fifield, *Americans in Southeast Asia* (New York: Crowell, 1973), pp. 142–147. Fifield has recalled that at the time of the Griffin mission, "Southeast Asia's potential as a bigger market for the industralized areas of the free world was widely accepted" (p. 250).

86 Fifield, *Americans in Southeast Asia,* pp. 247, 250, 251. For an analysis of the decision to intervene in Indochina by the Truman Administration, see Seigen Miyasato, "The Truman Administration and Indochina: Case Studies in Decision Making," *Japanese Journal of American Studies* 1 (1981): 119–149.

Chapter 4

1 Acheson to Embassy in Moscow, June 26, 1950, *FRUS,* 1950, VII, pp. 176–177.
2 Allison memo, July 27, 1950 *FRUS,* 1950, VI, p. 122; Dulles to Acheson, July 19, 1950, ibid., pp. 1243–1244. For American views on Japanese psychological vulnerability to Communism, see *FRUS,* 1950, VII, p. 151; Dulles to Acheson, November 30, 1950, *FRUS,* 1950, VI, p. 162. For Japanese views of China, see *Contemporary Japan,* 1952, pp. 311–312, and daily comments in the *Nippon Times.* The influence of John W. Dower's knowledge of the 1950–54 period is considerable in Chapters 4 and 5 of this work. His *Empire and Aftermath: Yoshida Shigeru and the Japanese Experiment, 1878–1954* (Cambridge: Harvard Univ. Press, 1979) presents the best overview of the period in English and reflects a rich understanding of Japanese sources.
3 Shigeru Yoshida, *The Yoshida Memoirs* (London: Heinemann, 1961), p. 192. Dodge advised MacArthur that since Gordon Gray had been appointed to study the dollar gap, "the issue of increasing foreign military aid has arisen. This promises to be a more extensive program than the initial disclosures indicate, and will directly affect the dollar gap. It will be necessary to have some integration of the two. . . . Our financial and economic commitments in the military area versus economic aid in Europe and, in the area of economic aid to the Far East versus Europe (including in the latter some military aid), seem to be on the move toward much larger totals" (Dodge to MacArthur, May 8, 1950, p. 4, Dodge Papers, Dower Collection). It is unknown if the deliberations on the dollar gap and military aid in Washington influenced Yoshida's thinking on using Japanese arsenals for American military intervention in Asia. For MacArthur's authorization of procurement, see Green to Allison, July 19, 1950, *FRUS,* 1950, VI, pp. 1244–1246.
4 "Korean War and the Japanese Economy," *Oriental Economist,* July 22, 1950, p. 746; "War Demand Rising," ibid., September 9, 1950, p. 947; "Japan's Export Will Mount," ibid., August 12, 1950, pp. 833–834; Economic Stabilization Board, *Monthly Economic Review,* August and September 1950, records of SCAP 8105; Economic Stabilization Board, "Recent Trend of Japan's Economy," October 1950, records of SCAP, 8105.
5 Economic Stabilization Board, "Impact on the Japanese Economy of Direct Procurement," November 16, 1950, records of SCAP, 8105; *Bank of Japan Monthly Review,* August through December 1950, and February 1951.

6 *U.S. News and World Report,* December 15, 1950, p. 22. For Japanese citing the war as a "savior," see *Oriental Economist,* May 5, 1951, p. 342; "Korean War and Foreign Trade," *Oriental Economist,* August 1953, pp. 381–384; and editorial in the *Mainichi Shimbun,* June 11, 1951, records of SCAP, 5977, "Economic Cooperation Missions."

7 Chalmers Johnson, *Conspiracy at Matsukawa* (Berkeley: Univ. of California Press, 1973), p. 23.

8 Asahi Shimbun, *The Pacific Rivals* (New York: Weatherill Asahi, 1972), pp. 179, 195.

9 *Oriental Economist,* February 3, 1951, p. 89; Asahi Shimbun, *The Pacific Rivals,* p. 193.

10 *Oriental Economist,* January 6, 1951, p. 6. See also *Oriental Economist,* February 10, 1951, p. 118; *Nippon Times,* November 5, 1950, p. 1; SCAP Monograph, "Foreign Trade," p. 228 (for economic growth).

11 *Nippon Times,* October 14, 1950, p. 8.

12 Fearey to Allison, August 18, 1950, *FRUS,* 1950, VI, p. 1266; William G. Jones, "The Impact of the Korean War on the Japanese Economy," summer 1950, Dodge Papers, Dower Collection.

13 Gordon Gray, "Report to the President on Foreign Economic Policy," November 11, 1950 (Washington, 1950). See *New York Times,* editorial, November 22, 1950, commenting on the optimism in Japan expressed by the Gray report; Trezise to Kauffman, August 21, 1950, records of the Commission on Foreign Economic Policy, Eisenhower Library, box 60, "Gray Report (2)"; secretary of the Army, Office of Occupied Areas, memo to White House, "Impact of Korean Developments on GARIOA FY 51 Budget, "records of SCAP, 7689, "FY51"; Garvin memo, August 8, 1950, and Garvin memo, "Economic Aid Requirements, Japan, FY 51," both in Dodge Papers, Dower Collection; Edward Mason to Carter Magruder, October 4, 1950, cites Magruder to Gray, September 29, 1950, and Hamblen to Mason, October 6, 1950, records of SCAP, 7692, "Dollar Gap." For Japanese pessimism about the misleading Gray report, see *Nippon Times,* November 15, 1950, p. 8, and Economic Stabilization Board, *Monthly Economic Review,* November 1950, p. 3.

14 Omar Bradley memo, October 15, 1950, *FRUS,* 1950, VII, p. 956; Acheson to Marshall, December 13, 1950, *FRUS,* 1950, VI, p. 1365. U. Alexis Johnson, of the Far East division of the State Department, wrote: "Dollars received by Japan, whether from GARIOA or PAYG would be equal to the estimated dollar deficit in the Japanese balance of payments but no more" (Johnson to Merchant, December 29, 1950, ibid., pp. 1393–1398). Dodge memo, "Post-Treaty Partial Pay-As-You-Go

Policy for Japan," Dodge Papers, Dower Collection. See also Rusk to Acheson, January 25, 1951, *FRUS,* 1951, VI, pt. 1, p. 809.

15 Dodge, "Press Statement to Yokohama," October 7, 1950, Dodge Papers, Dower Collection; Dodge, "Press Statement on U.S. Aid," ibid.; Dodge memo, "Equipment Import Trust Account," November 22, 1950, ibid.; "Comments on Dodge-Ikeda Conference," October 25, 1950, ibid.

16 Economic Stabilization Board, "Impact of the Korean War on the Japanese Economy," n.d., Dower Collection; Yoko Shigemi (minister of international trade and industry) to Marquat, January 31, 1951, records of SCAP, 6712, "Japan 1951." Economic Stabilization Board, "Basic Ideas Underlying Economic Self-Support Program," October, 1950, Dower Collection; Economic Stabilization Board, "Economic Self-Support Program," January 20, 1951, ibid. See also Self-Supporting Economy Council, "Report on Self-Support Program," January 20, 1951, records of SCAP, 8105.

17 Fearey to Dulles, January 25, 1951, *FRUS,* 1951, VI, pt. 1, p. 810.

18 Sebald to Marquat, "Comment on ESS Staff Study," December 28, 1951, records of SCAP, 5976, "Diplomatic Section."

19 Morrow to Marquat, "SCAP Washington Representatives," February 16, 1951, records of SCAP, 8348, "Reading File Classified—1951."

20 Dodge memo, "Japan–United States Economic Cooperation," n.d., Dodge Papers, Dower Collection.

21 Morrow to Marquat, "Japan's Industrial Potential, Vol. II," records of SCAP, 8110, "Secret Correspondence 1951–1952"; ESS, programs and statistics division, "Japan's Industrial Potential," February 21, 1951, Dower Collection.

22 ESS, "Japan's Industrial Potential." This is not to say that there was not concern on the part of strategic planners about Japan's obvious military vulnerability to an all-out Russian invasion of Japan.

23 Ibid. The State Department warned that production of arms in Japan for use other than in Korea was prohibited by the FEC in its "Prohibition of Military Activity in Japan," February 12, 1948, and "Reduction of Japanese War Potential," August 14, 1947 (Cabot to Burns, March 9, 1951, *FRUS,* 1951, VI, pt. 1, pp. 905–906). See also Burns to Matthews, February 22, 1951, ibid., p. 887.

24 ESS, "Japan's Industrial Potential."

25 ESS, programs and statistics division, "Coordination of U.S. Procurement under a U.S.-Japan Economic Cooperation Program," April 6, 1951, records of SCAP, 5977, "Economic Cooperation Mission"; "Marquat Mission Agenda," records of SCAP, 5977, "Economic Cooperation U.S.-Japan."

26 *Nippon Times,* May 17, 1951, p. 1; "Marquat Press Release," May 16, 1951, Dower Collection. On the change in procurement, see Russell Brines in *Nippon Times,* March 31, 1951; on increased procurement, see *Oriental Economist,* March 29, 1952, p. 242.

27 NSC 48/5, May 17, 1951, *FRUS,* 1951, VI, pt. 1, p. 38. See also Joint Strategic Plans Committee to Joint Chiefs, "Japan as a Source for Supply of U.S. Military Requirements," Joint Chiefs of Staff papers, National Archives, box 27, sec. 25, "Japan 1951–1953."

28 Marquat memo, "An Agency to Coordinate U.S. Procurement and Industrial Mobilization Activities in Japan," n.d., records of SCAP, 5977, "Marquat Mission."

29 Morrow to Harriman, December 21, 1951; Morrow to Marquat, December 26, 1951, records of SCAP, 6799, "U.S. Policy"; Morrow to Marquat, October 12, 1951, records of SCAP, 7693, "P&S"; Morrow report to Interdepartment Committee on Far East Mobilization (ICFEM), November 28, 1951, records of SCAP, 6799, "ICFEM Documents."

30 Minutes of ICFEM meeting, November 9, 1951, records of SCAP, 6799, "ICFEM Documents." The ICFEM cited a Department of Defense estimate that procurement orders for Japan would be cut. For the "Wilson Plan," see *New York Times,* July 22, 1951, pp. 1, 4.

31 Dulles testimony, Senate Foreign Relations Committee, *Executive Sessions,* Historical Series, vol. III, pt. 1, p. 273; Wilson to Lovett, November 15, 1951, Matthew Ridgway Papers, Army War College, Carlisle, Pa. (I am grateful to Howard Schonberger for copies of documents from the Ridgway Papers); Foster to Ridgway, November 21, 1951, ibid.; Ridgway to Lovett, December 8, 1951, ibid.; SCAP to the Department of Army, March 27, 1952, records of Joint Chiefs of Staff, Modern Military Branch. National Archives, box 26, 383.21, "Japan."

32 Morrow to Marquat, October 12, 1951, records of SCAP, 7693, "P&S." Dodge memo, "Japan—Post-Treaty Relationship," Dodge Papers, Dower Collection.

33 Sebald to Emmerson, September 30, 1951, *FRUS,* 1951, VI, pt. 1, pp. 1365, 1366, 1369. Morrow to Marquat, December 27, 1951, records of SCAP, 5980, "P&S." For Sebald critique, see Sherwood Fine memo, on Diplomatic Section memo, "Future Problems of U.S.-Japan Relationship," December 4, 1951, records of SCAP, 5976, "Diplomatic Section."

34 Fine memo, on Diplomatic Section memo.

35 Ernest Tupper to Marquat, April 17, 1951, records of SCAP, 7688, "Mladek Report"; Tupper memo, "Utilization of the Japanese Economic Potential," April 1951, records of SCAP, 8109, "15. memo PS/ADM 1951."

36 NSC 125/1, "U.S. Objectives and Courses of Action with Respect to Japan," July 28, 1952, pp. 1,5,7, records of the National Security Council. See also NSC 125, "Interim Policy with Respect to Japan," February 21, 1952, ibid. On plans to use offshore procurement in Japan, see Archie McLeod to SCAP, January 31, 1952, "Offshore Procurement in Japan from MSP in 1952," records of SCAP, 6799, "Offshore Procurement." For Administrative Agreement, see Ridgway to Joint Chiefs, April 19, 1952, records of the Joint Chiefs of Staff, box 25, "Japan, folder 2." The need to assure the legality of Japanese arms production for Southeast Asia, in order to convince Japanese investors that arms production would be ongoing, was a main argument of "Japan's Industrial Potential, Vol. III," by the ESS (February 21, 1952, Dower Collection). "Japan's Industrial Potential, Vol. II," is a still-classified breakdown of the use of Japanese industrial capacity to support American military efforts during a global conflict. It was completed in October 1951.

37 See embassy to Department of State, September 19, 1952, Department of Treasury, 59-A-5918, box 52, "Economic Development, General, Vol. I." For SCAP/ESS mission staying in Japan, see Morrow to Marquat (for Department of Army), December 27, 1951, records of SCAP, 5980, "P&S"; Reed to Marquat, March 22, 1952, records of SCAP, 6810, "300"; Morrow to King, June 6, 1952, records of SCAP, 6810, "400"; H. R. Garrett to Marquat, April 26, 1952, "Status of Publications and Retention of Japanese Personnel," records of SCAP, 6810, "500." With the end of the Occupation, many U.S. agencies, including the National Planning Agency, the Office of International Trade (Department of Commerce), the Defense Materials Planning Agency, and the General Services Administration, were involved in assisting Japan to procure American machinery and helping Japan to obtain markets and materials in Southeast Asia. See Army to SCAP, April 12, 1952, records of SCAP, 6810, "400."

38 Chitoshi Yanaga, *Big Business in Japanese Politics* (New Haven: Yale Univ. Press, 1968), pp. 240–241.

39 Masataka Kosaka, *100 Million Japanese* (Tokyo: Kodansha International, 1972), pp. 88–115. Kosaka gives credit to Yoshida for winning the peace. The *Oriental Economist* discusses Yoshida's diplomacy, March 10, 1951, p. 194. See also Yanaga, *Big Business in Japanese Politics,* pp. 233–239; Shigeto Tsuru, *Essays on the Japanese Economy* (Tokyo: Kinokuniya Bookstore, 1958).

40 Kozo Yamamura, *Economic Policy in Postwar Japan* (Berkeley: Univ. of California Press), p. 43; see Kamekichi Takahashi, "Problems of Post-Treaty Economy," *Contemporary Japan,* July–September 1951, pp. 309–

316; UN, *Economic Bulletin for Asia and the Far East* 2, no. 1, 3d quarter, 1951; *Bank of Japan Monthly Review,* March, April, May, June 1951; on "new special procurements," see *Mitsubishi Monthly Economic Circular,* May 1951, p. 3. *Oriental Economist,* June 23, 1951, p. 487; *Oriental Economist,* July 28, 1951, p. 580; Federation of Economic Organizations (FEO), "An Opinion on the U.S.-Japan Economic Cooperation," records of SCAP, 8054.

41 ESS, "Japan's Industrial Potential, Vol. III"; *Oriental Economist,* July 21, 1951, p. 564.

42 Frank A. Waring, "Economic and Financial Reports," June 16, 1952, Department of Treasury, 69-A-5918, box 47.

43 Economic Stabilization Board, "Basic Ideas Underlying Economic Self-Support Program," October, 1950, Dower Collection. See also "Economic Self-Support Program," January 20, 1951, ibid.; Self-Supporting Economy Council, "Report on Self-Support Program," January 20, 1951, records of SCAP, 8105, "ESB."

44 Economic Stabilization Board, "How to Cope with the Present Dollar Deficit of Japan," February 1952, Dower Collection; Suto to Marquat, January 12, 1952, ibid.; Economic Stabilization Board, "On Viable Economy of Japan," June 3, 1952, ibid.

45 On Yoshida's desire for foreign capital, see *Oriental Economist,* March 29, 1952, p. 241; see also Economic Stabilization Board, "Foreign Credits for Power Development and Construction of Industrial Roads," February 1952, Dower Collection. On loan request, see Yoshida to Dulles, December 22, 1951, *FRUS, 1951,* VI-I, p. 1465; Yoshida to Dodge, November 21, 1951, "1951," Dodge Papers, Nanto Collection.

46 See Dodge memos of November 20 and November 24, 1951, Dodge Papers, Nanto Collection. On the importance of capital accumulation and exports, see Dodge memo, "The Importance of Exports to Japan," October 20, 1951, Dodge Papers, Dower Collection; for American critique of Japanese financing, see Hutchinson to Dodge, October 9, 1952, Dodge Papers, Eisenhower Library, box 9, "Japan 1954." For tax rates, see Harold Moss to Marquat, January 27, 1951, Dodge Papers, Dower Collection, and Moss to Marquat, June 23, 1951, Dodge Papers, Nanto Collection, vol. 13.

47 Dodge to Reid, September 17, 1951 (on the need to support the conservative government), Dodge Papers, Nanto Collection, vol. 13; Dodge meeting with MITI, November 29, 1951 (for Dodge's opposition to the coordination of procurement), ibid. For further discussion of coordination of procurement, see Riichi Takahashi, "Security Forces Procurement," *Oriental Economist,* September 1952, pp. 31–33; Commission

on Foreign Economic Policy, "Staff Report on Off-Shore Procurement," November 23, 1953, pp. 17–18, records of the Commission on Foreign Economic Policy, Eisenhower Library, "Area 5, No. 2." For further discussion of Dodge's opposition to the depurge of Hatoyama and Ishibashi, see Dodge to Marquat, August 27, 1951, Dodge Papers, Nanto Collection, vol. 13., and Marquat to Dodge, July 22, 1951, ibid.

48 Shigeo Horie, "International Economic Situation," *Oriental Economist,* September 1952, pp. 18–22. See also *Oriental Economist,* January 5, 1952, pp. 4–5, April 12, 1952, p. 290; Paul Einzy, "The Future of the Dollar," ibid., September 1952, p. 29. *Far East Economic Review,* July 3, 1952, p. 34, comments on the British hope that American inflation would strengthen sterling competitiveness. "The Growing Japanese-German Competition in World Markets," *Magazine of Wall Street,* March 8, 1952, p. 207; "A Scramble for World Markets," ibid., May 17, 1952, p. 631.

49 T. Takemori and POLAD, memo, October 4, 1954, Dodge Papers, Nanto Collection, "Dodge, 1951"; Yanaga, *Big Business,* pp. 156–157.

50 Yanaga, *Big Business,* pp. 74, 251, 253–256, 248–249. Yanaga credits the "alertness of business and its ability to convert defeat into a triumph of cooperation with the United States" (p. 234). On arms plants, see "Revival of Munitions Industry," *Oriental Economist,* October 1952, pp. 68–69.

51 John Allison, *Ambassador from the Prairie,* (New York: Houghton Mifflin, 1973), p. 267.

52 Shigeto Tsuru, *Essays on the Japanese Economy,* p. 36.

Chapter 5

1 *Bank of Japan Monthly Review,* January through December 1952, and May 1953; "U.S. Forces Expenditures in Japan," July 13, 1954, Suzuki Papers, Nanto Collection, "1953"; "An Outlook of the Japanese Economy and Some of the Problems It Faces" (by the Japanese delegation to the Ikeda-Robertson talks in 1953), ibid. See also "International Accounts to Worsen," *Oriental Economist,* November 1952, p. 111; "Problems of Business Recession in Japan," *Far Eastern Economic Review,* September 11, 1952, p. 328; Shigeto Tsuru, "Business Cycles in Postwar Japan," Science Council of Japan, Division of Economics and Commerce, Economic Series, no. 1 (Tokyo, January 1953), p. 34.

2 *Oriental Economist,* May 1953, p. 224.

3 *New York Times,* August 4, 1953, p. 4, January 5, 1954, p. 45.

4 Dodge memo, n.d., Dodge Papers, Eisenhower Library, box 9, "Japan 1953–1954: The Postwar Economy"; "Kano's memo," April 3, 1953, ibid.; Jerome Cohen, "Japan's Foreign Trade Problem," *Far Eastern Survey,* November 19, 1952, pp. 167–170.

5 Merrill Gay, "The Special Problem of Japan," December 9, 1952, records of the Commission on Foreign Economic Policy, Eisenhower Library, box 63, "Studies, DOS Documents."

6 Campbell to Marquat, "Post, Colliers Complain Japan Goods Flood U.S.," February 16, 1952, records of SCAP, 5976, "Briefings for SCAP." American shipping interests felt Japan should be allowed to carry 50 percent of its foreign trade. They told Ridgway they feared Scandinavian competition more than Japanese ("Memorandum of Conversation with American Shipping Executives," February 6, 1952, Ridgway Papers). The State Department concluded by 1949 that the dollar gap meant foreign shipping would have to compete with American shipping, and this would require subsidies to keep American shipping in business, which remains American policy (October 28, 1949, memo, DOS, 894.50). For gloves, mittens and toys, see "UP Daily Financial and Economic World News Review," records of SCAP, 6703, "Complaints."

7 Bidwell to Dulles, January 11, 1952, Dulles Papers, Seeley G. Mudd Manuscript Library, Princeton University, Princeton, N.J., box 61; Steelman to Truman, "Memo on Tuna Problem," president's confidential file, Truman Library, box 52, "State Department Trade Agreements, 1951–1952 Negotiations," folder 26; Ridgway statement, Senate Foreign Relations Committee, *Executive Sessions,* Historical Series, 1953, V, p. 422; Ridgway to Joint Chiefs of Staff, February 9, 1952, records of the Joint Chiefs of Staff, box 24, "092 Japan, 1951–1953," sections 8–10.

8 Harold Linder testimony, House Foreign Affairs Committee, Subcommittee on Foreign Economic Policy, *Hearings,* 1953, 83:1, p. 3; Dulles to Millikan, August 1, 1953, enclosed in Leddy to Hague, August 4, 1953, Gabriel Hague Papers, Eisenhower Library, box 1, "J. F. Dulles"; Commission on Foreign Economic Policy, "Japanese Exports to the West," October 1953, records of the Commission on Foreign Economic Policy, box 65, "Studies 23"; Commission on Foreign Economic Policy, "Staff Report on Off-shore Procurement," November 23, 1953, ibid., box 46, "Area 5–No. 2."

9 Council on Foreign Relations, *The United States in World Affairs, 1953,* ed. Hollis W. Barber et al. (New York: Harper, 1955), pp. 262–263. General Olmstead explained to the Congress how Japan's unused military capacity could be used to produce military goods and replace economic aid (House Foreign Affairs Committee, *Mutual Security Act of 1953,* 82:1, p. 2).

10 Yanaga, *Big Business,* p. 263.
11 Federation of Economic Organization (FEO), "General Recommendations Regarding Reception of MSA Benefits," July 23, 1953, Department of Treasury, 69-A-5918, box 54, "JAP/9/11 Military Aid"; Takeo Godo, "Reference Views Concerning MSA," July 28, 1953, and "Military Aid and Production for Special Procurement," June 29, 1953, Nanto Collection; Tokuju Uchiyama, "Defense Production and the Economy," *Oriental Economist,* July 1953, p. 346 (see also p. 349 for further praise of procurement); Yanaga, *Big Business,* p. 260, discusses the FEO studies.
12 *Oriental Economist,* June 1953, p. 276; House Foreign Affairs Committee, *Mutual Security Act of 1953,* pp. 15–16; Yanaga, *Big Business,* p. 260.
13 G. H. Willis to A. N. Overby, September 29, 1953, Department of Treasury, 69-A-5918, box 47, "0/0/700." For Japanese pressure for orders, see Japan Ordnance Association, "Desires Regarding Receiving MSA Assistance from Technical Point of View," September 1, 1953, Suzuki Papers, 70, Nanto Collection. The United States sent relatively little in "offshore procurement" of the European variety to Japan (see Commission on Foreign Economic Policy, "Staff Report on Off-Shore Procurement"). For insights into the business of international arms procurement, see Michael Sapir, "Trans-Pacific Consultants Occasional News Letter," no. 1, August 10, 1953, and no. 7, October 12, 1953, Suzuki Papers, 72, Nanto Collection; and see *Oriental Economist,* August 1953, p. 384, for discussion of Japan's need for procurement aid.
14 *Oriental Economist,* September 1953, p. 427, November 1953, p. 533.
15 See papers presented by the Ikeda mission: "An Outlook of the Japanese Economy and Some of the Problems It Faces," October 5, 1953, Suzuki Papers, Nanto Collection; "Statement of Korean Procurement," ibid.; "New Phases in the Far East," ibid.; Suzuki notes on October 5 and October 8 meetings, ibid.
16 See Ikeda mission papers, Nanto Collection, "1953"; American paper, "U.S. Military Assistance to Japan," ibid.; "Japanese Summary," October 18–19, 1953, ibid; and notes of October 5 and 8, 1953, meetings, ibid; for anti-American feeling in Japan, see Richard Stebbins, in Council on Foreign Relations, *The United States in World Affairs, 1954* (New York: Harper, 1956), pp. 291–293. A memo in the Ridgway Papers (October 21, 1951) explains the opposition of the Diet to the security treaty system: Japan was pressured into the security treaty, pressured to recognize Taiwan, pressured to rearm (in violation of the Japanese constitution), and, most importantly, Japan had to invite American troops to Japan, but the bases could be terminated only upon mutual agree-

ment. Whereas the Japanese could justifiably complain about American
diplomatic heavy-handedness, the Yoshida government successfully exploited Japan's economic fragility to avoid rearmament. Lawrence Olson recalled, from the American viewpoint, the Japanese attitude toward
rearmament: "Grim diagnoses of the future were common at this time. . . .
Every argument that could be devised for Japan's own weakness would
be advanced to avoid commitment to others" (*Japan in Postwar Asia*
[New York: Praeger, 1970]).

17 John Allison, *Ambassador from the Prairie* (New York: Houghton Mifflin, 1973), p. 233.

18 Clark to Joint Chiefs, July, 20, 1953, records of the Joint Chiefs of
Staff, 383.24 "Japan, Sec. 3." "Dodge reply to Ikeda," October 14, 1953
(meeting of October 12), Suzuki Papers, Nanto Collection; Allison, *Ambassador from the Prairie*, p. 234.

19 Allison, *Ambassador from the Prairie*, p. 233; Dodge to Marquat, August 27, 1951, Dodge Papers, Nanto Collection, "1951."

20 See United States document, "Statement on U.S. Assistance," Suzuki
Papers, Nanto Collection; "U.S. Statement on Reparations," ibid.; "Japanese Summary," October 18–19, ibid.; "U.S. Reply to Japanese Summary," October 21, 1953, ibid.

21 Chitoshi Yanaga concluded that the Mutual Defense Assistance Agreement "stimulated the growth of the defense industry in precisely the way
envisaged by organized business and led the nation out of the doldrums
brought by the end of the Korean War" (*Big Business,* pp. 261–262).
New York Times, June 15, 1953, p. 1.

22 Jerome Cohen, "International Aspects of Japan's Economic Situation,"
in Council on Foreign Relations, *Japan between East and West,* pp.
116–117. See also *Oriental Economist,* April 1954, p. 165; Kishi speech
of January 27, 1954, Dodge Papers, Eisenhower Library, box 9, "Japan
Postwar Economy."

23 Cabinet meeting of June 21, 1954, Hagerty diary, Eisenhower Library,
box 1. See also meetings of June 23 and June 28, 1954, ibid.; "Legislative Leadership Meeting," June 21, 1954, Whitman Legislative Meeting Series, 1954, Eisenhower Library, box 1. Council on Foreign Relations, *The United States in World Affairs, 1954,* p. 290. "Supplemental
Report to the President on Japan," July 9, 1954, by Governors Thorn-
ton, Fine, and Shivers, Suzuki Papers, Nanto Collection.

24 Department of Commerce, "General Considerations Regarding Trade
Agreement Negotiations with Japan," Jacoby Papers, box 6, "Japanese
Trade Negotiations."

25 "U.S. Procurement in Japan: Recent Trends and Requested Countermea-

sures" Suzuki Papers, Nanto Collection. "U.S. Force Expenditure in Japan," July 13, 1954, ibid. There were five types of procurement earnings: yen sales to American military personnel; yen sales of goods and services to the United States Forces, Japan, the American military forces assigned to Japan; offshore procurement and Southeast Asian aid by the Foreign Operations Administration; Okinawa construction; and UN Korean rehabilitation aid.

26 Two versions of the August 6, 1954, cabinet meeting were recorded: Hagerty diary, Eisenhower Library, box 1, "August 1954," and Ann Whitman Cabinet Series, Eisenhower Library, box 3. Hagerty version is quoted here.

27 August 6, 1954, cabinet meeting, Hagerty diary.

28 Ibid. See "Failing Economy of Japan Receives Top U.S. Priority," *New York Times,* August 9, 1954, p. 1, which predicted Japan would suffer economic collapse within a year if no trade solution was found; and *New York Times,* August 11, 1954, p. 1, which cites Japan's request for a Marshall Plan to avoid collapse and Dulles's statement that the United States would seek to avoid direct economic aid.

29 "Importance of Successful Trade Agreement Negotiations with Japan," Jacoby Papers, Eisenhower Library, box 6, "Japanese Trade Negotiations." "Reactions of GATT Countries to U.S. Proposals for Multilateral Tariff Negotiations with Japan," ibid.; "Japanese Trade Negotiations: A Summary," ibid.; W. L. Hubbard, "The Problem of Japan," ibid. A Brookings Institute study cited the intractability of the American problem in Japan in 1954: economic aid was unpopular in Congress and in Japan; Japanese dependence on the Korean War was critical: "If hostilities are terminated, Japan will be confronted by serious economic difficulties"; trade concessions would arouse protectionists and would not solve Japan's problems, but the Japanese demanded them in return for limiting trade with China (Brookings Institute, *Major Problems of United States Foreign Policy, 1954* [Menasha, Wis.: George Banta, 1956], pp. 322, 328).

30 "Terms of Reference—U.S.-Japan Consultative Group," August 6, 1954, Suzuki Papers, Nanto Collection, box 73. "Interim Report of Consultation on Special Procurement," September 3, 1954, ibid.

31 See Yanaga, *Big Business,* pp. 264–265; see Japanese documents: "Special Procurement," Suzuki Papers, Nanto Collection, folder 116; "Outline of Japanese Defense Industry Buildup," ibid.; "Yoshida Speech to Japanese Chamber of Commerce in New York," ibid.; "Kiichi Aiichi Statement," ibid. Diehl to ambassador in Japan (through Waring), May 22, 1954, Department of Treasury, 68-A-5918, box 48, JAP/0/76,

"Yoshida Trip 1954"; "USIA Study on Japanese Public Opinion," Whitman International Series 30, "Japan 1953–1954."

32 Japanese documents, "Japan-U.S. Trade Relations" and "Yoshida Speech to Japanese Chamber of Commerce in New York," Suzuki papers, folder 116, Nanto Collection. American documents: "Statement on U.S.-Japanese Economic Questions," October 29, 1954, Suzuki Papers, Nanto Collection; "U.S. Paper on Special Procurement," ibid.; "Background Notes on the Japanese Economy," November 1954, ibid.

33 U.S. memo, "Present Status of PL 480, November 9, 1954, Suzuki Papers, Nanto Collection.

34 Minutes of October 12, 1954, Interdepartmental Committee on Agricultural Surplus Disposal meeting, Clarence Francis Papers, Eisenhower Library box 1, "ICASD Meetings, 1954–1957"; November 5, 1954, cabinet meeting, Whitman Cabinet Series, Eisenhower Library.

35 See Japanese documents: "Basic Concepts of the Government concerning Japanese Acquisition and Disposal of U.S. Surplus Agricultural Commodities," Suzuki Papers, Nanto Collection, folder 116; "Surplus Agricultural Commodities," November 8, 1954, ibid.; "Purchase of Surplus Agricultural Commodities with Yen," ibid.; November 12, 1954, meeting on "PL 480," ibid. See also Jerome Cohen, "International Aspects of Japan's Economic Situation," Council on Foreign Relations, ed., *Japan between East and West* (New York: Harper, 1957), pp. 126–127.

36 Japanese government, "Basic Concepts of the Japanese Government on Surplus Agricultural Commodities," Suzuki Papers, Nanto Collection, folder 116; "Purchases of U.S. Surplus Agricultural Commodities with Yen," ibid. See also "Press Release," November 13, 1954, ibid.

37 Jerome Cohen, *Japan's Postwar Economy* (Bloomington: Univ. of Indiana Press, 1958), p. 141; Robert Marks, "The Role of Japan in U.S. Surplus Agricultural Commodity Disposal," seminar paper, University of Wisconsin, 1974, in possession of the author.

The importance of Japan's role as the primary market for American agriculture, as well as its contribution as an industrial and financial partner for American corporations, cannot be overstated. The United States subsidized its own agricultural exports and created its greatest agricultural market in Japan. This market has sustained American agricultural prosperity since World War II. To the extent that overproduction was a serious problem after the war, that problem would have been many times more grave were it not for Japanese consumption. This work focuses on the tremendous efforts of American officials to help Japan and Europe. Readers should not conclude that the only gains to the United States were in preserving a favorable balance of power with the Soviet Union. Sustaining American exports, especially agricultural products, lay at the foundation of modern American prosperity, which many Americans do not understand. As State Department official Philip H. Trezise explained in 1962: "It is demonstrable that our trade with Japan would exist independently of any political requirements. It would do so because it makes the United States more prosperous, because it creates jobs and wealth, and because it coincides with our interest in promoting our own economic well-being." Japan was the second largest market for the United States (behind Canada), and thus instrumental in preserving income and employment and suppressing political conflict between agricultural and nonagricultural interests in the United States. Philip H. Trezise, "United States Trade with Japan," *Department of State Bulletin*, February 19, 1962, p. 183. See also the testimony of the American Farm Bureau Federation before the Subcommittee on Disposal of Agricultural Surpluses, Senate Committee on Agriculture and Forestry, 84:1, pp. 373, 375, 376; Robert L. Tontz, ed., *Foreign Agricultural Trade* (Ames, Iowa: Iowa State Univ. Press, 1966), p. 139.

38 Joint communiqué of the 1954 Yoshida mission, Yoshida and Eisenhower, *Oriental Economist*, December 1954, p. 586. See also Allison, *Ambassador from the Prairie*, p. 271.

39 Hagerty diary, December 10, 1954, Eisenhower Library; Randall to president, December 7, 1954, cabinet meeting of December 10, 1954, Whitman Cabinet Series, Eisenhower Library, box 4.

40 Statement of Raymond Moyer, Senate Foreign Relations Committee, *Mutual Security Act of 1955*, May 1955, 84:1, p. 210; Mansfield and Moyer, ibid., p. 216; FOA, ibid., p. 200. Yanaga comments on the great value of technological cooperation with the United States to Japan's industrial modernization (*Big Business*, p. 266).

41 Council on Foreign Relations, The United States in World Affairs, 1955, pp. 143–144; *Japan Report*, November 18, 1955, citing the threat by fourteen nations to invoke GATT article 35 against Japan; "Briefing Paper No. 3" states that eleven nations would invoke the article, records of the Council on Foreign Economic Policy, Dodge file, Eisenhower Library, box 3, "Japan: Shigemitsu Visit." For American trade concessions to Japan, see *New York Times*, April 10, 1955, p. 6; Stassen and George in Senate Foreign Relations Committee, *Mutual Security Act of 1955*, 84:1, p. 243. On trilateral deals, see Miriam Farley, "Mr. Shigemitsu in Washington," *Far Eastern Survey*, September 1955.

42 U.S. memo, March 17, 1955, Suzuki Papers, Nanto Collection, folder 70; H. Struve Hensel to Ichiro Ishikawa, May 18, 1955, ibid; Tetsuya

Senga, "Defense Production," *Oriental Economist,* April 1955, pp. 180–181.

43 Frederick P. Rich to Tetsuji Atarashiya, June 30, 1955, Suzuki Papers, Nanto Collection, folder 70.

44 H. Frazier Kammeyer to Gengo Suzuki, June 29, 1955, Suzuki Papers, Nanto Collection, folder 70. On November 23, 1955, the Defense Department issued a directive on Mutual Defense Assistance Program/Offshore Procurement to replace the April 15, 1953, procurement policy ("Japan as a Source for Military Equipment and Supplies," ibid.).

45 Economic Planning Agency, *Economic Survey of Japan 1956 to 1957* (Tokyo, 1957), pp. 31–34, 54–55. For an account of "Jimmu Prosperity," see Yanaga, *Big Business,* p. 269. On ships, see Council on Foreign Relations, *The United States in World Affairs, 1955,* p. 143. On trade expansion, see *Japan Report,* February 17, 1956, p. 9. On cartels, see Koza Yamamura, *Economic Policy in Postwar Japan* (Berkeley: Univ. of California Press, 1967), p. 63. On boom, see "Shigemitsu Briefing Papers," no. 1, August 30, 1955, no. 4, n.d., and no. 3, "Japan's Relations with South and Southeast Asia," August 23, 1955, Records of the Commission on Foreign Economic Policy, Dodge file, Eisenhower Library, box 3, "Japan."

46 Saburo Okita, "The Future of Japan's Foreign Trade," *Oriental Economist,* August 1955, pp. 407–409.

47 *Japan Report,* April 30, 1956, "Eisenhower Cites Japan's Problems."

48 *Japan Report,* April 17, 1956, p. 1, October 2, 1956, pp. 2–3.

Chapter 6

1 "Notes on Speech by Mr. Morrow," September 9, 1951, Dodge Papers, Nanto Collection.

2 Allison memos, January 11 and January 12, 1951, *FRUS,* 1951, VI, pt. 1, p. 791; Allison memo, January 18, 1951, ibid., p. 804. Dulles told *U.S. News and World Report* that the Korean War had temporarily cast the Southeast Asian problem into the background (April 27, 1951, p. 33). Dulles's scheme was partly based on the psychological insecurity of Japanese leaders about the threat of Asian revolution to Japan's economic interests. The chargé in Tokyo, Parsons, warned the State Department to maintain an optimistic public attitude on the situation in Indochina in order to avoid alarming the Japanese (Parsons to Department of State, February 18, 1954, *FRUS,* 1952–1954, XIII, pt. 1, pp. 1058–1059).

3 ESS, programs and statistics division, "Japan's Industrial Potential, Vol. III," February 21, 1952, Dower Collection. Leon Hollerman, a one-time SCAP economist, summarized the thinking of American officials and observers in 1951: "The only self-sustaining way in which normal peacetime trade between Japan and the Far East region can be restored to high levels is through full Japanese participation in the programs for rehabilitation and economic development." Hollerman suggested that the United States had to restore Japan as the creditor nation of Asia so Japan could "gain financial leverage in efforts to secure stable future resources of food and industrial raw materials. The integration of Japan within the total economy of the Far East would afford the sole means of long-term compensation for Japanese poverty in natural resources" ("Japan and Far Eastern Development," *Pacific Affairs*, December 1951, pp. 381, 383). For additional American thinking on Japanese integration with Southeast Asia, see Jerome Cohen, "Economic Problems of Free Japan," Princeton University Center for International Studies, *Memo No. 2*, 1952, pp. 88–89. For a Japanese view of Japan's role as the dominant industrial economy in Asian trade, see Kenji Katayama, "Japan's Role in Asiatic Trade," Institute of Pacific Relations, *11th Conference Proceedings* (Lucknow, 1950), vol. 2, pp. 41–43.

4 "Minutes of ICFEM Meeting #8," November 28, 1951, records of SCAP, 6799, "U.S. Policy." On ECA, see Griffin to Marquat, November 2, 1950, and November 14, 1950, records of SCAP, 5987, "Griffin Mission"; *Oriental Economist*, August 11, 1951, p. 625. The ECA pledged to continue giving business to Japan (see Reid to Bissell, May 3, 1951, and Bissell to Reid, May 18, 1951, records of SCAP, 6810, "300," 312.1A).

5 Acheson to diplomatic officers, December 21, 1951, records of SCAP, 6799, "U.S. Policy."

6 *New York Times*, July 22, 1951, pp. 1, 4.

7 On August 11, 1951, the *Oriental Economist* reported the establishment of the Interdepartmental Committee on Far East Mobilization (ICFEM) to "exploit the unused industrial capacity of Japan in the defense program of the free world" (p. 625). For Office of Defense Management interest in cooperation with Japan, see Office of Defense Management memo, 1551–1552, *Third Report to the President*, October 1951, chap. 4, p. 15, president's confidential file, Truman Library, box 16; "Minutes of ICFEM Meeting," October 3, 1951, and November 14, 1951, records of SCAP, 6799, "U.S. Policy." See also Morrow report to ICFEM, November 28, 1951, ibid. For sources of financing, see Morrow to Marquat, December 27, 1951, which discusses the December 6 meeting

with the U.S. Export-Import Bank, records of SCAP, 5980, "P&S"; minutes of November 9 and December 11, 1951, ICFEM meetings, and "Paper no. 12, Possible Sources of Dollar Financing of Raw Material Projects in the Area," records of SCAP, 6799, "U.S. Policy." On Goa deal, see Dodge memo, October 17, 1951, Dodge Papers, Nanto Collection, "1951"; ICFEM meeting of November 14, 1951, records of SCAP, 6799, "U.S. Policy"; Economic Stabilization Board, "Interim Progress Report on Southeast Asian Development," January 14, 1952, Dower Collection. For $91 million commitment, see Brookings Institute, *Major Problems of United States Foreign Policy, 1952–1953* (Menasha, Wis.: George Banta, 1952), p. 287. Japanese Ministry of Foreign Affairs memo, "Proposed SCAP-Japanese Mission to Southeast Asia," Dower Collection; Marquat, "Briefing for Alexander," June 1951, records of SCAP, 8351, "Briefing for Alexander." For nine contracts, see Michisuki Sugi, "Trade and Cooperation with Southeast Asia," *Contemporary Japan*, September 1957, pp. 60–61. See also Saburo Okita, "The Rehabilitation of Japan in Asia," Japanese Ministry of Foreign Affairs, Tokyo, 1954.

8 Senate Foreign Relations Committee, *Mutual Security Act of 1951*, 82:1, pp. 532–533; see also p. 412 for statement by Henry Bennett, head of the Technical Cooperation Administration, and pp. 578, 584 for R. Allen Griffin statement, which both discuss Southeast Asia's importance as a raw materials source for Japan and the West. Dulles statement, Senate Foreign Relations Committee, *Mutual Security Act of 1955*, 84:1, p. 22. For further evidence of Western and Japanese need for Southeast Asian resources, see CIA, NIE-43, November 13, 1951, *FRUS, 1951*, VI, pt. 1, pp. 108, 111, 112.

9 NSC 125/1, "U.S. Objectives and Courses of Action with Respect to Japan," July 28, 1952, pp. 1, 5, 7, records of the National Security Council. See also NSC 125, "Interim Policy with Respect to Japan," February 1952, ibid.

10 Joint Chiefs of Staff to secretary of defense, July 28, 1952, records of Joint Chiefs of Staff, 042, Japan, 12–12–50, sec. 14.

11 UN, *Economic Bulletin for Asia and the Far East* 2, no. 2, 1951; "Japan's Industrial Potential, Vol. III."

12 Webb to diplomatic officers, September 22, 1951, records of SCAP, 5976, "Diplomatic Section"; Cowen to secretary of state, August 8, 1951, *FRUS, 1951*, VI, pt. 1, p. 1248; Department of State, "Southeast Asia: Critical Area in a Divided World," June 1955, Far East Series, no. 65, p. 6.

13 House Foreign Affairs Committee, Subcommittee on Foreign Economic Policy Hearings, 83:1, 1953, p. 4.

14 *New York Times,* October 5, 1950; Dulles to Acheson, August 5, 1950, *FRUS,* 1950, VI, pp. 128–129. By 1951 American policy debates focused on how best to intervene in Southeast Asia. As it sought an elusive nationalist, yet pro-Western, solution to the Indochina conflict, the United States was caught between weak Premier Bao Dai and the arrogant French. Acheson warned Bao patronizingly that Americans had "misinterpreted" Bao's lengthy holiday on the Riviera as a lack of patriotism (Acheson to Heath, October 18, 1950, ibid., p. 898). The French, inspired by American boldness in Korea, tried to convince the United States that China had intervened in Indochina in order to lure the United States to intervene directly. They termed such joint Western military initiatives a "multilateral approach," or the "internationalization of the problem" (Bruce to Acheson, December 29, 1951, *FRUS,* 1951, VI, pt. 1, p. 580). Earlier the opportunistic French had sought a modus vivendi with China to preclude Chinese intervention, but Acheson opposed such approaches to Mao, as dictated by the NSC 68 philosophy (Heath to Acheson, October 15, 1950, *FRUS,* 1950, VI, pp. 894–896). The Western military alliance met in May 1951 to plan tactics for holding Southeast Asia ("Conference Report on Tripartite Military Talks on Southeast Asia," May 5–15, 1951, ibid, p. 64; Bruce to Acheson, December 26, 1951, ibid., p. 576).

15 Kennan statement, Senate Foreign Relations Committee, *Executive Sessions,* Historical Series, vol. 4, "MSA of 1952," pp. 200–202; Kennan speech before Economic Club of the Century, November 8, 1951, Kennan Papers, Seeley G. Mudd Manuscript Library, Princeton University, Princeton, N.J., box 18.

16 Charlton Ogburn, "Further Aspects of the Basic Difficulty in the Far East," *FRUS,* 1951, VI-I, pp. 6–9.

17 Ibid.

18 Ibid.

19 Fine memo, June 29, 1950, attached to Marquat to Lokanathan, June 29, 1950, records of SCAP, 7692, "ECAFE Correspondence." David Wightman, *Toward Economic Cooperation in Asia* (New Haven: Yale Univ. Press, 1963), p. 235. See also SCAP to Lokanathan, September 13, 1951, records of SCAP, 6715, "ECAFE"; Acheson to Sebald, February 2, 1951, ibid. ECAFE considered trade with Japan in the third session of the Committee on Industry and Trade (Lahore, Pakistan, February 1951). No decision was reached, and each nation was left with the

choice of how to promote trade with Japan. Pakistan was the most willing to be a trade partner for Japan with her cotton and grain production
and need for an industrial partner to avoid dependence on arch-enemy
India. See Hassan Habib, "Japanese Economic Recovery and Pakistan,"
mentioned in *Pacific Affairs,* June 1951.

20 NSC 141, p. 29, records of the National Security Council. See also
Wightman, *Toward Economic Cooperation in Asia,* on the 1953 ECAFE
conference, at which the International Chamber of Commerce superseded
the ECAFE Committee on Industry and Trade with its Commission on
Asian and Far Eastern Affairs. See also "The 2nd ECAFE Conference
on Trade Promotion," ECAFE records, Memorial Library, Madison,
Wisconsin, Industry and Trade, 1953.

21 Leon Hollerman, *Japan's Dependence on the World Economy* (Princeton: Princeton Univ. Press, 1963), p. 73.

22 Allison to Cleveland, November 27, 1951, *FRUS,* 1951, VI, pt. 1, p.
118. Allison cites Bissell's speech of October 29, 1951, before the Far
East Council of Trade and Industry in New York.

23 Stassen statement, Senate Foreign Relations Committee, *Mutual Security Act of 1955,* p. 237 (see also pp. 242–243); Moyer statement, ibid.,
p. 211; Leon Hollerman, *Japan's Dependence on the World Economy,*
pp. 102, 136. *Japan Report,* March 16, 1956, p. 8.

24 Fearey memo, April 17, 1951, *FRUS,* 1951, VI, pt. 1, p. 980; Acheson
meeting with Yoshida, September 3, 1951, Acheson memos of conversations, Truman Library, box 266. Emmerson Ross explained how the
reparations formula was established ("ICFEM Meeting," October 18,
1951, records of SCAP, 6799, "ICFEM Documents").

25 Lawrence Olson, *Japan in Postwar Asia* (New York: Praeger, 1970),
pp. 16–19. See also Yanaga *Big Business,* pp. 202–228.

26 Moyer and Mansfield statements, Senate Foreign Relations Committee,
Mutual Security Act of 1955, p. 216. Chitoshi Yanaga has vividly por-
trayed the "frantic efforts" of Japanese business "to obtain contracts and
get their slice of the one-billion dollar reparations pie. . . . There was
no doubt in the business community that it represented an investment in
the economic development of Southeast Asia that would result in economic cooperation, the reopening of markets, and the revival of sources
of much-needed raw materials." When Philippine ambassador Luanza
landed in Tokyo in March to reopen talks, he was besieged by agents
from several hundred Japanese firms. Reparations were treated as coordinated aid; Japanese taxes paid for orders from corporations, which
were shipped to recipient countries. Since they were designed to serve

business, the government allowed businessmen to handle the negotiations.

Japanese reparations to South Vietnam proved a fascinating example of coordinated aid and economic cooperation. Yanaga wrote that after the fall of Dien Bien Phu, American aid flowed in to prop up the Diem regime: "Organized business, which had been feeling the effects of the termination of the United States special procurement program in Japan for the Korean War, saw new opportunities . . . to derive sizeable profits from United States aid funds . . . [and] concluded that it would be best in the long run to make a fairly large reparations payment, which would over a period of time pay off handsomely." American ICA funds financed a technical cooperation agreement between Japan and South Vietnam in 1957, and a reparations agreement for $55.6 million was signed in May 1959. Yanaga concluded that the deal was "promoted by business leaders close to the Prime Minister because they saw an excellent opportunity to realize profits while cooperating with the United States in its policy of resisting communism in Southeast Asia" (*Big Business,* pp. 204–205, 222, 224–225, 227).

27 Allison, *Ambassador from the Prairie,* pp. 165–166; Ridgway, memo of conversation with Sebald, Dulles, Sparkman, and Smith, December 14, 1951, Ridgway Papers; Acheson to Sebald, December 18, 1951, *FRUS,* 1951, VI, pt. 1, pp. 1448–1450; Sebald memo, December 18, 1951, ibid., pp. 1445–1447. Acheson memo, meeting with Truman, Churchill, and Eden, January 16, 1952. Acheson Papers, box 66; Acheson meeting with Franks, April 2, 1951, ibid. Dulles advised MacArthur that the only threat to the Japanese-American alliance was that Japan would approach China for lack of economic opportunities. He assured MacArthur that British opposition to the peace treaty would ultimately be inconsequential (Dulles to MacArthur, March 18, 1951, *FRUS,* 1951, VI, pt. 1, p. 931). On this issue see Roger Buckley, *Occupation Diplomacy: Britain, the United States and Japan, 1945–1952* (Cambridge: Cambridge Univ. Press, 1982).

28 *Parliamentary Debates,* Hansard, 5th Series, vol. 173, *House of Lords,* 39:2, July 3, 1951, sections 74–75.

29 "Time to Say No," *New Statesman and Nation,* September 1, 1951; *Times,* August 15, 1951, Dulles Papers, box 15. *London Sunday Pictorial,* September 9, 1951, ibid., featured a quote by Australian statesman Evatt, who described the treaty as "an open, unashamed abandonment of all the standards of international justice."

30 *House of Commons,* vol. 49, statement by Mr. Ellis Smith, July 31,

1951, sections 1359–1360. Britain's "deep seated fear" of Japanese competition is explained by her commercial minister in Tokyo, N. S. Roberts, in *Overseas Economic Surveys: Japan* (London, 1953).

31 *House of Commons,* vol. 492, sections 490–491; *House of Lords,* vol. 174, November 29, 1951, sections 648–649, 653, 683–684.

32 *Time,* August 13, 1951, p. 27.

33 Senate Foreign Relations Committee, *Executive Sessions,* Historical Series, vol. 4, p. 124: Dulles explained that Britain's dollar gap greatly intensified the fear of Japanese competition in Southeast Asia. Statement by Eugene Dooman, Council on Foreign Relations meeting, January 22, 1951, Dulles Papers, box 48.

34 British aide-mémoire on limiting Japanese shipping capacity, March 12, 1951, *FRUS, 1951,* VI-I, p. 913; Babcock memo on meeting with Allison, Dulles, and Dening, *FRUS, 1950,* VI, p. 1307. Gifford (ambassador to Britain) to Acheson, February 26, 1951, *FRUS, 1951,* VI-I, pp. 896–897.

35 Marquat to chief of staff, records of SCAP, 6727, "Post-Treaty Extension of Agreement." The Army ordered Marquat to insist on Japanese privileges, SAOOA (secretary of the Army, Office of Occupied Areas) to Marquat, and Marquat to Army, May 16, 1951, records of SCAP, 6718, "Sterling Area Confidential." Boehringer to POLAD, April 20, 1951, records of SCAP, 8355, "Trade."

36 Minutes of the "Sterling Financial Conference, Tokyo," statements by Thomas and Shirasu, March 18 and 25, and May 24, 1951, records of SCAP, 6726, "Sterling Financial Conference." For the results of the conference, see UN, *Economic Bulletin for Asia and the Far East,* 1951, 3d quarter, p. 12. Japan appealed to members of the sterling area to grant most-favored-nation status to Japan on an individual basis (India was a particular target) (M. Yukawa memo, September 13, 1951, records of SCAP, 6726, "India"). For business pressure on the Japanese government, see briefing for SCAP, February 25, 1952, records of SCAP, 7692, "Briefing Materials." For British admission of higher prices, see Campbell to Marquat, March 27, 1952, records of SCAP, 6718, "Sterling Area Review Conference, 1952."

37 Minutes of Interdepartmental Committee on Far East Mobilization meeting, October 18, 1951, p. 4, records of SCAP, 6799, "ICFEM Documents"; Stevens to Morrow, March 7, 1952, records of SCAP, 6810, "300." Stevens cites a Reuters dispatch of February 27, 1952, for information on visas. Leon Hollerman felt the plan was designed to freeze Japan out ("Japan and Far Eastern development").

38 Japanese request, see Morrow to Marquat, March 21, 1952, records of

SCAP, 5976, "Colombo Plan," and Morrow meeting with Stevens and Kerr, February 1, 1952, ibid; Morrow to Marquat, February 6, 1952, records of SCAP, 7693, "P&S"; "Capture of Asian Markets by Japan: Apprehension in London," *Hindustan Times,* May 31, 1951, records of SCAP, 6726, "Sterling Area Conference."

39 Boehringer to POLAD, April 26, 1951, records of SCAP, 8355, "Trade"; Riichi Inagaki, "America's Japanese Dilemma," *New Statesman and Nation,* September 6, 1952. The British challenged SCAP's analysis of prewar Sino-Japanese trade, charging that SCAP had understated Japan's dependence on China. See Diehl memo, August 4, 1951, on American concern about British appeals to Japan (Department of Treasury, 67-A-245, box 23, "Trade Vol. II").

40 Council on Foreign Relations meeting, October 23, 1950, p. 10, Dulles Papers, box 48, "Japan." For American fear of Japan's attraction to China, see Council on Foreign Relations meeting, January 22, 1951, Dulles Papers; Perkins to Rusk, October 30, 1951, *FRUS,* 1951, VI-I, p. 1389; Johnson memo, August 29, 1951, ibid., p. 1307. For the inability of Southeast Asia to absorb Japanese exports, see UNESCO, ECAFE, Committee on Industry and Trade, 2d session, Bangkok, May 9, 1950. Memorial Library, Madison, Wisconsin. All agreed that increased intraregional trade would ease the regional dollar gap, but that Southeast Asia could not absorb Japanese production. For Sebald, see Fine memo on Diplomatic section memo, "Future Problems of U.S.-Japan Relationship," December 4, 1951, records of SCAP, 5976, "Diplomatic Section."

41 Robertson statement before Commission on Foreign Economic Policy, November 9, 1953, on Foreign Economic Policy records, Eisenhower Library, box 9, "1953–1954."

42 *Oriental Economist,* "Murphy on Japan," June 21, 1932. The *New York Times,* in a December 28, 1952, editorial, echoed the American line that Southeast Asia "can be more important than China" for Japan, and that the importance of China was overemphasized.

43 Marquat to Ridgway, "Japan–Communist China Trade," September 21, 1951, records of SCAP, 5976, "Briefings of SCAP." See embassy in Tokyo to Department of State, July 24, 1952, which advised that Southeast Asian development was five to ten years away, and that "few" Japanese businessmen did not want trade with China (Department of Treasury, 58-A 5918, box 50, JAP/5/000). C. L. Sulzberger cites the threat of the Soviets and Chinese either "wooing or scaring" Japan out of the American alliance (*New York Times,* February 17, 1953, p. 4).

44 Dodge meeting with Ichimada, September 3, 1951, Dodge Papers, Nanto Collection, vol. 13.

45 Takeshi Yamazaki, "The Asian Economy and Japan," Japanese Ministry of Foreign Affairs, Tokyo, 1954. On August 10, 1954, Ikeda announced that Japanese would be allowed to trade with China in order to "soothe the frayed nerves of business circles" about U.S. policy. See the *New York Times,* July 4, 1954, p. 2, which cites Japanese anxiety about being stuck on the losing side in Asia. Walter Judd declared that the United States had to "liberate China" or Japan would "have to go to the Communist world" (*New York Times,* July 9, 1954, p. 8). On the pressure from Osaka for China trade, see "The Outlook in Japan," *Economist,* September 8, 1951, p. 568.

46 Dulles to Allison (within Sebald to Acheson), December 14, 1951, *FRUS,* 1951, VI-I, pp. 1438–1439. When the Korean war slackened in August 1951, the ESS sought to return to pre–Korean War controls on Sino-Japanese trade (Campbell to Marquat, August 3, 1951, records of SCAP, 7690, "China Trade," and Marquat to Department of Army, records of SCAP, 5976, "Battle Act"). For changes in controls, see UN, *Economic Bulletin for Asia and the Far East,* 1951, 3d quarter, pp. 11–12. The American position did return to allowing nonstrategic trade to help Japan (NSC 125/1, p. 14, and "Draft Outline for NSC Study: Japanese Trade with the Soviet Bloc," records of SCAP, 6799, "U.S. Policy"). Congressional anti-Communism flourished in 1951, and the Battle Act strictly limited East-West trade for all nations receiving American aid, even though SCAP and the National Security Council advocated limited trade. See ESS, Finance Division, "Appraisal of Japan Foreign Exchange Control," June 21, 1951, Dodge Papers, Nanto Collection, "1951," which argued that Japanese steel would be more competitively priced if Japan could trade with China.

47 UN, *Economic Bulletin For Asia and the Far East,* 1953, 1st quarter, p. 46; Olson, *Japan in Postwar Asia,* pp. 74–76; *Fortune,* April 1957, p. 429. For American warning, see *Oriental Economist,* April 1955, p. 194; Yamaichi Yamamoto, "Trade Problems with China," *Contemporary Japan,* September 1958, pp. 363–398; Shigeyoshi Takami, "Prospects for Trade with Continental China," ibid., April 1958, pp. 208 ff.; Council on Foreign Relations, *Japan between East and West* (New York: Harper, 1957), p. 138.

48 Jerome Cohen, "International Aspect of Japan's Economic Situation," in Council on Foreign Relations, *Japan between East and West,* p. 134; Aiichiro Fujiyama, "Southeast Asia and Japanese Economic Diplomacy," *Contemporary Japan,* April 1958, pp. 180–185.

49 Olson (*Japan in Postwar Asia,* p. 31) cites Yoshida statement. Hollerman, *Japan's Dependence on the World Economy,* p. 73.

50 Everett Drumwright (assistant secretary of state for Far East affairs) statement before House Foreign Affairs Committee, *Mutual Security Act of 1954*, 83:2, p. 247; Allison, *Ambassador from the Prairie*, p. 267; Dulles statement before Senate Foreign Relations Committee, *Mutual Security Act of 1955*, p. 22. Dulles also advised the Senate that the United States must "help Japan maintain its economy without dependence upon the Communist Areas; that the United States was not in a position to go on doing it indefinitely or absorbing Japanese goods, and that the proper place for Japanese goods was . . . in this Southeast Asian area" (Senate Foreign Relations Committee, *Executive Sessions*, Historical Series, vol. VII, pp. 392–393). See also Saburo Okita, "Japan's Economy and the Rehabilitation of Asia," Japanese Ministry of Foreign Affairs, Tokyo, 1954. The cabinet seemed to agree in 1954 that Asians were "backwards," their nations were difficult to "stabilize," and that Vietnamese nationalism was equivalent to German and Japanese aggression in the 1930s. Dulles explained that other nations failed to recognize that there was no difference between overt and "internal aggression" (James Hagerty diary, cabinet meetings of March 26, April 24, February 8, and May 14, 1954, Eisenhower Library, box 1).

51 Japanese paper, "Trade and Investment Relations with Southeast Asia," Department of Treasury, 68-A-5918, box 47, JAP/0/71.

52 Yoshida speech before the National Press Club, November 8, 1954, Suzuki Papers, Nanto Collection, folder 115.

53 Yanaga, *Big Business*, pp. 264–265. For approach to MacDonald, see Masataka Kosaka, *100 Million Japanese*, p. 126.

54 Japanese government documents: "Proposal for a Southeast Asian Payments Union"; "Japanese Export-Import Bank"; "On Japan's Economic Independence and Her Economic Cooperation in Asia"; "A Survey of the Conditions to Facilitate the Economic Development of Southeast Asia," October 12, 1954; and "Japanese Position Paper"; Suzuki Papers, Nanto Collection, folder 115.

55 Miriam Farley, "Mr. Shigemitsu in Washington," *Far Eastern Survey*, September 1955; "Briefing Paper No. 3," Commission on Foreign Economic Policy, Eisenhower Library, Dodge Papers, box 3, "Japan: Shigemitsu Visit." See also Olson, *Japan in Postwar Asia*.

56 Fujiyama; "Southeast Asia and Japan's Economic Diplomacy"; "Kishi Visit to Washington," *Oriental Economist*, July 1957, pp. 333–334; "Press Release," June 21, 1957, Department of Treasury, 68-A-5918, box 48, JAP/0/76; Sidney Weintraub, "Background Paper for Kishi Visit," June 6, 1957, ibid. See also Lalita Prasad Singh, *The Politics of Economic Cooperation in Asia* (Columbia: Univ. of Missouri Press, 1966); Japa-

nese document, "Economic Desires of South and Southeast Asia," September 25, 1956, Department of Treasury, 68-A-5918, box 42, JAP/0/00, vol. 1; Diehl memo, August 10, 1956, ibid., JAP/0/80.

57 See Japanese document, "A Proposal for U.S.-Japanese Cooperation in the Economic Development of South and Southeast Asia," and Don Paarlberg memo of May 27, 1959 (within Diehl memo of June 2, 1959), both Department of Treasury, 68-A-5918, box 52.

58 *Mainichi* article, found in Tokyo embassy letter to secretary of state, March 9, 1957, Department of Treasury, 68-A-5918, box 52, JAP/5/60, "Trade and Payments Agreements, vol. 1."

59 Walter S. Robertson, "U.S. Policy towards Japan," *Department of State Bulletin,* February 15, 1954, p. 232. See also Raymond Moyer, statement, House Foreign Affairs Committee, *Mutual Security Act of 1954,* 83:2, pp. 260–261. Moyer discusses getting officials in Southeast Asia involved in helping Japan.

60 John Halliday and Gavan McCormick, *Japanese Imperialism Today* (New York: Monthly Review, 1973), p. 11; Russell Fifield, *Southeast Asia in U.S. Policy* (New York: Praeger, 1963), pp. 383–384.

61 Halliday and McCormick, *Japanese Imperialism Today,* pp. 26–27; Raul S. Manglapus, *Japan in Southeast Asia: Collision Course* (New York: Carnegie Endowment, 1976), pp. 3, 8, 105, 116. Irwin Isenberg, ed., *Japan: Asian Power* (New York: Wilson, 1971), p. 143. On the growth and significance of Asian trade for Japan, see Saburo Okita, *Japan in the World Economy* (New York: Japan Foundation, 1975), p. 140.

Conclusion

1 Shigeto Tsuru, *Essays on the Japanese Economy,* p. 47. For procurement figures in first paragraph, see Hollerman, *Japan's Dependence on the World Economy,* p. 136; Cohen, *Japan's Postwar Economy,* p. 113; Halliday and McCormick, *Japanese Imperialism Today,* p. 11.

2 Cohen, *Japan's Postwar Economy,* p. 108; Hollerman, *Japan's Dependence on the World Economy,* p. 135, mentions that all postwar Japanese recessions were triggered by balance of payments constraints. See also Hugh T. Patrick, "Cyclical Instability and Fiscal and Monetary Policy in Postwar Japan," which asserts that "the major importance of exogenous events both for growth and for cyclical fluctuation must be emphasized" (William Lockwood, ed., *State and Economic Enterprise in Postwar Japan* [Princeton: Princeton Univ. Press, 1965], pp. 558, 565).

3 G. C. Allen, *Japan's Economic Recovery* (London: Oxford, 1958), pp. 19–31. Allen cites Japan's "fortune" for the war boom, p. 181. Edwin O. Reischauer, in *The United States and Japan* (Cambridge: Harvard Univ. Press, 1965), p. 49, blithely attributes Japan's recovery to the good "fortune" of war. The thrust of this study is that American policy was largely responsible for establishing the environment which enabled Japan to capitalize on Asian hostilities and American intervention. Tsuru, *Essays on the Japanese Economy,* p. 45.

The revival of the steel industry was the key to Japanese trade recovery. The Dodge Plan "immediately" put the industry in "financial trouble." Price subsidies for steel products were to end June 30, 1950, which would have increased prices by 30–50 percent and "curtail[ed] the demand even further. The little rationalization that had been achieved was not very helpful, and the outlook for the industry was gloomy. The Korean War . . . changed the whole picture. The steel industry was revitalized not only by a large volume of direct Special Procurements on its products but also by a sharp rise in demand from other domestic industries that stepped up production in response to Special Procurements and a surge in the general level of income. Moreover, the war intensified the rearmament drive throughout the world, and the resulting worldwide prosperity brought a sizable volume of additional orders. The boom generated a high profit for the industry. The debt-equity ratio improved substantially. Attractive dividends were distributed to stockholders, and stock prices of steel companies climbed sharply. . . . [The Korean boom] generated the basis for a continuous rise of demand for steel for many years to come, and it provided the industry with funds to be used for modernization" (Kiyoshi Awahato, *The Japanese Steel Industry* [New York: Praeger, 1972], pp. 14, 17, 18, 21, 26).

4 On dualism, see Fumio Moriya, "The Character of Japanese Imperialism," Science Council of Japan, Economic Series, no. 26, Tokyo, February 1961. For an explanation of the imperative of exports for stimulating the oligopolistic industrial sector and avoiding the socialistic consequences of building a planned domestic market, see Theodorio Dos Santo, in Ronald H. Chilcote and Joel C. Edelstein, eds., *Latin America: The Struggle with Dependency and Beyond* (New York: John Wiley, 1974), p. 471. It is, of course, important to remember that the Japanese subtly guided American policies with their strategy of *Makeru Ga Kachi,* to lose is to win (see Cohen, *Japan's Postwar Economy,* p. 108, and Kosaka, *100 Million Japanese,* p. 92). This study has shown that American concerns about Japan and Southeast Asia were neither isolated nor unfounded. Indeed, such concerns, and the larger global

dollar gap problem, guided American policy in Japan from 1946 to 1960. Critics who insist Japan did not require trade with Southeast Asia to recover lose sight of several points: Japan's trade and investment in Southeast Asia were small only relative to her massive global expansion, which could not be foreseen by American planners or Japanese businessmen and diplomats from 1948 to 1956. Japan's stake in Southeast Asia has been significant, thus bearing out American hopes that Japan would not be drawn into an alliance with China. Global multilateral expansion was salient in Japan's recovery, but American policy in the postwar decade to integrate Japan and Southeast Asia was the only logical course, given the attempt to isolate China and the antipathy to long-term economic aid. It also, of course, meshed with global multilateralism and the reintegration of European industry with Third World primary producing areas.

Bibliography

Primary Materials

Dean G. Acheson Papers. Harry S. Truman Memorial Library, Independence, Missouri.

Stanley Andrews Papers. Harry S. Truman Memorial Library, Independence, Missouri.

Joseph M. Dodge Papers. Dwight David Eisenhower Memorial Library, Abilene, Kansas.

John Foster Dulles Oral History Collection. Firestone Library, Princeton University, Princeton, New Jersey.

John Foster Dulles Papers. Seeley G. Mudd Manuscript Library, Princeton University, Princeton, New Jersey.

Dwight David Eisenhower Papers (various presidential files). Dwight David Eisenhower Memorial Library, Abilene, Kansas.

George Elsey Papers. Harry S. Truman Memorial Library, Independence, Missouri.

Clarence F. Jacoby Papers. Dwight David Eisenhower Memorial Library, Abilene, Kansas.

George Frost Kennan Papers. Seeley G. Mudd Manuscript Library, Princeton University, Princeton, New Jersey.

Douglas MacArthur Papers. MacArthur Memorial Library, Norfolk, Virginia.

Records of the Commission on Foreign Economic Policy. Dwight David Eisenhower Memorial Library, Abilene, Kansas.

Records of the Department of State. RG 59. National Archives, Washington, D.C.

Records of the Japanese Ministry of Finance. In the collections of John W. Dower and Dick K. Nanto.

Records of the Joint Chiefs of Staff. Modern Military Branch, National Archives, Washington, D.C.

295

Records of the National Advisory Council on International Financial and Monetary Affairs. National Archives, Washington, D.C.

Records of the National Security Council. Modern Military Branch, National Archives, Washington, D.C.

Records of the Office of the Assistant Secretary of the Treasury for International Affairs. Department of Treasury, Washington, D.C.

Records of the Office of the Under Secretary of the Army. Modern Military Branch, National Archives, Washington, D.C.

Records of the Political Advisor to SCAP. RG 694. Washington National Records Center, Suitland, Maryland.

Records of the Supreme Command for Allied Powers. RG 331. Washington National Records Center, Suitland, Maryland.

Records of the United Nations Economic and Social Council, Economic Commission for Asia and the Far East, Committee on Industry and Trade. Memorial Library, University of Wisconsin, Madison, Wisconsin.

Matthew B. Ridgway Papers. Army War College, Carlisle, Pennsylvania.

Walter S. Salant Papers. Harry S. Truman Memorial Library, Independence, Missouri.

John Snyder Papers. Harry S. Truman Memorial Library, Independence, Missouri.

Gengo Suzuki Papers. In the collections of Dick K. Nanto and John W. Dower.

Harry S. Truman Oral History Collection. Harry S. Truman Memorial Library, Independence, Missouri.

Harry S. Truman Papers (including various presidential files). Harry S. Truman Memorial Library, Independence, Missouri.

Government Documents

British House of Commons. *Debates*. Hansard, 1948–1953.

British House of Lords. *Debates*. Hansard, 1948–1953.

Department of State. *Commercial Series, Economic Cooperation Series, Far Eastern Series*. 1946–1960.

Department of State. *Foreign Relations of the United States*. 1946–1954. All available volumes on Japan, Southeast Asia, Europe, and economic affairs.

Department of State. *Foreign Relations of the United States: Japan, 1931–1941*. Vol. II. Washington, D.C., 1943.

Economic Cooperation Administration. *Report to Congress on the European Recovery Program*. 1948–1952.

Economic Report of the President. Washington, D.C., 1948–1954.

Foreign Operations Administration. *Report to Congress.* 1954–1955.

House Appropriations Committee. *Hearings.* 1949–1954. On foreign aid appropriations.

House Foreign Affairs Committee. *Hearings.* 1947–1956. On the European Recovery Program, the Mutual Security Program, the Mutual Defense Assistance Program, foreign aid, and the North Atlantic Treaty.

House Foreign Affairs Committee. Subcommittee on Foreign Economic Policy. *Hearings.* 1953–1954.

Joint Economic Committee. United States Congress. *Hearings.* 1948–1954.

Mutual Security Agency. *Report to Congress.* 1951–1953.

Mutual Security Agency. *Report to the Public Advisory Board.* 1951–1953.

Organization of European Economic Cooperation. *Report on the European Recovery Program.* Paris, 1948–1952.

Senate Appropriations Committee. *Hearings.* 1949–1954. On foreign aid appropriations.

Senate Foreign Relations Committee. *Executive Sessions.* Historical Series. Vols. 1–9 (published in the 1970s).

Senate Foreign Relations Committee. *Hearings.* 1947–1956. On the European Recovery Program, the Mutual Security Program, the Mutual Defense Assistance Program, and foreign aid.

Newspapers and Periodicals

Bank of Japan Quarterly (originally *Monthly*) *Review,* 1947–1954
Business Week, 1949–1951
Contemporary Japan, 1947–1960
Department of State Bulletin, 1946–1958
Economist, 1947–1955
Far Eastern Economic Review, 1949–1955
Far Eastern Survey, 1948–1958
First National City Bank Monthly Letter on Economic Conditions and Government Finance, 1947–1954
Japan Report, 1956–1960
Magazine of Wall Street, 1948–1954
Mitsubishi Monthly Economic Circular, 1950–1953
Monthly Economic Review (Economic Stabilization Board), 1950–1955
New York Times, 1947–1955
Nippon Times, 1947–1952
Oriental Economist, 1948–1960
Pacific Affairs, 1948–1954

Selected Secondary Sources

Acheson, Dean. *Present at the Creation*. New York: Norton, 1969.

Allen, George C. *Japan's Economic Recovery*. London: Oxford University Press, 1958.

Allison, John. *Ambassador from the Prairie*. New York: Houghton Mifflin, 1973.

Asahi, Shimbun. *The Pacific Rivals*. New York: Weatherill Asahi, 1972.

Asian Development Bank. *Southeast Asia's Economy in the 1970s*. London: Longman, 1972.

Backman, Jules. *War and Defense Economics*. New York: Rinehart, 1952.

Baldwin, David A. *Economic Development and American Foreign Policy, 1943–1962*. Chicago: University of Chicago Press, 1960.

Ball, W. MacMahon. *Japan: Enemy or Ally*. New York: John Day, 1949.

Ball, W. MacMahon. *Nationalism or Communism in East Asia*. Carlton, Victoria: Melbourne University Press, 1962.

Balogh, Thomas. *The Dollar Crisis: Causes and Cures*. London: Oxford University Press, 1950.

Blakeslee, George. *The Far Eastern Commission*. Department of State Publication 5138. Far East Series 60. Washington, 1953.

Blyth, C. A. *American Business Cycles, 1945–1950*. London: George Allen and Unwin, 1969.

Brookings Institute. *Major Problems of United States Foreign Policy*. Annual. Menasha, Wis.: George Banta, 1949–1955.

Brown, W. Adams, Jr. *The United States and the Restoration of World Trade*. Washington: Brookings Institute, 1950.

Brown, W. Adams, Jr., and Redvers Opie. *American Foreign Assistance*. Washington: Brookings Institute, 1954.

Cohen, Jerome. *Economic Problems of Free Japan*. Princeton University Center for International Studies, 1952.

Cohen, Jerome. *Japan's Economy in War and Reconstruction*. Minneapolis: University of Minnesota, 1949.

Cohen, Jerome. *Japan's Postwar Economy*. Bloomington: University of Indiana Press, 1958.

Committee for Economic Development. *Economic Aspects of North Atlantic Security*. 1951.

Council on Foreign Relations. *Japan between East and West*. New York: Harper, 1957.

Council on Foreign Relations. *The United States in World Affairs*. Annual. New York: Harper, 1949–1955.

Diebold, William A. *Trade and Payments in Western Europe*. New York: Harper, 1952.

Dower, John W. *Empire and Aftermath: Yoshida Shigeru and the Japanese Experience, 1878–1954*. Cambridge: Harvard University Press, 1979.

Elliott, William Y., et al. *The Political Economy of American Foreign Policy*. New York: Holt, 1955.

Ellsworth, P. T. *The International Economy*. New York: Macmillan, 1958.

Fearey, Robert. *The Occupation of Japan, Second Phase, 1948–1950*. New York: Macmillan, 1950.

Feis, Herbert. *Contest over Japan*. New York: W. W. Norton, 1967.

Fifield, Russell, *Americans in Southeast Asia: The Roots of Commitment*. New York: Crowell, 1973.

Fifield, Russell. *Southeast Asia in U.S. Policy*. New York: Praeger, 1963.

Fine, Sherwood. *Japan's Postwar Industrial Recovery*. Tokyo: Foreign Affairs Association of Japan, 1953.

Flash, Edward S. *Economic Advice and Presidential Leadership: The Council of Economic Advisors*. New York: Columbia University Press, 1965.

Freeland, Richard. *The Truman Doctrine and the Origins of McCarthyism*. New York: Schocken, 1970.

Gardner, Lloyd C. *Architects of Illusion*. Chicago: Quadrangle, 1970.

Gardner, Lloyd C. *Economic Aspects of New Deal Diplomacy*. Boston: Beacon, 1964.

Gayn, Mark. *Japan Diary*. New York: William Sloane, 1948.

Geertz, Clifford. *Agricultural Involution*. Berkeley: University of California Press, 1968.

Gimbel, John. *The Origins of the Marshall Plan*. Palo Alto: Stanford University Press, 1967.

Goodman, Grant, ed. *The American Occupation of Japan: A Retrospective View*. Lawrence: University of Kansas Press, 1968.

Gray, Gordon, et al. *Report to the President on Foreign Economic Policy*. Washington, 1950.

Halliday, John, and Gavan McCormick. *Japanese Imperialism Today*. New York: Monthly Review, 1973.

Harris, Seymour, ed. *The Dollar in Crisis*. New York: Harcourt Brace and World, 1961.

Harris, Seymour, ed. *Postwar Economic Problems*. Cambridge: Harvard University Press, 1944.

Harrod, Roy. *The Dollar*. New York: W. W. Norton, 1963.

Hayes, Samuel P. *The Beginning of American Aid to Southeast Asia: The Griffin Mission of 1950*. Lexington, Mass.: D. C. Heath, 1971.

Horowitz, David, ed. *Corporations and the Cold War*. New York: Monthly Review, 1969.

Hudson, Michael. *Global Fracture*. New York: Harper, 1977.

Huh, Kyung Mo. *Japan's Trade in Asia*. New York: Praeger, 1966.

Husberger, Warren. *Japan and the United States in World Trade*. New York: Council on Foreign Relations, 1964.

Institute for Pacific Relations. *Problems of Reconstruction in the Far East*. New York, 1949.

Institute for Pacific Relations. *11th Conference of the IPR, 1950*. New York, 1951.

Institute for Southeast Asian Studies. *Japan as a World Power and Its Implications for Southeast Asia*. Singapore: Singapore University Press, 1976.

Isenberg, Irwin, ed. *Japan: Asian Power*. New York: Wilson, 1971.

Japan, Economic Planning Agency. *Economic Survey of Japan, 1956–1957*. Tokyo, 1958.

Johnson, Chalmers. *Conspiracy at Matsukawa*. Berkeley: University of California Press, 1973.

Jones, Joseph M. *The Fifteen Weeks*. New York: Harcourt Brace and World, 1955.

Kennan, George F. *Memoirs, 1925–1950*. Boston: Little, Brown, 1967.

Kindleberger, Charles. *The Dollar Shortage*. New York: MIT,-Wiley, 1950.

Kindleberger, Charles. *The International Economy*. Homewood, Ill.: Erwin, 1958.

Kolko, Joyce, and Gabriel Kolko. *The Limits of Power*. New York: Vantage, 1973.

Kosaka, Masataka. *100 Million Japanese*. Tokyo: Kodansha, 1972.

Lockwood, William, ed. *Japan's New Capitalism*. Princeton: Princeton University Press, 1965.

Lockwood, William, ed. *State and Economic Enterprise in Postwar Japan*. Princeton: Princeton University Press, 1965.

MacDougal, Donald. *The World Dollar Problem*. London: Macmillan, 1957.

Mandel, Ernest. *Decline of the Dollar*. New York: Monad Press, 1972.

Manglapus, Raul S. *Japan in Southeast Asia: Collision Course*. New York: Carnegie Endowment, 1976.

Marjolin, Robert. *Europe and the United States in the World Economy*. Durham: Duke University Press, 1953.

Martin, Edwin W. *The Allied Occupation of Japan*. Palo Alto: Stanford University Press, 1948.

Matsumara, Yataka. *Japan's Economic Growth, 1945–1960*. Tokyo: Tokyo News Service, 1961.

McClellan, David. *Dean Acheson*. New York: Dodd Mead, 1976.

McCormick, Thomas J. *China Market*. Chicago: Quandrangle, 1967.

Millis, Walter. *Arms and the State*. New York: Twentieth Century Fund, 1958.

Millis, Walter, ed. *The Forrestal Diaries*. New York: Viking, 1951.

Mintz, Ilse. *American Exports during Business Cycles*. New York, 1951.

Nagae, Yonosuke, and Akira Iriye. *Origins of the Cold War in Asia*. New York: Columbia University Press, 1977.

Nourse, Edwin G. *Economics in the Public Service*. New York: Harcourt, 1953.

Okita, Saburo. *Japan in the World Economy*. New York: Japan Foundation, 1975.

Olson, Lawrence. *Japan in Postwar Asia*. New York: Praeger, 1970.

Patterson, Thomas G. *Soviet-American Confrontation*. Baltimore: Johns Hopkins University Press, 1973.

Polanyi, Karl. *The Great Transformation*. Boston: Beacon, 1944.

Price, Harry. *The Marshall Plan and Its Meaning*. Ithaca: Cornell University Press, 1955.

Randall, Clarence. *A Foreign Economic Policy for the United States*. Chicago: University of Chicago Press, 1954.

Roberts, N. S. *Overseas Economic Surveys: Japan*. London, 1953.

Schilling, Warner; Paul Y. Hammond; and V. Glenn H. Snyder. *Strategy, Politics, and Defense Budgets*. New York: Columbia University Press, 1962.

Sebald, William J., and Russell Brines. *With MacArthur in Japan*. New York: Norton, 1965.

Selden, Mark, ed. *Remaking Asia: Essays on the American Uses of Power*. New York: Pantheon, 1974.

Singh, Lalita Prasad. *The Politics of Economic Cooperation in Asia*. Columbia: University of Missouri Press, 1966.

Smith, Gaddis. *Dean Acheson*. American Secretaries of State Series. New York: Cooper Square, 1972.

Stein, Herbert. *The Fiscal Revolution in America*. Chicago: University of Chicago Press, 1969.

Stone, I. S. *The Hidden History of the Korean War*. New York: Monthly Review, 1952.

Stone, I. S. *The Truman Era*. New York: Vintage, 1972.

Stueck, William. *The Road to Confrontation*. Chapel Hill: University of North Carolina Press, 1980.

Supreme Command for Allied Powers. Monograph Series on the Occupation of Japan. Vol. 22: "Reparations and Property Administration." Vol. 50: "Commerce, Foreign Trade."

Times (London). *The Dollar Gap*. London: 1949.

Triffin, Robert. *Gold and the Dollar Crisis*. New Haven: Yale University Press, 1960.

Tsuru, Shigeto. *Business Cycles in Postwar Japan*. Tokyo: Science Council of Japan, 1953.

Tsuru, Shigeto. *Essays on the Japanese Economy*. Tokyo: Kinokuniya Bookstore, 1958.

Tucker, Robert. *The New Left and the Origins of the Cold War*. Baltimore: Johns Hopkins University Press, 1974.

United Nations Economic Commission for Europe. *Economic Survey of Europe since the War*. Paris, 1953.

United Nations Economic Commission for Europe. *Europe in 1949*. (Annual Series through 1953.) Paris, 1950.

Vandenburg, Arthur, Jr. *The Private Papers of Senator Vandenburg*. Boston: Houghton Mifflin, 1952.

Ward, Robert, and Frank J. Shulman. *Bibliography of the Occupation of Japan*. Chicago: American Library Association, 1974.

Wightman, David. *Toward Economic Cooperation in Asia: The Economic Commission for Asia and the Far East*. New Haven: Yale University Press, 1963.

Wildes, Harry Emerson. *Typhoon in Tokyo*. New York: Macmillan, 1954.

Yamamura, Kozo. *Economic Policy in Postwar Japan*. Berkeley: University of California Press, 1967.

Yanaga, Chitoshi. *Big Business in Japanese Politics*. New Haven: Yale University Press, 1968.

Yoshida, Shigeru. *The Yoshida Memoirs*. London: Heinemann, 1961.

Index

Acheson, Dean G.: relationship with Congress, 9, 12–31, 30, 242–43n49; and military Keynesianism, 12; European austerity, 35–36; dollar gap memo of, 37, 38; anti-Communism, 39; cold war ideology of, 43, 72–73, 211, 242n49, 244n65; with defense budget/NSC 68, 45; on Soviet ideology, 46, 242n47; on ERP, 47, 53, 245n74; on Korean War, 50, 143–44; mentioned, 56, 158, 197, 198, 239n27, 263n43; on Japanese trade recovery, 64, 119, 148, 175; on workshop concept, 73; on Japanese reparations, 82, 203; blaming Soviets for peace treaty delay, 88; on Southeast Asia, 119–20, 123–24, 194; on China and Japan, 120–21; on Tokyo Conference, 132; on Russian threat, 244n65

Action Program for Asia, 201

Advisory Board on Economic Growth and Stability, 59

Africa, 7, 11, 16, 120

Agency for International Development, 202

Agricultural aid, U.S., 182–85

Agricultural exports, U.S., 36, 37, 40, 41, 75, 182–85, 240n30, 280–81n37

Agricultural Trade and Development Act of 1954. *See* Public Law 480

Aiichi, Kichi, 183–84

Allen, G. C., 221

Allied Council for Japan, 78

Allison, John: on Southeast Asian trade, 109, 201–2; and Yen Fund proposal, 137–39; on Korean War, 144; on China-Japanese trade, 174–75, 205, 213

Almond, General, 138

Alsop, Joseph, 123–24

American Council on Japan, 84

American Farm Bureau Federation, 183

American Management Association, 27

Americans for Democratic Action, 52

Anderson Clayton Corporation, 248n81

Anderson, Clinton, 36, 40

Andrews, Stanley, 126–28, 240, 247, 265n56

Anti-Communism: 8, 9, 10, 16, 47, 82, 144, 195, 198, 290n46

Appropriations Committee, Senate, 247n79

Army, U.S. Department of: occupied Japan, 14–15; aid for Japan, 75, 77; and reparations, 82; on recovery policies, 86, 87; on austerity in Japan, 90, 99, 139, 254n56; mentioned, 91, 96, 101, 119, 154, 209; on Southeast Asian trade, 108, 115–16; on China, 121; and coordinated aid, 125; on pay-as-you-go, 126, 148; and procurement, 129, 156; and most-favored-nation status for Japan, 131; and GARIOA aid, 138; on Korean War boom, 147

Asahi Shimbun, 99, 146

Asian Development Bank, 217, 219

303

COMPOSED BY GRAPHIC COMPOSITION, INC.
ATHENS, GEORGIA
MANUFACTURED BY MALLOY LITHOGRAPHING, INC.
ANN ARBOR, MICHIGAN
TEXT AND DISPLAY LINES ARE SET IN TIMES ROMAN

Library of Congress Cataloging in Publication Data
Borden, William S., 1951–
The Pacific alliance.
Bibliography: pp. 295–302.
Includes index.
1. United States—Foreign economic relations—Japan—.
History.   2. Japan—Foreign economic relations—United
States—History.   I. Title.
HF1456.5.J3B67   1984   337.73052   83-14541
ISBN 0-299-09550-9